A Guide to the Lakes

of Cumberland, Westmorland and Lancashire

by
Thomas West

Unipress Cumbria

Published with the support of the University of Cumbria

This edition of 700 softback copies first published in 2008

ISBN   978-1-8699-7925-6   softback

British Library Cataloguing-in-Publication Data applied for
A catalogue record for this book is available from the British Library

Text typeset in 9/12pt Sabon on Cyclus Offset. Plates on Mohawk Options.
Both are 100 per cent recycled papers.
Printed by **hpm**group, County Durham

With thanks to
The Wordsworth Trust for permission to reproduce John Smith's aquatints
Jeff Cowton, Curator, The Wordsworth Trust, for help with the prints
Martin and Jean Norgate, Portsmouth University, for permission to use
data from their website

Designed by Anna Danby
Proofread by Much Better Text
Project managed by Karen Bassett
Text transcribed by Karen Graham, Miranda Jenkins, Linda Shore,
Olivia Toppin and Kathy Woods

A Guide to the Lakes

of Cumberland, Westmorland
and Lancashire

by

Thomas West

edited by
Gerard M-F Hill

with an introduction by
Mark Haywood

and photographs by
Niki Thomas and John Darwell

Unipress Cumbria

Contents

Foreword

Three Cumbrians first made this book: Thomas West, its original author, lived in Furness; William Cockin, his rather bumptious and opinionated reviser, was a Westmorland man; and John 'Warwick' Smith, the talented landscape artist, was born and educated in Cumberland.

This edition is based on the 10th edition of 1812, which has all eleven addenda of the final version. It has been lightly restyled for the modern reader, mainly by pruning the punctuation and standardising spellings. Some long footnotes that continue the narrative have been taken into the main text. The numbered endnotes fill in background or explain references that might now be obscure.

Niki Thomas, in the plates at the end, shows the present-day view from each of West's 'viewing stations'; John Darwell's photographs in the next few pages correspond to Smith's landscapes. The aquatints are reproduced by kind permission of The Wordsworth Trust. Other contributors to this edition are credited on page ii.

The University of Cumbria has the same concerns – ecology, tourism and the outdoors, art, history and literature – as Thomas West's Guide. Indeed, it was West's vision, observation and research that enabled the early tourists to look at the Lake District in new ways. If we are to cherish and explore our heritage, we too must first study and understand it.

Professor Christopher J. Carr
Vice Chancellor, University of Cumbria

Shifting the Scenery

Mark Haywood

The heart of West's *Guide* – and its most innovative feature – is his 'viewing stations'. He tells the visitor to the Lakes exactly how to find each viewpoint and what they will see, illustrated in the book by 16 prints. As a contemporary artist interested in the history and theory of visual culture, I offer here some ideas and understandings gained from reflections on the Lakes. I examine the views and viewpoints that West so carefully chose and the way Smith and other artists have represented those scenes.

In this book, Niki Thomas's and John Darwell's photographs illustrate two types of change that have occurred since John 'Warwick' Smith painted the scenes described in Thomas West's *Guide to the Lakes*. Not only has the appearance of the landscape changed; there have been changes in how artists view the Lakes and also in what they choose to emphasise in a landscape.

In the next few pages I look at the idea of the Picturesque – now seen as unfashionable and artificial – using it to look at the Lakes in a post-modern light. Whereas West and his readers chose to view the landscape through devices like the Claude mirror and telescope, we choose to see it through a camera lens. Perhaps we see much the same view – but do we see the same things in it?

After that, I consider each of Smith's 16 illustrations in turn, comparing it with West's description and with other artists' versions of the same landscape. Finally, I draw conclusions and add some technical notes on the way the prints were produced.

Changing aesthetic terrain

'Then and now' photographs are popular features in local newspapers: photographs become indexical devices with which to measure the changing appearance of a place. Thomas's and Darwell's photographs also function as indices, but in differing ways.

Thomas's views have been taken from West's viewing stations and are a contemporary photographer's aesthetic response to an 18th-century description. While it is interesting to see 18th-century words rendered into 21st-century images, much can also be learned by comparing, empirically and iconologically, their pictorial conventions. Even more striking is the effect of using colour, rather than relying on tone. In these photographs, as in the tinted windows at Claife Station (see 'Windermere Isle', below), colour at once helps to identify the season, whereas in Smith's aquatints the time of year (and day) is often indeterminate. Colour photography shows the hues of the sky reflected in the lake, an effect also seen in paintings and often intensified by the higher viewpoints favoured by later artists, making more of the lake surface visible.

In such views the sky is usually further enlarged by lowering the horizon; but, as this is also found in many lakeshore depictions, it must be an aesthetic shift rather than just the result of a raised viewpoint. This greater emphasis on sky emerged as 19th-century artists began to understand clouds and weather much better, following the pioneering work by the proto-meteorologist Luke Howard* and the studies of Constable, Goethe, Turner and Ruskin. Now cameras can capture, as no sketch artist could, dramatically-lit instants in continually changing skies, and wide-angle lenses can exaggerate panorama and depth, in a way that evokes the cinema rather than the Claude mirror.

By contrast, Darwell's photographs were taken from the viewpoints corresponding to Smith's aquatints in West's *Guide* (often not exactly the same as West's stations) to learn how the views were 'constructed'. Darwell eschewed an aesthetic approach using dramatic composition or lighting; and he used a fixed-length lens, whose field of view is similar to that of the human eye. His methodology allows us to compare historical autographic transcriptions with present-day photographic records of these views.

Later editions of West were enriched by essays and poems as addenda to his main text. The present volume similarly seeks to complement the 18th-century account and views with present-day scholarship and images. Taken together, these writings and images from the two eras act as an index not merely of physical changes, but also of perceptual changes: *how* artists and travellers have perceived these views.

* Howard's 1802 Linnaean-inspired classification of cloud types also recognised the transitory nature of individual clouds (especially important for Lake District artists) and ultimately provided the foundations for much of modern meteorology (Hamblyn, 2001).

Questions of taste

Booksellers in 18th-century England stocked a succession of aesthetic manuals. Most of these differed from earlier works on judgements of taste in being directed at aspirant connoisseurs and collectors, rather than practising artists. The rapid growth in manufactured and imported items matched the expansion of the bourgeoisie, who strove to imitate the self-confident English aristocracy, whose possessions were largely inherited and who, as a class, were either already highly informed about, or wholly uninterested in, matters of taste. By contrast the *nouveau riche* were eager for aesthetic instruction to ease their social, consumerist and intellectual anxieties.

The English aesthetic phenomenon began with publication of the 3rd Earl of Shaftesbury's *Characteristicks of Men, Manners, Opinions, Times* (1711) and Joseph Addison's *Pleasures of the Imagination* (1712), followed by Francis Hutcheson's *An Inquiry into the Original of Our Ideas of Beauty and Virtue* (1725). Many of their ideas on beauty, harmony, order and design were refined in mid-century works, two in particular: William Hogarth's *The Analysis of Beauty* (1753) and Edmund Burke's *A Philosophical Enquiry into the Origin of Our Ideas of the Sublime and the Beautiful* (1757). Burke employed Hogarth's ideas on the properties of Beauty in a series of contrasts with a long-recognised (but previously vague) quality, the Sublime.

The result was a new, binary system of aesthetic qualities that prompted the emergence of an intermediate category, the Picturesque. This was sketched by a Cumberland man, William Gilpin, in his *Essay on Prints* (1768); he and others, such as Uvedale Price, developed Picturesque theory and criteria further over the following decades.

Enter Thomas West

Tours in search of the Picturesque were a by-product of this new phenomenon. West's *Guide to the Lakes* (published in 1778) was not the first in the field, but it soon became the most popular, an essential accessory for the tourist aesthete. This was in large part because it was the region's first modern guidebook. It put the Lake District on the map.

Who was West? William Cockin's Preface seems to be deliberately vague, but it gave strong clues that were easily decoded. After his "education on the Continent" (where? why?), he became "a professor in some of the branches of natural philosophy" (which?) only to turn up in Ulverston. "Having … much leisure time on his hands" he decided to write a guidebook. We learn nothing of his family, where he was born or how he lived.

His parentage is unknown, but he was born Thomas Daniel in Inverness, about 1720, and went to school in Edinburgh.† In the 1740s he changed his name to West and became a commercial traveller on the Continent,‡ possibly because he was a Jacobite being hunted after the 1745 rising. To an 18th-century English reader, education abroad would at once suggest papist parents – Thomas West was in fact a Jesuit priest, and Furness was his parish. He was also a member of the Society of Antiquaries, in demand among visiting gentry as a guide to the Lakes. This seems to have triggered his interest in what he called 'landscape studies' and led to this highly original book.

Changing views

After the author's death in 1779, the book ran to eight editions over the next 25 years, and tourists went on buying it into the 1820s before it was superseded by Wordsworth's *Guide*.¶ Even today, West's *Guide* still subtly informs the aesthetic values of Lakeland tourists and residents alike. Far from being abstruse, its 18th-century attitudes to the Lake District are part of our mind-set, both aesthetic and economic.

West's many references to 'fine new inclosures' remind us that not only were ways of viewing the landscape changing, but so was

† T. West, *The Antiquities of Furness* (1805 edn), p. 409.

‡ 'West [formerly Daniel], Thomas (1720?–1779)', *Oxford Dictionary of National Biography* (2004).

¶ Wordsworth's text appeared in a variety of guises, titles and editions before stabilising in its 5th edition (1835), which was titled *A Guide Through the District of the Lakes in the North of England, with A Description of the Scenery, etc. For the Use of Tourists and Residents* (Wordsworth, 1810: iii–vi).

the very appearance of the land itself. This was nothing new, because over the past several thousand years the Lake District had been largely deforested by intentional and unintentional tree clearance, soil erosion and later coppicing for charcoal burning. By the year of West's death, the tree population may have been at an all-time low, though the many Enclosure Acts around this time had begun slightly to reverse this trend by encouraging private plantations.

Cumbria has since changed dramatically in countless other ways, yet many of the scenes depicted by Smith remain surprisingly similar today. Of course this is partly because his views focused mainly on the mountains, which have remained uninhabited, and away from lowland or lakeshore settlements, which are visible only in the far distance.

For the Lake District, the changes that followed the Enclosure Acts were less significant than the change in 18th-century attitudes to mountains. Up till then, Western cultures had regarded mountains as unpleasant, unimportant, useless features – 'warts, pimples, blisters, or other such ugly deformities on the earth's surface.'* This long-held view was increasingly repudiated during the 18th century, but its legacy lingered on into West's time and even occasionally surfaces in his account, slightly undermining the value he places on 'awefulness' as part of that newly emergent aesthetic quality, the sublime. For instance, looking north-west from Coniston Station II, West notes that

> the range of naked rocks that cross the head of the lake appear now awful, from their sable hue, and behind them the immense mass of Cove, Rydal Head and many *nameless* mountains have a most stupendous appearance and seemingly inaccessible height.†
> [my italics]

The Picturesque artist and 'scenery'
John Smith (1749–1831) was the son of a gardener in the village of Irthington in north-east Cumberland. He studied under John Gilpin in nearby Scaleby and later under his son, the writer – artist William Gilpin, chief theoretician of the Picturesque movement, in which Smith himself, Uvedale Price and Richard Payne Knight became the leading figures.

In about 1775, his tutor's younger brother, the painter Sawrey Gilpin, introduced Smith to the 2nd Earl of Warwick, who became his patron and the origin of his 'middle name'. Over the following decades John 'Warwick' Smith became a prominent aesthetician of the Picturesque topographical tradition, and eventually one of its last exponents. Today we lack an exact equivalent of this concept,‡ and so these artists' values and intentions are worth exploring in some detail.

Almost two centuries after Smith, 'land artists' in remote parts of the United States were making huge artworks – like Robert Smithson's *Spiral Jetty* or Michael Heizer's *Double Negative* – by moving or refashioning

* Nash, 2001: 45.

† West, 1778: 50.

‡ The Picturesque practice of constructing a picture from ideal elements has a parallel in computer-aided retouching and collaging practices that seek to flatter the subject and deceive the viewer.

thousands of tons of earth and rock. Yet the scale of their ambitions was quite limited when compared to the Picturesque imagination and its remodelling of terrain. Despite 'Warwick' Smith's reputation as a fine topographical artist, when his aesthetics deemed it necessary he would change the course of rivers and move whole mountains across the skyline as if they were but stage scenery.

Should shifting scenery seem an over-fanciful analogy, it is worth noting that the earliest recorded use of the word 'scenery' was of a backdrop in the theatre, not of a landscape outdoors. That was in 1770;¶ seven years later, the term was being used of Picturesque landscape. There are illuminating points of correspondence between the proscenium arch and a painting's frame, between stage sets and landscape paintings, and between the Claude mirror and the scene painter's manipulation of depth and perspective.

The origin of the word 'scenery' usefully reminds us of the intentional artifice of the Picturesque and the way its artists constructed a landscape. They took from the theatre the foreground-framing *coulisses*,* but these were merely the foremost of a series of planar-spatial waves that washed towards the spectator, from the mountains of the backdrop over a succession of painted flats.†

The artifice of the Picturesque combined landscape elements in a prescribed manner to make the composition conform to a particular aesthetic trope. Although by the third quarter of the 18th century many artists had already painted the Lakes, and a great many more have done so since, the significance of Smith's work for West's *Guide* lies above all in its direct relationship to burgeoning aesthetic tourism. Almost equally importantly, it marks a turning point in our increasingly complex relationship with the landscape, when theoretical, theatrical and classical ideas were only partly replaced by a new emphasis on direct observation of landscape.

By the end of the century, the practice of constructing landscapes was being questioned from a number of standpoints. Timothy Wilcox observes that 'in 1794 Richard Payne Knight's didactic poem *The Landscape* and Uvedale Price's *Essay on the Picturesque* ... challenged the formulaic dictums of Rev. William Gilpin'‡ – and in 1798 the Reverend James Plumptre wrote *The Lakers*, a satirical opera that lampooned both Price and the vogue for aesthetic tourism.¶ Another, more painterly challenge came from artists who placed a new emphasis on 'realism' and vaunted their topographical accuracy – probably often achieved with the aid of a *camera obscura*.* In the 20th century, the implicit values of the realistic approach were exemplified by Wainwright's precise illustrations to his fell-walkers' guides.

In contrast to the literal attitude to landscape, an even more imaginative development can be seen in the early works of J.M.W. Turner, who first visited the Lake District in 1797. Whilst, like the Picturesque artists, he was pragmatically capable of shifting the

¶ The word 'scenery' was derived from the much older *scena*, 'scene', with its origins in the Roman stage.

* In Picturesque repertoire, these theatrical side-screens often took the form of a pair of bushes whose foliage drew the eye inwards from the outer edges of the painting.

† This was an era of expanding empire, so the aesthetic conventions of the Picturesque and those of Romanticism manifested the colonial gaze. The former translated dangerous, exotic wilderness into safe, familiar landscape (Bunn, 1994); the latter turned uninhabited landscape (in northern Europe, a trope of the sublime) into empty land that could be 'legitimately' colonised (Bordo, 2002; Haywood, 1999).

‡ Wilcox, 2006: 3.

¶ *The Lakers*' popularity probably prompted Rowlandson and Combe's satirical poem *The Tour of Dr. Syntax in Search of the Picturesque*, first published in the *Poetical Magazine* in 1809 and in turn also much imitated.

* See Wilcox, 2006: 8–9.

† Turner's landscapes, even his studies, though ostensibly recording the view from a single vantage point, were actually complex constructions achieved by composing and adjusting elements of the landscape. Ruskin described Turner's landscape studies as 'being both commemorative and determinant' (Ruskin, 1860: 241–2).

‡ Boime (1991), *The Magisterial Gaze: Manifest destiny and American landscape painting, c.1830–1865* (Washington, Smithsonian Institute).

scenery when necessary,† he raised the depiction of landscape and the atmospheric effects of light to far higher levels. This elevation was both aesthetic and physical.

Most 18th-century artists preferred low-level views, from the lake shores, heightening the distant mountains of the background. In West's prints the mountains are usually flat areas of aquatint tone, featureless apart from their (often exaggerated) jagged skyline. By contrast the foregrounds contain many minor details of Picturesque piquancy, such as shaggy Highland cattle or peasant figures whose diminutive size is contrasted with the vastness of their surroundings. Mountains, when not safely in the background, were dark peaks, 'awe-full' and sublime, that loomed over the spectator.

By contrast, 19th-century Romanticism drove the artist–hero to the dramatic solitude of the mountain tops. The archetypal Romantic viewer, epitomised in Caspar Friedrich's *Wanderer Gazing over a Sea of Mist*, saw the scene from the Olympian perspective of the Almighty, with what Alfred Boime was to later term the 'magisterial gaze'.‡

Over the past two centuries a succession of aesthetic models has been imposed on the Lake District and its landscapes. The artists of the Picturesque prescribed aesthetic formulae by the lakeshore; the Romantics imaginatively invested the mountaintops with the full-blown sublimity of Kant; today we link the environmental and the social. Far from being impregnable and remote, Cumbrian landscapes have now become fragile and highly contested sites, managed or reconstructed to meet conflicting demands for conservation and preservation, re-forestation and re-wilding, more tourists and fewer tourist vehicles. Our attitudes are post-modern hybrids with earlier tropes and values.

Millions of people now care very much about the Lake District and its landscapes; yet, before the aesthetic tourists came, the reverse was true. The rich pastures of the Eden Valley, Lakeland's eastern neighbour, were literally so. Their richness was evidenced in Eden's wealth of castles, halls and manor houses, indices of its status in earlier centuries when the beauty of a landscape was measured by its utility and fertility.

The Picturesque and its accompanying revaluation of the Lake District's scenery are part of a much greater aesthetic watershed, from which a whole system of ideas still supplies many of our contemporary landscape values. I would argue that the principles of the Picturesque are some of the most significant because they are among the earliest sources of our present mind-set, the headwaters of present-day landscape aesthetics.

John 'Warwick' Smith's Views of the Lakes

1 *The Vale of Lonsdale*

West advised his readers to make a detour east before entering the Lakes in order to visit a viewing station mentioned in Gray's Journal (included in the Addenda to West's *Guide*). 'Every feature which constitutes a perfect landscape of the extensive sort is here not only boldly marked, but also in its best position.'¶ A footnote in later editions gives more detailed directions as 'several mistakes have been made respecting this station'.*

Gray's original directions had been slightly vague, but perhaps the resulting confusion was not wholly dispelled because what is now called Gray's Seat is on top of a hill to the south of the road, not in a field on the north side as the footnote says. Today foliage obscures the view in summer, but in winter one can see that the prospect from here is the principal element in Smith's composition despite the proximity, profile and height of Ingleborough being greatly exaggerated (in his day it was believed to be a mile high).

The view from Gray's Seat is also known as the 'Crook o' Lune', though the dramatic nature of this feature immediately below the station is not apparent in Smith's work, where the foreground figures appear to be standing on the outcrop that created the Crook.† Yet another name is 'Turner's View', from his famous 1817 watercolour, *Crook o' Lune, Looking towards Hornby Castle*.

The two artists' compositions show up significant differences between the Picturesque and Romantic aesthetics. Smith chose to emphasise the gentle meanders of the Lune, which 'serpentizes' through the flat-bottomed glaciated valley. The aesthetic qualities of the serpentine had been set out in Hogarth's *Analysis of Beauty* of 1753 wherein the artist claimed that the properties of beauty could be reduced to a single mnemonic device,‡ the serpentine 'Line of Variety'.¶ By contrast, Turner sites the viewer on the edge of a dizzying precipice, looking down on the sharp elbow of the Crook, which dominates the foreground. In Turner's painting, the mellow valley which fills the fore and middle ground of Smith's work is used to heighten the sense of pictorial space beyond the eyrie. Equally dramatic and highly inventive is the composition, which transforms Smith's gentle, meandering Lune by fragmenting it into three foaming, sickle-shaped reaches that wheel around the outside of the Crook.

2 *Coniston Hall*

Turner had also made a view of Coniston, in the same decade as Smith, but their very different treatments emphasise the fact that Turner's *Morning among the Coniston Fells* is a seminal work of the next century, whereas Smith's *Coniston Hall* is firmly grounded in the conventions of the 18th. In Smith's foreground, the picturesque peasants of the Vale of Lonsdale are replaced by a couple of shaggy Highland cattle.*

¶ West, 1778: 26.

* For instance, West (10th edn), 1812: 25 fn.

† It is usually said that such figures provided scale and local colour. But, given Picturesque artists' idealisation of landscape, we may consider Jonathan Bordo's suggestion in the context of wilderness painting that they function as 'witnesses'. They tell the viewer that the artist witnessed the scene, and testify from within to its 'authenticity' by asserting 'we were there' (Bordo, 2002).

‡ See Ronald Paulson's 1997 foreword to Hogarth's *Analysis of Beauty*, pp. xiii, xxxvi, xxxviii and 22n; also Hogarth, pp. 121–2 and 153.

¶ Hogarth's work was controversial at the time and has since been much misunderstood. Elsewhere (Haywood, 2002/2007) I have proposed that Hogarth's theory of the appeal of the arabesque was based on its capacity to evoke aspects of the post-pubescent female body. His ideas were later adopted by Ingres, who distorted his models' bodies to maximise the number of sensual, serpentine elements in the composition. The most extreme example is his *Grande Odalisque*, whose spine was given an extra vertebra to achieve a serpentine curve. Another example of contemporary fondness for the serpentine is the eponymous lake in Kensington Gardens, a by-product of the 19th-century Rococo revival.

* Turner's painting was not just a description, but a symbolically paradisal interpretation of the view over Coniston. The shepherd and shepherdess in the foreground are Adam and Eve witnessing their first dawn, as was made clear by a verse from *Paradise Lost* beside the painting at the Royal Academy in 1798.

† Sandby was also a founder member of the Royal Academy; his godson, the painter Paul Sandby Munn, was more closely associated with the Lakes.

‡ Darby, 2000: 58; see also Schama, 1995: 466–71. Maillard has suggested that the origin of the English term 'picturesque' may lie in the 17th-century Italian *pittoresco* (Maillard, 2004: 260n.8), and the OED supports his hypothesis, citing 'F. Redi (1684), "in the style of a painter"'.

¶ 'View across Windermere-water, looking over the great island, from the hill above the ferry-house'; it was No. 17 of Farington's *Twenty Views of the Lakes* published between 1784 and 1789.

* West, 1778: 67.

Diminutive local figures and Highland cattle in the foreground were both common tropes of the Picturesque. The invention of the latter is credited to Paul Sandby, one of the movement's founders.† He and his brother had begun as draughtsmen for Surveyor General William Roy's mapping of the Highlands, in the years after the suppression of the Forty-Five Rebellion. Ironically, the experience of erasing wilderness by making it knowable and controllable gave Sandby a rich stock of imagery which he and others later employed in Picturesque depictions of other 'wildernesses'. Highland dress, stunted trees and hirsute Highland cattle were liberally incorporated into Picturesque landscapes, to distance them from the sterile order of the older Palladian landscape, adding a *frisson* of wildness and pleasing irregularity.

This practice was enthusiastically adopted by others and lasted through several decades of Lakeland landscapes. The plaid-swathed figures in Allom's 1832 depiction of Honister Crag are not early tourists from north of the border, but wild metonymic figures that Darby identifies as descendants of Salvator Rosa's *banditti*, who had been deployed to similar ends in Neapolitan scenes of the previous century.‡

3 *Windermere Isle*
In the 1780s Farington's version of the view over the island had been included in a folio of engravings;¶ they were advertised in the 5th edition of West's *Guide* (1793), which also contained an advertisement for Smith and Emes' aquatints.

West quoted Arthur Young: 'In landscapes, you are either on a level with the objects, or look up to them; the painter cannot give the declivity at your feet, which lessens the object as much in the perpendicular line, as in the horizontal one'.* Smith sought to overcome this limitation. His composition was centred on Belle Isle, which occupies the middle distance. The island is by far the largest on the lake, but the artist reduced its distance from the viewer (and its size) by adding an extra storey to the house† and exaggerating its scale, so its dark roof could be dramatically silhouetted against the pale slopes rising on the far shore, beyond what are now the resorts of Windermere and Bowness.

In 1800 a Gothick folly was built on the site of the viewing station; at first called Belle Vue, it later became known as Claife Station. The building's most notable feature was the first-floor drawing room: its six coloured windows functioned as large-scale Claude lenses so visitors could view lake and the landscape in simulations of the seasons.‡ Today it may seem strange or unnatural to go inside a building to view the landscape around it (though this is exactly what people do in visitor centres),¶ but the Picturesque was not primarily concerned with the 'natural'; it refined and applied an aesthetic perception that turned the natural into an idealised version of its mundane self.

In a similarly curious inversion of outdoors and indoors, Claife Station 'framed' the landscape in which it was set, while its windows aesthetically isolated and filtered the scenery. The Station is now a rather charming ruin; no longer merely a late by-product of the Picturesque, it has become its exemplar. The National Trust, who own Claife and its surrounding, long-overgrown pleasure gardens, are currently considering how best to maximise their possibilities.

4 *Winandermere Lake from Colgarth*

This is one of the most dramatic of Smith's depictions: the foreground trees and figures are picturesquely curled and bent in the wind, the conditions reiterated by the billowing sail of the small boat in the centre of the composition and the background illuminated through a sudden gap in the clouds. A stylistically interesting comparison can be made with Smith's view of Grasmere (discussed below), where a similar *coulisse* tree is reversed and placed on the right-hand side of the scene.

Earlier forms of the lake's name were still in use: Wordsworth in his 1810 *Guide* used both 'Windermere' and 'Winandermere', and Keats in a letter of 1818 refers to it as Winander.* The name's instability today lies in the tension between the undesirably tautological *Lake* Windermere and its usefulness in distinguishing between the lake and its eponymous resort.

5 *Elterwater*

Smith drew the lake from the south-east and, as with the River Lune in the Vale of Lonsdale, used a meander to lead the eye into the lake by a slightly circuitous route. However, unlike the Lune, the Brathay's meander seems to have required a certain amount of artistic licence to achieve the requisite serpentine aesthetic of 'variety'. The two scenes are remarkably similar in other compositional respects, from the position of their main topographical features down to the placing of such characteristic Picturesque devices as a near-identical *coulisse* tree on the left-hand side and the small conversing figures (who also generate a slight sense of narrative).

† Wordsworth's famous 1844 letter to the *Morning Post* opposing the projected Kendal & Windermere Railway contains a characteristically perceptive account of the origins and history of this house. The poet noted that it was 'the first to be built in the Lake district *[sic]* in order to appreciate the beauty of the countryside' (appendix in Wordsworth, 1810: 150; and Gage, 1972: 77).

‡ Pale green glass gave the appearance of Spring, yellow was used for Summer, orange for Autumn and pale blue for Winter; a dark blue window simulated moonlight and lilac an impending storm. The building (but not its windows) has a footnote in later editions (West, 1812: 55n).

¶ Another instance is some contemporary art museums, where the topmost storey is not the traditional, top-lit painting gallery, but a glass-walled restaurant where, after arduous ascents through windowless white-box galleries, visitors feast on a panorama of the metropolitan sublime.

* John Keats, letter to Tom Keats, 25–27 June 1818 (English History, on line).

† Other local 'forces' include Aira, Colwith, Scale, Rutter, Spout and Stanley Ghyll.

‡ Foster, 1994: 233n.24.

¶ West, 1778: 77.

* See Hebron et al., 2006: 94–5.

† The other is 'Derwentwater from Ormathwaite'.

6 *Stock-gill Force near Ambleside*

Waterfalls were popular with writers and artists and they were, after 'lofty mountains', probably the most common trope of the Romantic sublime. Falling or cascading water was a natural feature that generated flights of fancy and literary hyperbole. Unlike other eras, when poetic allusions emphasised the tinkling musicality of the English waterfall, at his time they were 'forces',† pumping fonts of masculinity that were often favourably compared to what were actually much larger, foreign rivals. Today, readings of this aqueous trope are more likely to locate its appeal in the realm of the feminine:

> When Kant writes of the 'delight in terror' provoked by the natural sublime, he refers to 'threatening rocks, thunderclouds …, hurricanes …, the boundless ocean …, the high waterfall of some mighty river', all so many tropes of the fragmentary and the fluid, i.e. of the fantasmatic feminine body that threatens to overwhelm the patriarchal subject – an overwhelming that is both desired and feared.‡

Smith probably sketched the waterfall from a point beneath the present viewing station, for today one gazes across at the falls. As with the Rydal Cascade (below), it may be that there was little room for manoeuvre and that he offers a largely faithful delineation of the scene. In fact I would argue that, in contrast to his customary practice, for once the drama is actually reduced, because Smith fails to convey the true, impressive height of the waterfall, particularly given his lower viewpoint. This uncharacteristic lapse may be the result of a combination of 18th-century pictorial convention, the image format required by the folio and, possibly, his proximity to the Force. In the event, verticality is sacrificed to breadth and Smith's waterfall looks slightly squashed.

Like present-day visitors, West probably viewed the scene from a slightly higher point for (with characteristic restraint) he describes the torrent as being 'precipitated into a dark gulph *[sic]*, unfathomable to the eye.'¶ It is slightly surprising that his account omits any description of the Force's considerable height (70 ft) and one must assume that this too is because the high viewpoint causes one to look across, rather than up, at the falls.

7 *Upper Cascade, Rydal*

The cascades at Rydal were a popular subject in the late 18th century but, as with many waterfalls, the number of possible viewpoints was limited and therefore so were artists' opportunities for compositional variety – though Constable later made some studies of Rydal that were contrastingly unfussy.* The print in the folio is one of a pair not drawn by Smith† and inscribed 'from a sketch by Laporte'. John Laporte (1761–1839) was a topographical artist who taught drawing at the

Addiscombe Mill Academy, contributed illustrations to several books of Picturesque tours and exhibited at the Royal Academy. Laporte may have used a Claude mirror, which artists sometimes employed in the way we use a wide-angle lens, to help compose a scene when they could not get sufficiently far back from the subject.

  The lower Rydal cascade could also be appreciated from the window of a stone summer house, whose construction pre-dated the Picturesque by a century and a half‡ – rather surprisingly, since viewing a waterfall from inside a building built for that very purpose was a characteristic pastime of the Picturesque aesthete. As Shannon Fraser notes in connection with the Hermitage above Black Linn Falls on the River Braan, in addition to the window's framing of the view, it is a safe *interior* from which to gaze upon the *exterior* roaring torrent.¶

  Besides being a conveniently warm, dry place from which to muse or paint, the station could incorporate devices with theatrical effects, such as Claude lenses (as at Claife Station, above) or multiple mirrors, that blurred the visual distinction between interior and exterior, effectively bringing the waterfall into the room. The Wordsworths were among the many visitors to the mirrored Hermitage, of which Dorothy wrote in her journal, 'and lo! we are at the entrance of a splendid room, which was almost dizzy and alive with waterfalls, that tumbled in all directions'.*

8 *Rydalwater*

Smith most probably constructed his scene from two adjacent sites on the north shore, one in front of and the other behind the large rocky outcrop on the extreme right-hand side of the picture. In this way the lake surface becomes a neutral ground across which pictorial elements such as islands† could be slid and realigned, much in the manner of the cut-and-paste layer techniques of present-day digital artists.

  Today, if one stands on the spot from which the outcrop probably was drawn, the lake shore in the foreground to its left is dominated, and partially hidden, by an old stone boathouse. Its exact age is difficult to judge, but it is interesting to speculate whether it also blocked West's view, inspiring him to replace it with the small rowing-boat, which may be both a compositional element and a cryptic allusion to the building's absence.

9 *Grasmere Lake*

Many editions of the *Guide* contain an earlier steel engraving of Grasmere, after John Feary RA, which sometimes replaced Farington's view of the Lowdore waterfall as the frontispiece.‡ Feary and Smith both drew the lake from Loughrigg Terrace, a slope that runs across the southern end of the lake. We may therefore conclude that Smith made a conscious effort to distance his depiction from that of his predecessor, though – since they shared both viewpoint and compositional formulae – they had to incorporate similar elements, even if they distributed them slightly differently.

‡ I am grateful to the garden archaeologist, Dr Sarah Rutherford, for this information.

¶ An early example dating from 1757 (Fraser, 2006).

* Ibid.

† Heron Island and Little Isle.

‡ The plate inscription reads 'Drawn by Jos^h Farington RA' *[sic]*.

This is noticeable in the use of foreground figures and detail, and dramatically evident in their differing positioning of the island, which in reality is almost equidistant from the lake's east and west shores. It is moved to just off the east shore by Feary, and a similar distance in the opposite direction by Smith. The latter also adopted a slightly higher viewpoint and, on the left-hand side, replaced Feary's side-screen house with a craggy rock topped by a stunted tree dramatically silhouetted against the sky.

There is a much stronger tonal range in Smith's version, whose *chiaroscuro* lighting plunges the foreground into deep shadow. Indeed, the lighting thoughout the scene is far more dramatic, with the Vale of Grasmere hidden beneath low cloud. The overall effect is to suggest one of those typical Lakeland days when the weather alternates between bright sun and sudden showers. It may therefore be significant that Smith's views are usually of more clement weather, with clear skies and the tops of mountains clearly visible. Even if low cloud had hidden the mountains when Smith sketched Grasmere, he could have added detail from Feary, and so this may be a further clever means of further distancing the two versions. In the event meteorological differences and the tonality of aquatint together imbue Smith's *Grasmere* with a much greater sense of space than can be achieved with the relentless detail of the engraver's *roulette* lines.

10 *Leathes Water*
A century after Smith drew Leathes Water, its name and appearance changed rather abruptly after a dam was built at its northern end. It became Thirlmere, a reservoir to supply the burgeoning industrial city of Manchester with further supplies of drinking water, conveyed there by a sophisticated system of tunnelled aqueducts.

In Smith's time the lake consisted of two sections, linked by a short channel. He drew it from Wythburn at the southern end of the lake, from where perhaps only half the lake's surface would have been visible, the northern section being almost entirely hidden behind the two promontories that faced each other across the centre of his composition. Because of the rise in water levels after the dam was built, these features are now much less significant; and the lake's two islands are now submerged, though two new ones have been created by patches of higher ground separated from the lake shore.¶

Smith drew the lake looking north, towards St Johns in the Vale, but much that one might expect to see is only suggested through a vague, weak indication of aquatinted mountains. However, the potentially impressive bulk of Helvellyn would be beyond the right-hand edge of the artist's field of view and perhaps other potentially dramatic detail was omitted because it was invisible through low cloud. This may also have hidden the possibilities otherwise suggested by combining it with a higher viewpoint, such as Smith used elsewhere; here such a strategy would have enabled him to see the length of the valley, thus including both lakes and the view beyond towards Blencathra.

11 *Derwent-water from Castle-crag*

This view is possibly the one in the folio that corresponds most closely to the optical index of the photograph: even the path up from the lake serpentizes in the prescribed manner towards the crest of the ascent. Furthermore, though there are a few significant divergences from the modern photographic record, they actually serve to give us a greater understanding of the spatial disposition of significant scenic elements.

Firstly, the two islands in the middle ground (which correspond to St Herberts and Rampsholme) have been brought closer to the viewer in order to visually separate them from the eastern lake shore and thus confirm their status as islands.

¶ See Tyler for a full and colourful account of the flooding of Haweswater, with before-and-after photographs of Thirlmere and a very helpful map showing the ensuing changes in water level (p. 120).

Secondly, the Derwent's meanders as it enters the lake are not directly visible, but are indicated by its tree-lined banks. Thus the simplified, treeless view of the river's meander through the moraine at the lake head gives form to the middle ground. This device is also employed in Smith's views of the Vale of Lonsdale and Elterwater.

The clouds over Derwentwater are more solidly drawn than in any of Smith's other scenes; this is in part a product of the higher-than-usual viewpoint, but it is interesting to note similar, though more developed, meteorological conditions in views from the far side of the lake by Laporte (then) and Thomas (now).

12 *Derwentwater from Ormathwaite*

Although there is a 1795 'Warwick' Smith print of Derwentwater,* the one in the Emes folio (from which the aquatints in West's *Guide* were taken) is the second of two contributed by John Laporte.

Like Smith, Laporte combined multiple viewpoints, but – as noted previously – Smith characteristically opted for a high viewpoint, looking down on the foreground, and then drew the background from a lower station, thus increasing the height of the mountains. By contrast, Laporte's study was made at some considerable distance from the lake, on the fell just above the hamlet of Applethwaite; then, to compensate for his much greater distance from the subject, he brought the lake closer to the viewer than it really appears from this position (which he probably achieved with the aid of a telescope).

To the left of the composition he added Ormathwaite Hall, which is out of sight below this station. Possibly he used it to replace a farmhouse, whose field pattern (in the foreground) is still visible today.

13 *Buttermere Water*

Smith's depiction of Buttermere melded two rather dissimilar views from the northern end of the lake. The tonally, and therefore spatially, 'neutral' surface of the water was used by the artist to seamlessly unite elements from topographically differing stations.

The foreground and fellside *coulisse* on the left of the picture were observed from high above the lake's north-east corner, looking down from an outcrop above St James's Church. The mountains on the far side of the lake were probably drawn from a spot about 200 m lower down, on the shore at the opposite corner of the lake about half a mile to the north-west. The result gives the spectator a commanding view over the foreground detail whilst looking up at the background from a low viewpoint, thereby making the height of the mountains ar more impressive.

14 *Loweswater*

Smith here employed a similar compositional strategy to that of *Buttermere Water*, but there are two disparities: despite the background

* Smith made a close-up study of the lake, titled 'Pocklington's or Vicar's Island'; it is dominated by a newly erected folly, later excoriated in Wordsworth's *Guide* under the heading 'The Country Disfigured' (Wordsworth, 1810: 71).

beyond the lake being a fairly accurate record of the view below Loweswater Hall, the foreground's elevated viewpoint is not available at that point by the lake shore, so Smith probably merged a lakeside study of the background with a foreground drawn from higher and further back from the lake.

More intriguingly, the craggy north end of Mellbreak, which rises some 500 m above the lake, is missing, having been merged with the slopes of Loweswater Fell to its left. The actual topography seen from this viewpoint is far more dramatic than depicted and the huge, seemingly isolated outcrop rising beyond the lake would have made a striking central compositional element. Instead it has been partially hidden behind the outcrop of Darling Fell.

15 and 16 *Ulleswater* and *Upper end of Ulls-water*
As with Windermere, the spelling of Ullswater had not yet stabilised, and we know from artists' titles (Tonge, 1847; Bulloch, 1857) that these forms endured well into the 19th century.

Smith concluded with a view halfway along the lake, looking towards Patterdale. This stretch has since become one of the most popular points from which to photograph the lake; indeed, it is possibly *the* definitive view of Ullswater. However, what is not apparent from a single drawing or photograph is that this spot is one of the few places where one can see both ends of the lake, which 'dog-legs' at this halfway point.

A second reason for this stretch of lake shore's present-day popularity is that, a decade after Smith's visit, it began a journey to eventual poetic immortality as 'Wordsworth Point', the place where on Thursday 15 April 1802 the poet and his sister came across those now world-famous daffodils.†

† Wordsworth, 2002: 84–5.

Concluding Reflections
One might expect an illustrated book called 'A Guide to the Lakes' to contain much on the subject of water. Not only is it the essential characteristic of lakes, but names in 'water' (along with 'mere' and 'tarn') are now preferred in the Lake District to those using the word 'lake'. Yet it is striking how little West's *Guide* and Smith's images add to our knowledge of water; indeed on the subject of water, with the notable exception of waterfalls, the otherwise descriptively effusive West remains as silent as the waters of the lakes themselves.

It is in keeping with West's silence on the subject that Emes' aquatints often indicated the presence of water by leaving the plate unetched, the engraver being unable to render water's qualities other than through blankness. Rather than depictions of water, we have only reflections, or else a significant absence, as both writer and artist instead directed their efforts to describing or showing the mirror's frame. These difficulties of representation also reflect the limitations of a largely scopic regime, that is, a particular set of visual ideas and practices. Today similar limitations persist and it is only by viewing lake and setting not as polar opposites of detail and reflection, but as the most visible elements in a far more complex ecosystem, that we can take our understandings much beyond those of the Picturesque. When contemporary attitudes to landscape are increasingly characterised by ecological concerns and longings for the 'natural', it is forgivable if we see the composed artifice of the Picturesque as outdated.

We might assume that we are separated from its aesthetic values by Romanticism, a movement which certainly continues to inform many aspects of contemporary mores. Yet the modern tourist's experience of landscape is often as packaged and artificial as that of any Picturesque tourist. Most people are probably more physically distanced from Nature than their ancestors were two centuries ago and, in the Lake District as elsewhere, a great many visitors (and locals) clearly prefer the 'leisure experience' of lakeside resort cafés and retail outlets to solitary trudging or cloud-like wandering over the high fells and mountain ridges.

Those who shun prepacked diversions may still find themselves distanced from the Romantic sublime by their own knowingness. A few years ago the sculptures of Tania Kovats – wonderful Lilliputian models of landscape features such as cliffs and gorges embedded in white plinths – prompted the art critic David Barrett to sadly conclude that we no longer really respond to Nature, unlike the Romantics who

> attributed meaning to landscape and man's spiritual encounter with the sublime. Today we have internalised the concept of Nature and simply read images of mountain vistas as sublime. That is to say the relation has become semiological; we know the cultural significance of mountains before we even see them. We already know what to think.‡

‡ Barret, 1998: 10.

Even if our culture did not distance us from the natural world, it turns out that the fells and mountains of Lakeland, so admired for the last couple of centuries as the epitome of wild, unspoilt Nature, are actually a 'degraded' landscape: their appearance now is the product of several millennia of human intervention, deforestation and soil erosion.

It may seem perverse to say so, but – in contrast to the eco-devastation of the fells – the velvety-green lower slopes now appear too 'manicured', at least to lovers of wilderness. Certainly most parts of the region are far less 'shaggy' than they were in the heyday of the Picturesque. For a glimpse of how it might have once appeared, it is worth visiting the largely tourist-free western Lakes.

Above Ennerdale Water – in an area that West passed through, but largely overlooked, reserving his superlatives for its lower, lakeside features such as 'the verdant bounds of Gillerthwaite'¶ – a gentle form of re-wilding* is being undertaken with assistance from the hooves of woodland-dwelling Galloway cattle. This writer hopes that future visitors to 'Wild Ennerdale' will one day rediscover the shaggy boskiness of earlier times.

Technical Notes

John 'Warwick' Smith's studies were made into etchings and reproduced by John Emes,† a London printer with whom he was already collaborating on another venture, *Select Views in Italy*. This publication was based on sketches Smith had made between 1775 and 1781 during a lengthy tour funded by his eponymous patron. After his return to England, Smith spent the next ten years working up the Italian sketches into larger, formal paintings; he also began two new bodies of work based on sketches taken on tours of Wales and the Lake District.

As part of this process it seems reasonable to assume that, like many artists before and since, Smith made use of a Claude mirror. Arnaud Maillet's recent excellent book makes clear that the instrument served various purposes, rather than simply making the reflection resemble the work of Claude (a common explanation). It not only unified the image, but provided a tonality that would have been particularly important for a study that was going to be translated into an aquatint.‡

Although Emes' plates display a variety of etching techniques, hard and soft grounds make a relatively minor contribution, with their etched lines largely confined to the foreground, where their main function was to add shaggy, irregular texture to areas of foliage and delineate the occasional figure. The image was almost entirely constructed through many subtly different depths of aquatint bite, which gave a wide range of tonal variations. It was this technique that enabled Smith's *grisaille* studies (studies in shades of grey, as they probably were) to be successfully turned into prints.

Emes employed a liquid aquatint ground that had been developed in the 1760s by Paul Sandby.¶ The technique of suspending aquatint resin in a volatile liquid (in this case, spirits of wine) differed from the earlier French (and later common) practice of dusting the etching plate with dry resin powder. In both liquid and dry aquatints, the resin is melted and fused to the surface of the plate by applying a flame to the underside of the copper plate; each resin grain then protects a minute area of the metal surface from the corrosive 'bite' of the mordant (the acid used to etch the plate).

¶ West, 1778: 294.

* The term 're-wilding' covers a range of land management practices, whereby cultivated land is deliberately allowed to revert to an earlier condition, usually through the re-introduction of indigenous, or formerly indigenous flora and fauna.

† The second of the two advertisements in the 5th edition of West describes the prints as having been 'engraved by S. Alken, from drawings by J. Smith and J. Emes.'

‡ Maillet 2004: 109–10.

¶ Although aquatint was of French origin, many important aspects of its early development occurred in England during the latter decades of the 18th century (Printmaking Dictionary, on line).

The area of the plate covered by the grain of resin remains smooth, is unable to retain ink when the plate is wiped and so prints out as a tiny speck of white, which gives the tonal areas of aquatints their characteristic granularity, though with fine resin or bitumen powders this may be visible only through a magnifying glass. In the 18th century, a possible advantage of Sandby's liquid aquatint medium was that it gave smoother, more consistent areas of tone.

The soft copper etching plates of the time eventually deteriorated with repeated printings. Often this resulted in a loss of fine linear detail, or in aquatints losing their sparkle and becoming muddy. In 1857 Salmon and Garner solved the problem by patenting steelfacing, an electroplating process which protected the surface of the plate with a thin coating of harder metal, and this method is still in use today.

Bibliography

David Barrett, 'No Damien No Gary No Tracy' in *Art Monthly*, No. 219, September 1998, pp. 7–10

Jonathan Bordo (2002) 'Picture and Witness at the Site of Wilderness' in Mitchell (ed.), pp. 291–315

David Bunn (2002) '"Our Wattled Cot": Mercantile and Domestic Space in Thomas Pringle's African Landscapes' in Mitchell (ed.), pp. 127–71

Wendy Joy Darby, *Landscape and Identity: Geographies of nation and class in England* (Oxford, Berg, 2000)

Steve Edwards, '"Profane Illumination": Photography and photomontage in the USSR and Germany' in Edwards and Wood (eds) *Art of the Avant Gardes* (New Haven, CT, Yale University, 2004), pp. 397–425

Hal Foster, *Compulsive Beauty* (Cambridge, MA, MIT Press, 1994)

Shannon Fraser, 'Capturing the Body in a Dangerous Theatre: Interpreting Sublime landscape in 18th-century Perthshire' (unpublished paper from *The Lie of the Land* conference, University of Stirling, 2006, generously made available by Dr Fraser)

John Gage, Turner, *'Rain, Steam and Speed': Art in Context* (London, Allen Lane Penguin, 1972)

Richard Hamblyn, *The Invention of Clouds: How an amateur meteorologist forged the language of the skies* (New York, Farrar, Strauss & Giroux, 2001)

Mark Haywood, *Outside Perspective* (Grahamstown, Rhodes University, 1999)

Mark Haywood (2002) 'From Desire to Design' in *twoninetwo: essays in visual culture*, ed. A. Patrizio (Edinburgh College of Art), Vol. 3, pp. 77–90

Mark Haywood, 'Morphologies of Beauty: Evolutionary psychology and the genetically relayed appeal of biomorphic design' in de Rijk and Druker (eds) *Design and Evolution* (Delft, Technical University, 2007)

Hebron, Shields and Wilcox, *The Solitude of Mountains: Constable in the Lake District* (Grasmere, Wordsworth Trust, 2006)

William Hogarth (1753) *The Analysis of Beauty*, ed. R. Paulson (New Haven, CT, Yale University, 1997)

Robert W. Jones, *Gender and the Formation of Taste in Eighteenth-Century Britain: The analysis of beauty* (Cambridge University, 1998)

Arnaud Maillet, *The Claude Glass: Use and meaning of the black mirror in Western art* (New York, Zone, 2004)

W.J.T. Mitchell (ed.) *Landscape and Power* (University of Chicago, 2nd edn, 2002)

Roderick Frazier Nash, *Wilderness and the American Mind* (Yale University, 4th edn, 2001)

John Ruskin (1860) 'Modern Painters, Vol. V' in Cook and Wedderburn (eds) *The Works of John Ruskin*, Vol. VII (London, George Allen, 1905, Library edn)

Simon Schama, *Landscape and Memory* (London, Fontana, 1995)

Robert Smithson (1973) 'Frederick Law Olmsted and the Dialectical Landscape' in Jack Flynn (ed.) *The Collected Writings of Robert Smithson* (New York University, 1996), pp. 157–71

Ian Tyler (1999) *'Thirlmere Mines' and 'The Drowning of a Valley'* (Keswick, Blue Rock, 2005 edn)

Thomas West, *A Guide to the Lakes* (Kendal, W. Pennington, 1778)

Thomas West, *A Guide to the Lakes*, ed. William Cockin (Kendal, W. Pennington, 1812, 10th edn)

Timothy Wilcox, 'Which Way to Watendlath', in Hebron, Shields and Wilcox (2006), pp. 1–10

Dorothy Wordsworth, *The Grasmere and Alfoxden Journals*, ed. P. Woof (Oxford University, 2002)

William Wordsworth (1810) *Guide to the Lakes*, ed. A. de Sélincourt 1906 (Oxford University, 1970 edn)

Electronic Sources
The checking of many final details of this essay has been greatly aided by
Martin and Jean Norgate (2008) *West's Guide to the Lakes, 1778/1821* at:
http://www.geog.port.ac.uk/webmap/thelakes/html/west/ws21fram.htm
[accessed 9 May 2008]

English History
http://englishhistory.net/keats/letters/thomaskeats2527June1818.html
[accessed 27 April 2008]

Printmaking Dictionary
http://www.polymetaal.nl/beguin/mapa/aquatint.htm
[accessed 27 April 2008]

http://www.polymetaal.nl/beguin/maps/steelfacing.htm
accessed 27 April 2008]

A Guide to the Lakes

of Cumberland, Westmorland and Lancashire

By the author of *The Antiquities of Furness*

——————————For Nature here,
Wanton'd as in her prime, and play'd at will
Her virgin fancies.————
Wild above rule or art—[and beauteous form'd]—
A happy rural seat of various view.
(Milton, *Paradise Lost*)[1]

THE TENTH EDITION

Kendal

Printed by W. Pennington

And sold by J. Richardson, Royal Exchange; and W. Clarke, New Bond Street, London

1812

Preface to the Second Edition

The speedy sale of the first edition of this work has induced the publishers to use their best endeavours to make the present one still more worthy of public encouragement, by subjecting it to such alterations and improvements as were judged necessary to complete its design—and of which it may be here proper to give some account.

The many imperfections of style and composition which but too evidently appeared in the first impression are attempted to be rectified in this. Some additional matter is introduced into the body of the text, and a few notes are inserted on incidental subjects which were thought to be properly allied to the leading one. An Addenda is subjoined, containing a collection of several valuable miscellaneous pieces which have occasionally appeared respecting the lakes. And a friend of the publishers has communicated an original article, called 'A Tour to the Caves', which, it is hoped, will not only entertain, but be found particularly accurate as to matter of fact. In short, the publishers have done everything in their power to make this Guide as complete and useful as its object is curious and popular.

Guides of every denomination should be well acquainted with the regions in which they exercise their vocation; and it must be natural for the purchasers of this manual to wish to know something of its author, and the pretensions he has to claim their implicit confidence in the character he assumes. This curiosity may *now* be properly indulged, as he is no longer within the reach of either praise or censure—but what we have to say on the subject will be very short.

Mr West, late of Ulverston, author of this tract and also of *The Antiquities of Furness*, is supposed to have had the chief part of his education on the Continent, where he afterwards presided as a professor in some of the branches of natural philosophy: whence it will appear that though, upon some account or other, he had not acquired the habit of composing correctly in English, he must nevertheless have been a man of learning. He had seen many parts of Europe, and had considered what was extraordinary in them with a curious, if not a judicious and philosophic eye.[2] Having in the latter part of his life much leisure time on his hands, he frequently accompanied genteel parties on the tour of the Lakes; and, after he had formed the design of drawing up his Guide, besides consulting the most esteemed writers on the subject (as Dr Brown, Messrs Gray, Young, Pennant, &c.), he took several journeys on purpose to examine the lakes and to collect such information concerning them, from the neighbouring gentlemen, as he thought necessary to complete the work, and make it truly deserving of its title.

* Mr West died the 10th of July 1779 at the ancient seat of the Stricklands, at Sizergh in Westmorland, in the 63rd year of his age; and, according to his own request, was interred in the choir or chapel belonging to the Strickland family, in Kendal Church. As he was a man of worth, as well as ingenuity, this further short memorial of his exit will not need an apology.

From these particulars, and the internal evidence of the following pages, it is presumed the reader will be satisfied that the author was, in the most essential respects, well qualified for his undertaking. And should some of his digressions into antiquity be thought too long, or a few descriptions want precision, and now and then a station be dubiously pointed out—if, on the whole, the matter be selected by no uniform plan—let it be remembered, few writers of tours have been able to avoid blemishes of this kind, and that the chief end of the work is accomplished if, along with due copiousness, it be authentic in the principal articles of local information.

Before the author's death (which happened very lately)* he had collected some new matter for this tract, which is introduced in the present edition in the manner he designed; but the revision of the language, &c., mentioned before, fell of course to another person and, in justice to him and the author, it is proper to say here in what manner it has been executed.

As there is something particular, and often pleasing, in the author's strokes of description and manner of thinking, care has been taken all along to preserve his ideas as much as possible in his own order, terms and mode of construction. A few needless repetitions and redundancies have indeed been retrenched, but little has been added which was not necessary to complete the sense. On this account, as the work is in itself more of a useful than entertaining nature, it is presumed the judicious reader will not yet expect elegance of language, but be satisfied if on the whole he find it decently perspicuous and correct.

William Cockin
September 28, 1779

Advertisement

The late ingenious Mr Cockin of Burton[3] wrote the Preface to the second edition of this work and revised the whole, after the death of Mr West: he also wrote all the articles marked with his initials. All who knew Mr C. will be satisfied how well he was qualified for the undertaking; and the internal evidence of the articles themselves and the sale of nine editions will, it is expected, be sufficient for others.

In this edition, such corrections and improvements are made as have appeared necessary since the publication of the former, in order to make the whole complete.

W. Pennington
Kendal, June 1, 1812

Table of the Lakes
In the order they are described

The Chief Towns
Described (or passed through) in this tour

Measurements

Articles contained in the Addenda

The taste of visiting the Lakes

Since persons of genius, taste and observation began to make the tour of their own country, and to give such pleasing accounts of the natural history and improving state of the northern parts of the kingdom, the spirit of visiting them has diffused itself among the curious of all ranks.

† The noble art being landscape painting.

Particularly the taste for one branch of a noble art† (cherished under the protection of the greatest of kings and best of men), in which the genius of Britain rivals that of ancient Greece and modern Rome, induces many to visit the lakes of Cumberland, Westmorland and Lancashire, there to contemplate in alpine scenery, finished in nature's highest tints, the pastoral and rural landscapes, exhibited in all their styles, the soft, the rude, the romantic and the sublime; and of which, perhaps, like instances can nowhere be found assembled in so small a tract of country. What may be now mentioned as another inducement to visit these natural beauties is the goodness of the roads, which are much improved since Mr Gray[4] made his tour in 1765 and Mr Pennant[5] his in 1772. The gentlemen of these counties have set a precedent worthy of imitation in the politest parts of the kingdom by opening, at private expense, carriage roads for the ease and safety of such as visit the country; and the public roads are equally properly attended to.

The design of the following sheets is to encourage the taste of visiting the lakes, by furnishing the traveller with a Guide; and, for that purpose, the writer has here collected and laid before him all the select stations and points of view noticed by those authors who have made the tour of the lakes, verified by his own repeated observations. He has also added remarks on the principal objects, as they appear viewed from the different stations; and such other incidental information as he judged would greatly facilitate and heighten the pleasure of the tour, and relieve the traveller from the burden of those tedious enquiries on the road or at the inns, which generally embarrass and often mislead.

The local knowledge here communicated will not, however, injure, much less prevent, the agreeable surprise that attends the first sight of scenes that surpass all description, and of objects which will always affect the spectator in the highest degree.

For such as spend their lives in cities

Such as wish to unbend the mind from anxious cares or fatiguing studies, will meet with agreeable relaxation in making the tour of the lakes. Something new will open itself at the turn of every mountain, and a succession of ideas will be supported by a perpetual change of objects, and a display of scenes behind scenes in endless perspective. The *contemplative* traveller will be charmed with the sight of the sweet retreats that he will observe in these enchanting regions of calm repose;

and the *fanciful* may figuratively review the hurry and bustle of busy life, in all its gradations, in the variety of unshaded rills that hang on the mountains' sides, the hasty brooks that warble through the dell, or the mighty torrents precipitating themselves at once with thundering noise from tremendous rocky heights; all pursuing one general end, their increase in the vale and their union in the ocean.

Such as spend their lives in cities, and their time in crowds, will here meet with objects that will enlarge the mind by contemplation, and raise it from nature to nature's first cause. Whoever takes a walk into these scenes, must return penetrated with a sense of the creator's power, in heaping mountains upon mountains and enthroning rocks upon rocks. Such exhibitions of sublime and beautiful objects cannot but excite at once both rapture and reverence.

When exercise and change of air are recommended for health, the convalescent will find the latter here in the purest state, and the former will be the concomitant of the tour. The many hills and mountains of various heights, separated by narrow vales, through which the air is agitated and hurried on by a multiplicity of brooks and mountain torrents, keep it in constant circulation, which is known to add much to its purity. The water is also as pure as the air, and on that account recommends itself to the valetudinarian.

Not inferior to the Alps or Apennines

As there are few people in easy circumstances but may find a motive for visiting this extraordinary region, so more especially those who intend to make the continental tour should begin here; as it will give, in miniature, an idea of what they are to meet with there in traversing the Alps and Apennines—to which our northern mountains are not inferior in beauty of line or variety of summit, number of lakes and transparency of water; not in colouring of rock or softness of turf; but in height and extent only. The mountains here are all accessible to the summit, and furnish prospects no less surprising and with more variety than the Alps themselves. The tops of the highest Alps are inaccessible, being covered with everlasting snow which, commencing at regular heights above the cultivated tracts of wooded and verdant sides, forms indeed the highest contrast in nature; for there may be seen all the variety of climate in one view. To this, however, we oppose the sight of the ocean, from the summit of all the higher mountains, as it appears intersected with promontories, decorated with islands, and animated with navigation; which adds greatly to the perfection and variety of all grand views.

Those who have traversed the Alps, visited the lake of Geneva and viewed Mont Blanc, the highest of the glaciers, from the valley of Chamonix in Savoy, may still find entertainment in this domestic tour.[6] To trace the analogy and difference of mountainous countries furnishes the observant traveller with amusement; and the travelled

‡ In truth, a more pleasing tour than these lakes hold out to men of leisure and curiosity cannot be devised. We penetrate the glaciers, traverse the Rhone and the Rhine, whilst our domestic lakes of Ullswater, Keswick and Windermere exhibit scenes in so sublime a style, with such beautiful colourings of rock, wood and water, backed with so tremendous a disposition of mountains, that if they do not fairly take the lead of all the views of Europe, yet they are indisputably such as no English traveller should leave them behind him.

(Mr Cumberland's Dedication to Mr Romney).

¶ Hugh, to whom William de Lancaster, 6th Baron of Kendal, gave a certain place called Askeleros and Ceoc, to look to his fishing in the River Loyn [or Lune].

(Burn's Westmorland, p. 31)

* Those however who love to see the variety of green and olive tints, which appear in the springing and decaying foliage, would be much pleased with a sight of the lakes either in May or September.

visitor of the Cumbrian lakes and mountains will not be disappointed of pleasure in this particular.‡

Prospects for the artist

This Guide may also be of use to the artist who may purpose to copy any of these views and landscapes, by directing his choice of stations, and pointing out the principal objects. Yet it is not presumed positively to decide on these particulars, but only to suggest hints, that may be adopted or rejected at his pleasure.

The late Mr Gray was a great judge of landscapes, yet whoever makes choice of his station at the three-mile stone from Lancaster, on the Hornby Road, will fail in taking one of the finest afternoon rural views in England.[7] The station he points out is a quarter of a mile too low and somewhat too much to the left. The more advantageous station, as I apprehend, is on the south side of the great or Queen's Road, a little higher than where Mr Gray stood; for there the vale is in full display, including a longer reach of the river and the wheel of Lune, forming a high-crowned isthmus, fringed with tall trees, that in time past was the solitary site of a hermit.¶[8] A few trees, preserved on purpose by the owner, conceal the nakedness of Caton Moor on the right and render the view complete.

By company from the south, the lakes may be best visited by beginning with Haweswater and ending with Coniston Water, or vice versa. Mr Gray began his tour with Ullswater, but did not see all the lakes. Mr Pennant proceeded from Coniston Water to Windermere Water, &c. but omitted Ullswater and Haweswater.

When to visit

Mr Gray was too late in the season for enjoying the beauties of prospect and rural landscape in a mountainous country; for in October the dews lie long on the grass in the morning, and the clouds descend soon in the evening and conceal the mountains. Mr Pennant was too early in the spring, when the mountains were mantled with snow and the dells were darkened with impenetrable mist; hence his gloomy description of the beautiful and romantic vale of St John, in his journey from Ambleside to Keswick. Flora displays few of her charms early in May, in a country that has been chilled by seven winter months.

The best season for visiting the lakes is from the beginning of June to the end of August.* During these months the mountains are decked in all the trim of summer vegetation and the woods and trees, which hang on the mountains' sides and adorn the banks of the lakes, are robed in every variety of foliage and summer bloom. In August nature has given her highest tints to all her colours on the enamelled plain and borders of the lakes. These are also the months favourable to botanic studies.

Some rare plants are then only to be found: such as delight in alpine heights, or such as appear in ever-shaded dells or gloomy vales.[9]

> Can Flora's self recount the shrubs and flowers,
> That scent the shade, that clasp the rocky bowers?
> From the hard veins of sapless marble rise
> The fragrant race, and shoot into the skies.
> Wond'rous the cause, can human search explore
> What vegetation lurks in every pore?
> What in the womb of diff'rent strata breeds?
> What fills the universe with genial seeds?
> Wond'rous the cause! and fruitless to enquire,
> Our wiser part is humbly to admire.†

† From the poem 'Killarney'.

Mr Young[10] visited the lakes in this fine season, and saw them all except Coniston and Esthwaite (both Lancashire lakes), which are on the western side of the others and lie parallel to Windermere.

Nothing but want of information could prevented that curious traveller from visiting the whole range of the lakes; which had he done—and described their scenery with that accuracy and glow of colouring he has bestowed upon the lakes of Keswick, Windermere, &c.—a copy of his account would have served for a Guide to all who make the same tour.

For visitors coming from the north

The course of visiting the lakes from Penrith is by Bampton to Haweswater, and from thence to Ullswater, and return to Penrith. Next set out for Keswick: seventeen miles good road. Having seen the wonders of Keswick and the environs, depart for Ambleside: sixteen miles of excellent mountain road, which afford much entertainment. From Ambleside, ride along the side of Windermere Water, six miles, to Bowness, and, having explored the lake, either return to Ambleside and from thence to Hawkshead, five miles, or cross Windermere at the horse ferry, to Hawkshead, four miles. The road, part of the way, is along the beautiful banks of Esthwaite Water.

From Hawkshead the road is along the skirts of the Furness Apennines to the head of Coniston Water, three miles, good road. This lake stretches from the feet of Coniston Fells, to the south, six miles. The road is on the eastern side, along its banks, to Lowick Bridge; from thence to Ulverston by Penny Bridge, or by Lowick Hall, eight miles— good carriage road everywhere. From Ulverston, by Dalton, to the ruins of Furness Abbey, six miles. Return to Ulverston, from thence to Kendal, twenty-one miles, or to Lancaster over the sands, twenty miles.

‡ An abridged view of the tour may be seen in a Table of the Roads at the end.

¶ As descriptions of prospects, greatly extended and variegated, are often more tedious than entertaining, perhaps the reader will not lament that our author has not anywhere attempted to delineate a view taken from either of these capital mountains, but rather wish he had shown the same judgement of omission in some other parts of his work. However, as an apology of the most persuasive kind for what may appear either prolix or too high coloured in some of the following descriptions, let it be noted by the candid reader at the outset that the lakes were his favourite object, and on which he thought enough could scarce ever be said, and that the seducing effects of an ardent passion are in any case easier to discover in others, than to rectify in ourselves. [Wm Cockin]

N.B. In this edition is given Mrs Radcliffe's description of the scenery in a ride over Skiddaw; see Addenda, Article XI.

For visitors coming from the south

This order of making the tour of the lakes is the most convenient for company coming from the north, or over Stainmore; but for such company as come by Lancaster, it will be more convenient to begin the visit with Coniston Water. By this course, the lakes lie in an order more agreeable to the eye and grateful to the imagination. The change of scenes is from what is pleasing, to what is surprising; from the delicate touches of Claude,[11] verified on Coniston lake, to the noble scenes of Poussin,[12] exhibited on Windermere Water; and from these to the stupendous romantic ideas of Salvator Rosa,[13] realised on the lake of Derwent.

This Guide shall therefore take up the company at Lancaster, and attend them in the tour to all the lakes,‡ pointing out (what only can be described) the *permanent* features of each scene: the vales, the dells, the groves, the hanging woods, the scattered cots, the deep mountains, the impending cliff, the broken ridge, &c. Their *accidental* beauties depend upon a variety of circumstances: light and shade, the air, the winds, the clouds, the situation with respect to objects, and the time of the day. For though the ruling tints be permanent, yet the green and gold of the meadow and vale, and the brown and purple of the mountain, the silver grey of the rock, and the azure hue of the cloud-topped pike, are frequently varied in appearance by an intermixture of reflection from wandering clouds or other bodies, or a sudden stream of sunshine that harmonizes all the parts anew. The pleasure therefore arising from such scenes is in some sort accidental.

An eyeglass and mirror desirable

To render the tour more agreeable, the company should be provided with a telescope, for viewing the fronts and summits of inaccessible rocks, and the distant country from the tops of the high mountains Skiddaw and Helvellyn.¶

The landscape mirror will also furnish much amusement in this tour.[14] Where the objects are great and near, it removes them to a due distance, and shows them in the soft colours of nature, and in the most regular perspective the eye can perceive, or science demonstrate.

The mirror is of the greatest use in sunshine; and the person using it ought always to turn his back to the object that he views. It should be suspended by the upper part of the case, holding it a little to the right or left (as the position of the parts to be viewed require) and the face screened from the sun.

The mirror is a plano-convex glass, and should be the segment of a large circle; otherwise, distant and small objects are not perceived in it. But, if the glass be too flat, the perspective view of great and near objects is less pleasing, as they are represented too near. These inconveniences may be provided against by two glasses of different convexity. The dark glass answers well in sunshine, but on cloudy and gloomy days the silver foil is better. Whoever uses spectacles upon other occasions must use them in viewing landscapes in these mirrors.

Lancaster*[15]

The castle here is the first object that attracts the attention of the curious traveller. The elevation of the site and magnificence of the front strike the imagination with the idea of a place of much strength, beauty and importance; and such it has been ever since its foundation, on the arrival of the Romans in these parts.

An eminence of swift descent, that commands the fords of a great tiding river, would not be neglected by so able a general as Agricola;[16] and accordingly he occupied the crown of this eminence in the summer of his second campaign, and of the Christian era 79, and here he erected a station to secure his conquest and the passes of the river, whilst he proceeded with his army across the bay of Morecambe, into Furness. The station was called Longovicum, and in process of time the inhabitants were called Longovices, that is, a people dwelling upon the Lon or Lune.

The station communicated with Overborough by exploratory mounts (some of them still remaining) on the banks of the Lune, which also answered the purposes of guarding the fords of the river and overawing the natives. The mounts of Halton, Melling and at the east end of the bridge of Lune, near Hornby, are still entire. The station at Lancaster was connected with that of Watercrook, near Kendal, by the intervention of the beacon on Warton Crag and the castellum on the summit of a hill that rises immediately above Watercrook, at present called Castle Steads.

The town that Agricola found here belonged to the western Brigantes,[17] and in their language was called Caer Werid, that is, 'the green town'. The name is still retained in that part of the town called Green Aer, for Green Caer; the British construction being changed, and Werid translated into English. The green mount on which the castle

* Named as *Longovicum* in the imperial *Notitia Dignitatum*.

stands, appears to be an artefactum of the Romans. In digging into it a few years ago, a Roman silver *denarius* was found at a great depth. The eminence has been surrounded with a great moat.

The castle of Lancaster

The present structure is generally supposed to have been built by Edward III, but some parts of it seem to be of higher date. There are three styles of architecture very evident in the present castle.†

† As seen in 1778.

1. Round towers, distant from each other about 26 paces, and joined by a wall and open gallery. On the western side there remain two entire, and from their distance and the visible foundation of others it appears they have been in number seven, and that the form of the castle was then a polygon. One of these towers is called Adrian's Tower, probably from something formerly standing there dedicated to that emperor. They are two stages high; the lights are narrow slits; the hanging gallery is supported by a single row of corbels, and the lower stages communicate by a close gallery in the wall. Each stage was vaulted with a plain pyramidal vault of great height. Those in the more southern towers are entire and called John of Gaunt's ovens, but the calling them so is as ridiculous as groundless.[18]

   Taillebois, baron of Kendal, is the first after the conquest who was honoured with the command of this castle; and William de Taillebois in the reign of Henry II obtained leave to take the surname of Lancaster. It is therefore probable that the barons of Kendal either built or repaired the ancient castle in which they resided, until they erected, upon the summer site of the station of Concangium, their castle at Kendal; for the remains of some of the bastions *there* agree in style with the towers *here*.

2. The second distinct style of building in Lancaster castle is a square tower of great height, the lower part of which is remote antiquity; the windows are small and round headed, ornamented with plain short pillars on each side. The upper part of this magnificent tower is a modern repair; the masonry shows it, and a stone in the battlement, on the northern side, inscribed

E.R.

1585 R A.

proves that the repair was made in the time of Queen Elizabeth. It is pretty evident that two towers, with the rampart, have been removed to give light and air to the lower windows on the outside of the great square tower; and it is joined by a wall of communication to Adrian's

Tower, that could not be there when the other two round towers were standing. There are two lesser square towers on the opposite side of the yard or court.

3. The third style of building is the front or gateway. This may be given to Edward III, or to his son John of Gaunt. It faces the east, and is a magnificent building in the Gothic style. It opens with a noble and lofty pointed arch, defended by overhanging battlements, supported by a triple range of corbels, cut in form of boultins. The intervals are pierced for the descent of missiles, and on each side rise two light watch-towers. Immediately over the gate is an ornamented niche, which probably once contained the figure of the founder. On one side is still to be seen on a shield France quartered with England; on the other side, the same with a label ermine of three points, the distinction of John of Gaunt, Duke of Lancaster, fourth son of Edward III, the first English monarch that quartered France and England on a shield— it was Henry V that reduced the lilies of France to three.‡

On the north side of the hill, below the churchyard, are some remains of the wall that encompassed the station. It retains part of the ancient name of the place, being called Wery wall. Those who suppose it to be that part of the priory-enclosure wall, which was situated on the north side of the churchyard, may be satisfied it is not so, by viewing the part of the enclosure wall yet standing, which is a thin mouldering fabric; whereas the Wery wall is a cemented mass, that nothing but great violence can injure. Another fragment of it stands at a stile on the footpath, under the west end of the churchyard.¶ It is frequently met with in the churchyard, and its direction is to the western side of the castle. The father of the late William Bradshaw esquire, of Halton, remembered the Wery wall projecting over Bridge Lane, and pointed directly to the river. This could never be the direction of the priory wall. To say nothing of the name which tradition has preserved, had Mr Pennant viewed both, he would not have doubted a moment to join Camden against Leland.[19] At Bridge Lane this wall makes an angle, and runs along the brow of the hill behind the houses, in a line to Church Street, which it crosses about Covell Cross. This is attested by the owners of the gardens, who have met with it in that direction, and always found blue clay under the foundation stones.

Though the station was one of the first which the Romans had in these parts and, from its importance, the last they abandoned, yet but few Roman British remains have been discovered at it.

The Caledonians, the unconquered enemies and greatest plague of the Romans in Britain, were particularly galled and offended with the garrison at Lancaster, it being always the first to oppose them as often as they invaded the empire by crossing the Solway Firth. For having taken the advantage of the spring tides, and the darkness of the nights

‡ The improvements lately made in the castle, under the direction of Mr Harrison, are very extensive, in the best style of Gothic architecture, and add greatly to the noble appearance of that building

¶ This fragment has been lately destroyed.

at the change of the moon, they escaped the garrison at Virosidium, Ellenborough, Arbeia and Moresby; and skulking along the Cumberland coast, they crossed the Morecambe bay, and were first discovered on the banks of the Lune. Here they were opposed by the townsmen, who kept the garrison; and if they did not return by the way they came, the alarm brought upon them the garrisons of Overborough, Watercrook and Ambleside, who surrounded and cut them off. Hence arose a particular hatred to the Lancastrians, which time and repeated injuries fomented into rage.

In the end, the barbarous clans, following close upon the heels of the flying Romans, in a particular manner satiated their desire of revenge upon the helpless Lancastrians, by sacking and destroying their town and fortifications, in order that they might at no future time oppose their invasions. The Saxons, arriving soon after, raised on these ruins the town that remains to this day. Hence it may be inferred that the present town of Lancaster stands on a magazine of Roman-British antiquities, and this is often verified by digging under ancient houses, where Roman remains are frequently found, and where it appears that the earth has been removed. Beside what Dr Leigh mentions,[20] there are many recent instances that prove the conjecture.

In the year 1772, in digging a cellar where an old house had stood, in a street or lane called Pudding Lane (almost in the centre of the town) there was found, reversed in a bed of fine sand, above 5 ft underground, a square inscribed stone, of 4 ft by 2½ ft dimensions: 1 ft 2 ins were broken off the lower corner on the right-hand side, so as to render the inscription obscure, but the remaining letters were very plain, elegantly formed, square and about 3 ins high. The inscription had consisted of eight or nine lines, of which six are entire and of easy explanation; the loss in the seventh is readily supplied; but the eighth must be made out by the common style of such votive stones. The elegance of the characters pronounces them to be the work of the best times; but the two small letters in the third and fifth lines reduce it to the age of Emperor Gordian; and, if the three small letters have been occasioned by the omission of the sculptor, then it will be of higher antiquity. It is known by inscriptions found at Olenacum (Old Carlisle) that the Augustan wing mentioned on this tablet was stationed there in the time of Gordian; and now, from this inscription, it seems also to have been at Lancaster. This memorable stone was in the rare collection of Sir Ashton Lever, knight.

A few years ago, in sinking a cellar in an old house in Church Street, great quantities of fragments of Roman earthenware were thrown out, urns, pateræ, &c. many of them finely glazed and elegantly marked with emblematic figures. Also some copper coins were found, and an entire lamp with a turned-up perforated handle to hang it by, the nozzle of which was black from use. At the depth of 2 yds were likewise discovered a great number of human bones, with burned ashes, a wall of great thickness and a well filled with rubbish of the same kind, probably leading to a vault where other human remains were deposited; but the curious must for ever regret that no further search was made into its use and contents.

What throws new light upon the station here is the late discovery of a Roman pottery, at Quarmoor, near Lancaster.[21] That these works have been very considerable may be supported from the space discoloured with broken ware, the holes from whence the clay has been taken, and the great variety of bricks, tiles and vessels that are found about them. But the greatest discovery is gathered from a tile with turned-up edges, impressed on each end with the words *Ale Sebusia*, which points out a wing of cavalry not heard of before. The same inscription is found on bricks, the label smaller and the letters *Ala Sebusia*. The shape of the second letter in the first word is like that in the inscription on the rock near Brampton, in Cumberland, supposed to have been cut in the time of the Emperor Severus, ad 207, and is the fifth L in Horsley's Alphabet.[22] On the brick the letters are square, from which it may be inferred that this wing was long stationed at Lancaster.

The town of Lancaster

This town, ever since the conquest, has been renowned for loyalty and attachment to established government; for which King John honoured it with as ample a charter as he had conferred on the burgesses of Bristol and Northampton. Charles II confirmed it with additional privileges. But Lancaster derived its greatest lustre and importance from the title it gave to Edmund, second son of Henry III, and to his issue, Dukes of Lancaster and Kings of England of the Lancastrian line. In the end, however, it suffered much by supporting their title to the crown in the contest with the house of York. And so little had it retrieved itself when Camden visited it in 1609, that he speaks of it as not populous, and that the inhabitants were all husbandmen. Since that time it is, however, much enlarged.*

The new houses are particularly neat and handsome; the streets are well-paved and thronged with inhabitants, busied in a prosperous trade to the West Indies and other places. Along a fine quay, noble warehouses are built. And when it shall please those concerned to deepen the shoals in the river, ships of great burthen may lie before them; for at present we only see, in that part of the river, such as do not exceed 250 tons.

The air of Lancaster is salubrious, the environs pleasant, the inhabitants wealthy, courteous, hospitable and polite. The church is a handsome Gothic structure, but the inside view of the beautiful east window is obstructed by a tall screen behind the altar, and the rest of the church is further hurt by its multiplicity of pews. The only remains it has of ancient furniture are a few turn-up seats, carved in the style of the times when it belonged to the priory of St Martin of Sayes, in France. Some of the carvings are fine, but the figures are either gross or

* The town has continued to increase. It has also been lately ornamented with a new town hall, or exchange, esteemed a handsome building, with a noble portico. An elegant steeple has been also lately built to the chapel (after a design of Mr Harrison) by a donation of the late Mr T. Bowes, which, with the turret on the exchange, adds much to the pleasing or rather striking appearance this town has at a distance, on account of the castle, church and the conspicuous situation of several good stone houses.

grotesque. This building stands on the crown of an eminence, below the castle, from which it is only separated by the moat. The views from the churchyard are extensive and pleasant, particularly the grand and much admired prospects of the northern mountains.

The chapel is a neat and convenient place of worship. There are also in this town presbiterian, quaker and methodist meeting houses, and a Romish chapel. When the present incommodious bridge was lately repaired, some brass pieces of money were met with under a foundation stone, from which it was conjectured to be of Danish origin. A more ancient bridge stood higher up the river, at Skerton town end—an eligible situation for a new one, which would make a fine and convenient entrance into Lancaster from the north, and which at present on many accounts it much wants.†[23]

Vale of Lonsdale: the prospect

Before you leave Lancaster, take a ride to the three-mile stone on the road to Hornby, and there have Mr Gray's noble view of the vale of Lonsdale, which he or his editor describes in these words, in the note, page 373 of his life.[24]

> This scene opens just three miles from Lancaster, on what is called the Queen's road. To see this view in perfection you must go into a field on the left.‡ Here, Ingleborough, behind a variety of lesser mountains, makes the background of the prospect; on each hand of the middle distance rise two sloping hills, the left clothed with thick wood, the right with variegated rock and herbage. Between them is the richest of valleys: the Lune serpentizes for many a mile, and comes forth ample and clear through a well-wooded and richly pastured foreground. Every feature which constitutes a perfect landscape of the extensive sort is here not only boldly marked, but also in its best position.

Crossing the sands

From Lancaster to Hest Bank, 3 miles: set out with the Ulverston carriers at the stated hour, or take a guide for the sands that succeed, called Lancaster Sands¶ and which are 9 miles over.* On a fine day there is not a more pleasant seaside ride in the kingdom.[25]

But those who wish to evade them may easily go in one day round to Ulverston by the head of estuary. The roads are in general very good, the ride about 37 miles and not wanting in the natural variety peculiar to the country. The route will be thus: From Lancaster to Burton 11 miles. (There observe Mr Atkinson's neat house of freestone. The odd venerable building on the right hand of the road, about two miles short of Burton, is Borwick Hall, formerly the residence of Sir Robert Bindloss, but now

Thomas West, A Guide to the Lakes

18

† A new bridge has since been erected on the site above pointed out. It is built after a design of Mr Harrison, consists of five equal elliptical arches, and is 549 ft long. The expense of the erection, which was paid by the county, amounted to £14,000. It is one of the handsomest bridges of its size in Europe, and does honour to the taste of the architect and to the public spirit of those who promoted the work on so liberal a plan.

In the year 1792 an act was obtained, chiefly promoted by the inhabitants of Lancaster, for making a navigable canal from Kendal, by way of Lancaster and Preston, to go through the great coal countries in the neighbourhood of Chorley and Wigan, and to join the canals in the south of Lancashire, its principal design being for the carriage of limestone and slate from the north, and to return with coals. It is carried over the River Lune by the largest aqueduct in the kingdom, which is an amazing grand object and is seen to advantage from Lancaster bridge, about two miles off.

‡ As several mistakes have been made respecting this station, it is necessary to point it out more precisely. About a quarter of a mile beyond the third milestone, where the road makes a turn to the right, there is a gate on the left which leads into a field, where the station meant will be found.

only a farmhouse.) From thence to Milnthorpe, 4 miles. (There see Dallam Tower, the seat of Daniel Wilson esquire, in which there are several elegancies and more capabilities. Also, see a bold waterfall of the river at Beetham Mill.) From Milnthorpe to Levens (an ancient seat of the Earl of Suffolk, where a curious specimen of the old style of gardening may be seen, as laid out by the gardener of King James II), 2 miles. From thence to the nearer end of the long causeway at Beathwaite Green, 1 mile.

Thence to the Black Bull in Witherslack, 3 miles (which takes you to the foot of Whitbarrow Scar, a remarkable precipice of limestone rock, formed in several places like a fortress). Thence to Newton (over the hill Tawtop), 4 miles. Thence to Newby Bridge, 3 miles, which is situated at the lower end of Windermere Water. From thence to Bouth, on the common turnpike, 3 miles. (But it might be worthwhile to go a little out of the way through the valley on the left hand, by Backbarrow cotton-spinning mills, the iron foundries and Low wood gunpowder mills, which are very romantically situated.) From Bouth to Penny Bridge, 2 miles, which there brings you into the tract of the tour by Ulverston, now only 4 miles distant.

If, on account of getting post-chaises &c., it be thought more convenient to go by Kendal to Ulverston, the journey will be about 7 miles more, all good turnpike road. From Burton (where the two roads part) to Kendal is 11 miles, and from Kendal to the above named Newby Bridge (where they meet again) is about 13 miles. This latter stage, which is mountainous and uneven, affords a great variety of prospects.

On the right a bold shore, deeply indented in some places and opening into bays in others; valleys that stretch far into the country, bounded on each side by hanging grounds cut into inclosures, interspersed with groves and woods, adorned with sequestered cots, farms, villages, churches and castles; mountains behind mountains, and others again just seen over them, close the fore scene. Claude has not introduced Soracte on the Tiber in a more happy point of view than Ingleborough appears in during the course of this ride.

At entering on the sands, to the left, Heysham Point rises abruptly and the village hangs on its side in a beautiful manner. Over a vast extent of sands Peel Castle, the ancient bulwark of the bay, rears its venerable head above the tide. In front appears a fine sweep of country sloping to the south. To the right, Warton Crag presents itself in a bold style. On its arched summit are the vestiges of a square encampment and the ruins of a beacon. Grounds—bearing from the eye for many a mile, variegated in every pleasing form by woods and rocks—are terminated by cloud-topped Ingleborough. A little further, on the same hand, another vale opens to the sands and throws a broken ridge of rocks, and beyond them groups of mountains towering to the sky. Castle Steads, a pyramidal hillthat rises above the station at Kendal, is now in sight. At the bottom of the bay stands Arnside Tower, once a mansion of the Stanleys.

¶ *Morecambe*, Ptol.

* Along with the proper guides, crossing of the sands in summer is thought a journey of little more danger than any other.

The Cartmel coast, now as you advance, becomes more pleasing. Betwixt that and Silverdale Nab (a mountain of naked grey rock) is a great break in the coast, and through the opening the River Kent rolls its waters to join the tide. In the mouth of the estuary are two beautiful conical isles, clothed with wood and sweet verdure. As you advance towards them, they seem to change their position and hence often vary their appearance. At the same time a grand view opens of the Westmorland mountains, tumbled about in a most surprising manner. At the head of the estuary, under a beautiful green hill, Heversham village and church appear in fine perspective. To the north, Whitbarrow Scar, a huge arched and bended cliff of an immense height, shows its storm beaten front.†
The intermediate space is a mixture of rocks and woods, and cultivated patches, that form a romantic view.‡

[Mr Cockin adds:]²⁶

> What most attracts the notice of the traveller is not the objects of the surrounding country (though they are fine) but the sands themselves. For when he has got a few miles from the shore, the nature of the plain on which he treads cannot but suggest a series of ideas of a more sublime kind than those of rural elegance, which will therefore gain a superior attention. The plain is then seemingly immense in extent, continued on in a dead level, and uniform in appearance.
>
> As he pursues his often trackless way, he will recollect that, probably but a few hours before, the whole expanse was covered with some fathoms of water, and that in a few more it will as certainly be covered again. At the same time he may also perceive, on his left hand, the retreated ocean ready to obey the mysterious laws of its irresistible movement without any visible barrier to stay it a moment where it is. These last considerations, though they may not be sufficient to alarm, must yet be able to rouse the mind to a state of more than ordinary attention; which, co-operating with the other singular ideas of the prospect, must affect it in a very sublime and unfamiliar manner. This the bare appearance of the sands will do.
>
> But when the traveller reaches the side of the Eau, these affections will be greatly increased. He there drops down a gentle descent to the edge of a broad and seemingly impassable river, where the only remains he can perceive of surrounding lands are the tops of distant mountains, and where a solitary being on horseback (like some ancient genius of the deep) is described hovering on its brink, or encountering its stream with gentle steps, in order to conduct him through it.
>
> When fairly entered into the water, if a stranger to this scene and he does not feel himself touched with some of the most pleasing emotions, I should consider him destitute of common sensibility.

† A little to the left of Whitbarrow is Castle Head, belonging to John Wilkinson esquire. The site is something curious, and the owner has made great improvements in the grounds about it. The house is seen to advantage as you cross the sands, and greatly enlivens the part of the coast where it is situated.

‡ The above description of this curious and pleasing ride is, as far as it goes, just, but not characteristic. [Wm Cockin]

For, in the midst of apparently great danger, he will soon find that there is really none at all; and the complacency which must naturally result from this consideration will be highlighted to an unusual degree by observing, during his passage, the anxious and faithful instinct of his beast and the friendly behaviour and aspect of his guide. All the fervours of grateful thankfulness will then be raised and if, with the useful perquisite to his venerable conductor, he can forget to convey his blessing, who would not conclude him to want one essential requisite for properly enjoying the tour of the lakes?

Having crossed the river, the stranger traveller (whom we will suppose at length freed from any petty anxiety) will now have more inclination to survey the objects around him. The several particulars peculiar to an arm of the sea (as fishermen, ships, sea-fowl, shells, weeds &c.) will attract his notice and new-model his reflections. But, if the sun shine forcibly, he will perhaps be most entertained with observing the little gay isles and promontories of land, that seem to hover in the air, or swim on a luminous vapour, that rises from the sand and fluctuates beautifully on its surface

In short, on a fine summer day, a ride across the estuary (and that of Leven mentioned a little further on) to a speculative stranger (or to anyone who is habituated to consider the charms of nature abstractedly) will afford a variety of most entertaining ideas. Indeed, the objects here presented to the eye are several of them so like in kind to what will frequently occur in the tour of the lakes, some of them are so much more magnificent from extent, and others so truly peculiar, that it seems rather surprising that this journey should not be considered by travellers from the south as one of the first curiosities of the tour, in beauty as well as occurrence.

And if the reader of this note be of a philosophic turn, this question may perhaps here offer itself to him and to which it is apprehended he may found a satisfactory answer on very evident principles, viz "Why a view so circumstanced as this and, when taken from the shore at full sea, so very like a lake of greater apparent extent than any in the kingdom, should never be brought into comparison with the lakes to be visited afterwards, and generally fail to strike the mind with images of any peculiar beauty or grandeur?"

At the side of the Eau¶ or river of the sands, a guide on horseback called the carter is in waiting to conduct passengers over the ford. The priory of Cartmel was charged with this important office, and had synodals and Peter's pence[27] allowed towards its maintenance. Since the dissolution of the priory, it is held by patent of the Duchy of Lancaster, and the salary, £20 per annum, is paid by the receiver general.

¶ Pronounced commonly Eea.

Cartmel

Cartmel is a small district belonging to Lancashire, but united to
Westmorland a little below Bowness, on Windermere Water, from
whence it extends itself betwixt the rivers Leven and Kent, and so
intersects the great bay at Morecambe. It is three miles across from
Cark Lane, where you quit the sands, to Sandgate. Pass through
Flookburgh,*[28] once a market town, by charter granted to the Prior
of Cartmel, lord paramount, from King Edward I.

The only thing worthy of notice in Cartmel is the church, a
handsome Gothic edifice. The large east window† is finely ribbed
with pointed arches, light and elegant; but the painted glass is almost
all destroyed. The preservation of this edifice reflects honour on the
memory of George Preston esquire of Holker, who at his own expense
new-roofed the whole and decorated the inside with a stucco ceiling.
The choir and chancel he also repaired, suiting the new parts to the
old remains of the canon's coats, and thereby giving them their ancient
uniform appearance. Persons uninformed of this always take it to be the
same as it was before the dissolution. The style of the building, like most
of its contemporaries, is irregular. The form is a cross, in length 157 ft;
the transept 110 ft; the height of the walls 57 ft. The tower on the centre
is of a singular construction, being a square within a square, the higher
set at cross angles with the lower. This gives it an odd appearance on all
sides, but may have some reference to the octagonal pillars in the church,
and both to the memory of something now forgotten.

According to some accounts, it was built and endowed with the
manor of Cartmel, by William Marischal the elder, Earl of Pembroke,
in 1188, but as in the foundation deed mention is made of Henry II,
Richard and Henry the younger, his lord the King, it appears rather to
have been founded in the beginning of that reign; for William the elder,
Earl of Pembroke, died in the fourth or fifth year of the reign of Henry
III. He gave it, never to be erected into an abbey, to the canons regular of
St Austin, reserving to himself and his heirs the right of granting them the
congé d'lire of a prior, who should be independent of all others. Under the
north wall, a little below the altar, is the tombstone of William de Walton,
Prior of Cartmel. He is mentioned in the confirmation diploma of Edward
II, and must have been one of the first priors.

Opposite to this is a magnificent tomb of a Harrington and his lady,
which Mr Pennant thinks may be of Sir John Harrington, who in 1305
was summoned by Edward I, "with numbers of other gallant gentlemen,
to meet him at Carlisle, and attend him on his expedition into Scotland".
But it agrees better with a John de Harrington, called John of Cartmel,
or his son, of Wraysholme Tower in Cartmel, as Sir Daniel Fleming's
account[29] of that family has it.‡ The head of the Harrington family,
Sir John Harrington, in the reign of Edward I, was of Aldingham, and
lived at Gleaston Castle in Furness, and died in an advanced age in 1347;
and is more probably the Sir John Harrington mentioned in Dugdale's

Baronage,[30] and said, as above, to be summoned by Edward I. There is not one vestige of the monastery remaining. There is indeed an ancient gatehouse, but whether this was connected with the cloisters or not, tradition is silent, and its distance from the church is unfavourable to the conjecture.

By Holker and Leven Sands

Proceed through rocky fields and groves to Holker, one mile, the seat of the Right Honourable Lord George Cavendish. The carriage road is by Cark Hall. At the top of the hill there opens a fine view of Furness. Holker Hall lies at your feet, embosomed in wood. On the left, Ulverston Bay opens into the great bay, and is three miles over. The coast is deeply indented, and the peninsulas are beautifully fringed with wood. On the right, a bold bending rock presents a noble arched forehead; and a fine slope of enclosed grounds, mixed with wood, leads the eye to Ulverston, the port and mart of Furness.

Conishead shows its pyramidal head, completely clothed in woods. At its feet is the priory, shielded by a wing of hanging wood, that climbs up the side of a steep hill. Bardsea, under its rocks and hanging woods, stands in a delightful point of view. In front, a sweet fall of enclosures, marked with clumps of trees and hedgerows, gives it a most picturesque effect. Also a white house on the sea bank, under the cover of a deep wood, has a most enchanting appearance. The coast from thence is of singular beauty, consisting of hanging wood, enclosed lands and pasture grounds, varied through a great extent of prospect in every pleasing form.

Descend to Holker, which adds to the surrounding scenes what is peculiar to itself, joined to the improvements of the noble owner, finished in a masterly style.¶[31] The traveller will here observe husbandry in a more flourishing situation than in the country he is soon to visit. The husbandmen in this part, as elsewhere, are slow in imitating new practices; but the continued success which has attended the improvements on his lordship's estates, has not failed to effect a reformation amongst the Cartmel farmers.

In crossing Leven Sands to Ulverston, you have on the right a grand view of alpine scenery. A rocky hill patched with wood and heath, rising immediately from the coast, directs the eye to an immense chain of lofty mountains, apparently increased in magnitude and height since they were seen from Hest Bank. On a fine morning this is a pleasant ride, when the mountains are strongly illuminated by the sunbeams and patched with shadows of intervening clouds that fall along their sides; or when they drag their watery skirts over the summits, and, admitting the streaming beams, adorn their rocky heads with silver, and variegate their olive-coloured sides with stripes of gold and green. This fairy scene soon shifting, all is concealed in a mantle of azure mist.

¶ The connoisseur in painting may here have the pleasure of seeing a good collection of pictures; amongst which are by Claude Lorrain, a very capital landscape, exhibiting a view of the Tiber, with the temple of Apollo, the nine muses &c., another representing the departure out of Egypt, and two small views. Also a large landscape by Rubens; two fine church pieces by B Neess (the figures by Elshamer); and several others by Woverman, Hobina, Teniers, Swanevelt, Zuccarelli, Rysdal and other eminent masters.

At the Eau, or ford of the River Leven, another carter conducts you over. On the dissolution of the Priory of Conishead, King Henry VIII charged himself and his successors with the payment of the salary, 15 marks per annum, which the guide received from the priory.

Ulverston

Ulverston, the London of Furness, is a neat town, at the foot of a swift descent of hills to the south-east. The streets are regular, and excellently well paved. The weekly market for Low Furness has been long established here, to the prejudice of Dalton, the ancient capital of Furness. The articles of export are iron ore in great quantities, pig- and bar-iron, oats, barley, beans, potatoes, bark and limestone. The principal inns are kept by the guides, who regularly pass to and from Lancaster, on Sunday, Tuesday and Friday in every week.

Make an excursion to the west, three miles, and visit the greatest iron-mines in England. At Whitriggs the works are carried on with much spirit, by driving of levels into the bosom of the mountain. The ore is found in a limestone stratum mixed with a variety of spars of a dirty colour. There is much quartz in some of the works, that admits of a high polish. At present the works in Stone Close and Aldgarly are the most flourishing that have been known in Furness. This mineral is not hurtful to any animal or vegetable. The verdure is remarkably fine about the workings, and no one ever suffered by drinking the water in the mines, though discoloured and much impregnated with the ore.

Furness Abbey

Proceed by Dalton to the magnificent ruins of Furness Abbey, and there

> See the wild waste of all devouring years,
> How Rome her own sad sepulchre appears,
> With nodding arches, broken temples spread,
> The very tombs now vanish like the dead.[32]

This abbey was founded by Stephen, Earl of Mortaign and Boulogne, afterwards King of England, AD 1127, and was endowed with the lordship of Furness and many royal privileges. It was peopled from the monastery of Savigny in Normandy, and dedicated to St Mary. In ancient writings it is styled "St Marye's of Furness". The monks were of the order of Savigny, and their dress was grey cloth; but on receiving St Bernard's form, they changed from grey to white, and became Cistercians; and such they remained till the dissolution of the monasteries.

The situation of this abbey, so favourable to a contemplative life, justified the choice of the first settlers. Such a sheltered site, in the bottom of a deep dell, through which a hasty brook rolls its murmuring stream, and along which the roaring west wind would often blow, joined with the deep-toned matin song, must have been very favourable to the solemn melancholy of a monastic life.

To prevent surprise and call in assistance, a beacon was placed on the crown of an eminence that rises immediately from the abbey, and is seen all over Low Furness. The door leading to the beacon is still remaining in the enclosure wall on the eastern side. The magnitude of the abbey may be known from the dimensions of the ruins; and enough is standing to show the style of the architecture. The round and pointed arches occur in the doors and windows. The fine clustered Gothic, and the heavy plain Saxon pillars stand contrasted. The walls show excellent masonry, are in many places counter-arched, and the ruins discover a strong cement. The east window has been noble; and some of the painted glass that once adorned it, is preserved in a window in Windermere church.

On the outside of the window, under an arched festoon, is the head of the founder, and opposite to it that of Maud his queen, both crowned and well executed. In the fourth wall, and east end of the church, are four seats adorned with Gothic ornaments. In these the officiating priest, with his attendants, sat at intervals during the solemn service of high mass. In the middle space, where the first barons of Kendal are interred, lies a procumbent figure of a man in armour, cross-legged.

The chapter house has been a noble room of 60 ft by 45. The vaulted roof, formed of twelve ribbed arches, was supported by six pillars on two rows, at 13 ft distance from each other. Now supposing each of the pillars to be 2 ft in diameter, the room would be divided into three alleys or passages each 13 ft wide. On entrance, the middle one only could be seen, lighted by a pair of tall pointed windows at the upper end of the room; the company in the side passage would be concealed by the pillars, and the vaulted roof, that groined from those pillars, would have a truly Gothic disproportionate appearance of 60 ft by 13.

The two side alleys were lighted, each by a pair of similar lights, besides another pair at the upper end, at present entire, and which illustrate what is here said. Thus, whilst the upper end of the room had a profusion of light, the lower end would be in the shade. The noble roof of this singular edifice did but lately fall in, and the entrance or porch is still standing, a fine circular arch, beautified with a deep cornice and a portico on each side. The only entire roof now remaining is of a building without the enclosure wall. It was the schoolhouse of the abbot's tenants, and is a single ribbed arch that groins from the wall.

There is a general disproportion remarkable in Gothic churches, which must have originated in some effect intended by all the architects; perhaps to strike the mind with reverential awe, at the sight of magnificence arising from the vastness of two dimensions, and a third seemingly disregarded; or perhaps such a determinate height and length was found more favourable than any other to the church song, by giving a deeper swell to the choir of chanting monks.

A remarkable deformity in this edifice, and for which there is no apparent reason or necessity, is that the north door, which is the principal entrance, is on one side of the window above it. The tower has been supported by four magnificent arches of which only one remains entire. They rested upon four tall pillars, whereof three are finely clustered, but the fourth is of a plain, unmeaning construction.

Furness

From the abbey, if on horseback, return by Newton, Stainton and Adgarly. See on the right a deep embayed coast, the islands of Walney and Foulney, Peel Castle and a variety of extensive views on all sides. At Adgarly the new iron ore works are carried on under the old workings. The richest ore is found here in immense quantities; 140 tons have been raised at one shaft in 24 hours. To the right, you have a view of the ruins of Gleaston Castle, the seat of the Flemings soon after the conquest, which by a succession of marriages went to Cansfield, then to Harrington, who enjoyed it six descents, after that to Bonville, and lastly to Gray; and was forfeited by Henry Gray, Duke of Suffolk, AD 1559.

Leaving Urswick behind, ascend Birkrigg, a rocky eminence, and from the beacon have a variety of extensive and pleasant views of land and sea, mountains and islands. Ulverston appears to the north-east, seated under a hanging wood, and beyond that Furness Fells in various shapes form the grandest termination that can be imagined. The back view is the reverse of this. When the tide is up, you see a fine arm of the sea stretching far within land, terminated by bold rocks and steep shores. Beyond this expanse, a far country is seen, and Lancaster town and castle, in a fine point of view, under a screen of high grounds, over which sable Clougha rears his venerable head. Ingleborough, behind many other mountains, has a fine effect from this station.

If in a carriage, return from the abbey by Dalton. This village is finely situated on the crest of a rocky eminence, sloping to the morning sun. At the upper end is a square tower, where formerly the abbot held his secular court, and secured his prisoners. The keep is in the bottom of the tower, and is a dismal dungeon.

Conishead Priory

Return to Ulverston, and from thence to the priory of Conishead, the paradise of Furness; a Mount Edgcumbe in miniature,[33] which well deserves a visit from the curious traveller. The house stands on the site of the priory of Conishead, at the foot of a fine eminence, and the ground falls gently from it on all sides. The slopes are planted with shrubs and trees in such a manner as to improve the elevation; and the waving woods that fly from it on each wing give it an airy and noble appearance. The south front is in the modern taste, extended by an arcade. The north is in the Gothic style, with a piazza and wings. The apartments are elegantly furnished, and the house is good and convenient.

But what recommends itself most to the curious is a plan of pleasure ground, on a small scale, containing beauties equal in number to gardens of the greatest extent in England. The variety of culminated grounds and winding slopes comprehended within this sweet spot furnish all the advantage of mountains and vales, woods and water. By the judicious management of these assemblages, the late owner performed wonders. Consulting the genius of the place, he called in, to aid his plan, and harmonized to this little spot, the features of a country vast in extend, and by nature highly picturesque* whose distant parts agreeing with what was immediately near him, form a most magnificent whole.

* The note intended for this place proving too long, it is inserted in the Addenda, and makes Article VIII. [Wm Cockin]

For, besides the ornamental grounds, the views from the house are both pleasing and surprising. They are at once grand and elegant, rural and marine. On the eastern side, you have a fine estuary, spotted with rocks, isles and peninsulas, a variety of shore, deeply indented in some places, in others composed of noble arched rocks, craggy, broken and fringed with wood; over these, hanging woods, intermixed with cultivated enclosures, covered with a background of stupendous mountains. As a contrast to this view, from the other end of the gravel walk (between two culminating hills, covered with tall wood) is seen, in fine perspective, a rich cultivated dale divided by hedgerow trees; beyond these, hanging grounds cut into enclosures, with scattered farms, and above them all a long range of waving pasture ground and sheep walks, shining in variety of vegetation. This sweet pastoral picture is much heightened by the deep shade of the towering, wooded hills, between which it is viewed.

Turn to the left, the scenery is all reversed. Under a range of tall sycamores, an example of water bursts upon the eye, and beyond it land just visible through the azure mist. Vessels traversing this bay are also seen in a most picturesque manner and, from the lower part of the house, appear sailing through the trees and approaching it till they drop anchor just under the windows. The range of sycamores has a fine effect in this sea view, by breaking the line in the watering plain and forming an elegant frame to a very excellent picture. By turning a little to the right, the prospect changes. At the head of a sloping enclosure and under the skirts of a steep wood, a sequestered cottage stands in the nicest point of beauty.

There is a great variety of pleasing views from the different meandering walks and seats in the wood: one at the hermitage, and another at the seat in the bottom of the wood, where Ulverston and the environs make a pretty picture. From under the shrubbery (on the eastern side of the house, and from the gate at the north end of the walk, behind the swell of green hills), if the afternoon sun shine, the conical summits of distant mountains are seen glistening like burnished gold and pointing to the heavens in noble style. But as this sweet spot is injured by description, I shall only add, that it is a great omission in the curious traveller to be in Furness and not to see so wonderfully pretty a place, to which nature has been so profuse in noble gifts and where art has lent its best assistance, under the regulation of an elegant fancy and refined taste.†

> Here hills and vales, the woodland and the plain,
> Here earth and water seem to strive again;
> Not chaos like, together crush'd and bruis'd,
> But, as the world, harmoniously confus'd.

Coniston

From Ulverston to Coniston water is 8 miles, either by Penny Bridge or by Lowick, both excellent carriage roads.‡ By Lowick the road is along a narrow vale, beautifully divided by hanging enclosures and scattered farms, halfway up the mountains' sides, whose various heads are covered with heath and brown vegetation. About three miles from Ulverston, observe a farmhouse on the left—stop at the gate[34] on the brow of the hill and have a distant view of the lake, finely intersected with high-crowned peninsulas. At the upper end, a snow-white house is seen, under a hanging wood, and to the north-east the lake seems to wind round the mountain's feet. The whole range of Coniston Fells is now in sight, and under them a lower sweep of dark rocks frown over the crystal surface of the lake.

Advancing on the left see Lowick Hall, once the seat of a family of that name. Behind this a dismal scene of barrenness presents itself; clustered grey rocky mountains, variegated with some few stripes of heath. After crossing the outlet of the lake, at Lowick Bridge, these dreary objects are found often intercepted by pieces of arable ground, hanging sweetly to the east and prettily situated under ancient oaks or venerable yews. The white houses in these parts, covered with blue slate, have a neat appearance. The thatched cot is esteemed a more picturesque object; and yet the other kind, seen under a deep green wood or covered with a purple background of heath, has a pleasing effect.

Reach the south end of the lake. Here it is narrowed by rocky prominences from both sides, forming between their curvatures, a variety of pretty bays. The whole length of the lake is about six measured miles, and the greatest breadth about three quarters of a mile. The greatest depth, by report, exceeds not 40 fathoms. A little higher the broadest part commences, and stretches, with small curvatures, to Waterhead. The shores are frequently indented, and one pretty bay opens after another in a variety of forms.

Station I[35]

A little above the village of Nibthwaite, the lake opens in full view. From the rock on the left of the road, you have a general prospect of the lake upwards. This station is found by observing where you have a hanging rock over the road on the east, and an ash tree on the west side of the road. On the opposite shore, to the left, and close by the water's edge, are some stripes of meadow and green ground, cut into small inclosures, with some dark-coloured houses under aged yew trees. Two promontories project a great way into the lake; the broadest is finely terminated by steep rocks and crowned with wood; and both are insulated when the lake is high. Upwards, over a fine sheet of water, the lake is again intersected by a far-projecting promontory, that swells into two eminences, and betwixt them the lake is again caught, with some white houses at the feet of the mountains. And more to the right, over another headland, you catch a fourth view of the lake, twisting to the north-east. Almost opposite to this station, stands a house, on the crown of a rock covered with ancient trees, that has a most romantic appearance.

The noble scenery increases as you ride along the banks. In some places, bold rocks (lately covered with wood) conceal the lake entirely, and when the winds blow, the beating of surges is heard just under you. In other places, abrupt openings show the lake anew, and there, when calm, its limpid surface shining like a crystal mirror reflects the azure sky or its dappled clouds, in the finest mixture of nature's clare-obscure. On the western side, the shore is more variegated with small inclosures, scattered cots, groves and meadows.

The road continues along the eastern banks of the lake; here bare, there sweetly fringed with a few tall trees, the small remains of its ancient woods that till lately clothed the whole.

Station II[36]

When you are opposite to the peninsula last described, proceed through a gate on the left hand. And from the rocky eminence you have a general view of the lake, both ways. To the south, a sweet bay is formed between the horns of two peninsulas, and beyond that a fine sheet of water appears, terminated by the promontories which form the straits, through which the lake has its outlet. From thence the coast is beautifully diversified by a number of green eminences crowned with wood and sequestered cottages interspersed among them, half concealed by yew trees; and, above them, a wave of rocky, spiral mountains, dressed in brown vegetation, form the most romantic scenes.

Between this and a wooded eminence, a green hill, cut into inclosures to the very top, in some parts patched with rock and little groves, has a beautiful appearance, especially when contrasted with the barren scenes on one hand and the deep shade of a waving wood on the other. At the foot of this cultivated tract, and on the margin of the lake, a few white houses, partly concealed in a grove, look like enchanted seats on fairy ground. Behind these, a barren bleak mountain frowns in sullen majesty, and down his furrowed side the Black Beck of Torver rolls its fretted torrent.

Just at your feet lies the oblong rocky isle of Peel; and near it the dark points of half-immersed rocks just show themselves by turns. Here is the finest picture of the lake, and when it is smooth the whole is seen reflected on the shining surface of the watery mirror. On the western side the coast is steep rocks. The eastern side is much embayed. The high end of the lake is here in view, yet it seems to wind both ways behind the opposite promontories. The range of naked rocks that cross the head of the lake appear now awful, from their sable hue, and behind them the immense mass of Cove, Rydal Head and many nameless mountains have a most stupendous appearance, and seemingly inaccessible height.

A succession of pretty bays open to the traveller as he advances; the banks become more wooded, and more cultivation appears. On the western margin stands the lady of the lake, Coniston Hall, concealed in a grove of tall trees, and above it the village of the same name. The hall has only changed masters twice since the conquest, and has belonged to the family of Fleming most of the time.

Station III[37]

After crossing the common, where grows a picturesque yew tree on the right hand, and a small peninsula rushes into the lake on the left, crowned with a single tree, enter the grove, and pass a gate and bridge that crosses a small rivulet. Look for a fragment of dark-coloured rock on the margin of the water, and near it will be found the best stand for the artist to take the finest view on the lake.

Looking across the lake, by the south end of the grove that conceals Coniston Hall and over the cultivated tract that rises behind it, between two swells of rocks a cataract will meet the eye, issuing from the bosom of the mountains. The side ground on the right is a wooded sloping rock, and over it the road is catched slanting along. The near foreground is the greatest extent of the lake; and, behind the immediate mountains, the Westmorland fells are seen towering to the clouds. This station will be found, by company coming down the lake, at the circular bay where the road first joins the level of the water.

The next grand view is had in the boat, and from the centre of the lake, opposite to Coniston Hall.[38] Looking towards the mountains, the lake spreads itself into a noble expanse of transparent water and bursts into a bay on each side, bordered with verdant meadows and inclosed with a variety of grounds, rising in an exceedingly bold manner. The objects are beautifully diversified amongst themselves, and contrasted by the finest exhibition of rural elegance (cultivation and pasturage, waving woods and sloping inclosures, adorned by nature and improved by art) under the bold sides of stupendous mountains, whose airy summits the elevated eye cannot now reach, and which almost deny access to human kind.

Following the line of shore from Coniston Hall to the upper end of the lake, the village of Coniston is in full view and consists of seats, groups of houses, farms and cots, scattered in a picturesque manner over the cultivated slope. Some are snow-white, others grey; some stand forth on bold eminences at the head of green inclosures, backed with steep woods; others are pitched on sweet declivities and seem hanging in the air; some again are on a level with the lake; and all are neatly covered with blue slate, the ornamental yews, hollies and tall pines or firs. This is a charming scene, when the morning sun tinges the whole with a variety of tints. In the point of beauty and centre of perspective, a white house, under a hanging wood, gives life to this picture. Here a range of dark rugged rocks rise abruptly, and deeply contrast the transparent surface of the lake and the stripe of verdure that skirts their feet. The eastern shore is not less bold and embayed.¶

It will be allowed that the views on this lake are beautiful and picturesque, yet they please more than surprise. The hills that immediately inclose the lake are ornamental, but humble. The mountains at the head of the lake are great, noble and sublime, without anything that is horrid or terrible. They are bold and steep, without the projecting precipice, the overhanging rock or pendant cliff. The hanging woods, waving inclosures and airy sites are elegant, beautiful and picturesque; and the whole may be seen with ease and pleasure. In a fine morning, there is not a more pleasant rural ride; and then the beauties of the lake are seen to the most advantage. In the afternoon, if the sun shines, much of the effect is lost by the change of light; and such as visit it from the north lose all the charms arising from the swell of mountains by turning their backs upon them.

The feeder of this lake, besides the Black Beck of Torver, is Coniston Beck. It descends from the mountains, or rather is precipitated, in a short course to the lake, which it enters on the western canton in a clear stream, concealed by its banks. The lake bends away to the east, and its immediate shore is a beach of pebble and sand. This beach is adorned with a cot, set under a full-topped tree. The char here are said to be the finest in England. They are taken later than on Windermere, and continue longer in the spring.

At Waterhead,* the road to the east leads to Ambleside, 8 miles; to Hawkshead, 3 miles. Ascend a steep hill surrounded with wood, and have a back view of the lake.[39] To the north is a most awful scene of mountains heaped upon mountains, in every variety of horrid shape. Amongst them sweeps to the north a deep winding charm, darkened by overhanging rocks, that the eye cannot pierce, nor the imagination fathom; from which turn your face to the east, and you have a view

¶ The slate brought down from the mountains is laid up here, till put on board boats that transport it to the waterfoot.

* A little to the west, and at the north end of the lake, stands the house of the late George Knott esquire, who made many handsome improvements on his estate here, which contrasted with the native rudeness of the surrounding hills have a pleasing effect.

of some part of Windermere. The road soon divides; the left leads to Ambleside, the right to Hawkshead, which stands under a mountain at the upper end of a narrow valley. The church is seated on the front of an eminence that commands the vale, which is floated with

Esthwaite Water

Two miles in length and half a mile in breadth, intersected by a peninsula from each side, jutting far into the lake, finely elevated, crowned with cultivation, and bordered with fringed trees and coppice wood. The lake is encompassed with a good carriage road, and over its outlet is a narrow stone bridge. On the banks are villages and scattered houses, sweetly situated under woods and hanging grounds, enamelled with delightful verdure and soft vegetation; all which is heightened by the deep shade of the woods and the strong background of rocky mountains. At the head of a gentle slope, with a just elevation, a handsome modern house, Belmount, is charmingly situated and commands a delightful view of the lake with all its environs.

The fish here are perch, pike, eel, and trout. No char are found in this lake, though it is connected with Windermere.

From Hawkshead to Ambleside, 5 miles; to the horse ferry on Windermere, 4 miles. On horseback, this latter is the more eligible route, as it leads immediately to the centre of the lake where all its beauties are seen to the greatest advantage.

Windermere

Windermere Water, like that of Coniston, is viewed to the greatest advantage by facing the mountains, which rise in grandeur on the eye and swell upon the imagination as they are approached.

The road to the ferry is round the head of Esthwaite Water, through the villages of Colthouse and Sawreys. Ascend a steep hill, and from its summit have a view of a long reach of Windermere Water, stretching far to the south till lost between two high promontories. The road serpentizes round a rocky mountain, till you come under a broken scar, that in some places hangs over the way, and where ancient yews and hollows grow fantastically amongst the fallen rocks. This brings you soon to

Station I[40]

Near the isthmus of the ferry point.† In front, Rampsholme or Berkshire Island presents itself in all its length, clothed in wood. To the left, the ferry point—closing with Crow Holme, a wooded island—forms a fine promontory. Just behind this, the mountain retiring inward makes a semicircular bay, surrounded with a few acres of the most elegant

† This station is now sufficiently pointed out by the elegant building lately erected thereon, belonging to John Christian Curwen esquire and called The Station, which, with the

verdure, sloping upwards from the water's edge, graced with a cottage in the finest point of view. Above it, the mountain rises in an agreeable wildness, variegated with scattered trees and silver-grey rocks. An extent of water of 12 miles in circumference spreads itself to the north, frequently intersected with promontories or spotted with islands.

Amongst them, The Holme or Great Island, an oblong tract of 30 acres, traverses the lake in an oblique line, surrounded by a number of inferior isles, finely formed and dressed in wood. The pointed dark rocks of Curlew Crags appear above the water, and others just concealed give a sable hue to the part of the lake. Rough Holme is a circular isle, covered with trees. Lady Holme, where in ancient times stood an oratory, is an isle of oval form, vested with coppice-wood. Hen Holme is a rock covered with shrubs. Grass Holme is shaded with a grove of oaks. And two smaller isles borrow their names from the lilies of the valley, which decorate them. These, with Crow Holme and Berkshire Island, form this Archipelago.

To the north of this magnificent scene, a glorious sheet of water expands itself to the right and left, in curves bearing from the eye; bounded on the west by the continuation of the mountain where you stand, whose bold lofty side is embellished with growing trees, shrubs and coarse vegetation, intermixed with grey rocks that group finely with the deep green of yews and hollies.

The eastern view is a noble contrast to this, adorned with all that is beautiful, grand and sublime. The immediate space is much cultivated. The variety of hanging grounds are immense, consisting of woods, groves and inclosures, all terminated in rocky uplands of various forms. It spreads above in a beautiful variety of waving inclosures, intermixed with hanging woods and shrubby circular spots, overtopped with wild grounds and rocky ridges of broken mountains. In some places it swells into spacious bays, fringed with trees, whose bushy heads wave beautifully over the crystal waters. The parsonage house is seen sweetly seated under a range of tall firs.

Following the same line of shore above, the east ferry point and, on the banks of the bay, the tops of the houses and the church of Windermere are just seen. Above that, Bannerigg and Orresthead rise gradually into points, cultivated to the top and cut into inclosures. These are contrasted by the rugged craggs of Biscot How. Troutbeck Park comes next in view, and over that Hill Bell rears his comic top and Fairfield swells in alpine pride, rivalled only by Rydal's loftier head.

The eastern coast, to the south of what has been described, is still more pleasing in variety of little groves, interposed inclosures and scattered houses, sweetly secreted. To the south, and from the western coast at 3 miles distance, Rawlinson's Nab, a high crowned promontory, shoots far into the lake; and from the opposite shore you see the Storrs, another wooded promontory, stretching far into the water, pointing at the rocky isle of Ling Holme. Over Rawlinson's Nab, the lake spreads out in a magnificent sheet of water; and, following the winding shore far

improvements made in the Ferry House inn and grounds adjoining, renders it one of the most delightful places near the lake.

to the south, it seems lost behind a promontory on the eastern side. Over two woody mountains, Park and Landen Nab, the blue summits of other distant mountains, indented in various forms, close the scene.

Return to the road, and at the gate leading to the ferry house, follow the path to the left, having a stone wall on the right, until you approach the farmhouse called Harrow.[41] Here a charming picture will present itself in an elegant style. The island, from this stand, appears with much variety of shore, indented and embayed; almost surrounded with islets, adorned with ancient oaks and scattered trees.‡ Here the lake is caught a second time over the island; and the village and church of Bowness hang on its banks. A sweeter picture than this, the lake does not furnish. The artist will find a proper stand on the inside of the stone wall.

Having from this station enjoyed these charming views, descend to the ferry house, and proceed to the Great Island, where you will again see all that is charming on the lake, or magnificent and sublime in the environs, in a new point of view. The island was long the property of the Philipsons, once a family of consequence in these parts.¶

‡ In the collection of *Views of the Lakes*, engraved by Messers Byrne &c., Mr Farrington's view from the hill above the ferry house represents this scene.

¶ This island is now the property of Mr Curwen, who finished the large mansion house begun by Mr English, laid the whole out in pleasure grounds in the modern style suitable to the place, and made it one of the sweetest places that can be imagined.

Station II[42]

The views from this delicious spot are many and charming. From the south side of the island you look over a noble extent of water, bounded in front by waves of distant mountains, that rise from the water's edge. The two ferry points form a picturesque strait: and beyond that, the Storrs on one side and Rawlinson's Nab on the other, shooting far into the lake, form a grand sinuosity, while the immediate shores are beautifully indented with wooded promontories, or ornamentated with elegant edgings of luxuriant trees.

Berkshire and Crow Holme islands break the line in this noble expanse of water. The eastern shore discovers much cultivation and the succeeding hills are much diversified and strangely tumbled about. Some are laid out in grass inclosures, others cut with hedges and fringed with trees; one is crowned with wood and skirted with the sweetest vendure; another waves with corn; and the whole is a mixture of objects that constitute the most pleasing of rural scenes. The upper grounds are wild, and pastured with flocks.

Station III[43]

From the north side of the island, the views are more sublime and vast. The lake is here seen both ways. To the south, an expanse of water spreads on both hands and, behind, you see a succession of promontories, with variety of shore, patched with islands, and the whole encircled by an amphitheatre of distant hills, rising in a noble style. Turning to the north, the view is over a reach of the lake, 6 miles in length and above 1 mile in breadth, interrupted with scattered islands of different figure and dress; which, on a calm day, may be seen distinctly reflected from the limpid surface of the water that surrounds them.

The environs exhibit all the grandeur of alpine scenes. The conic summits of Langdale Pikes and Hill Bell, the broken ridge of Wrynose and the rocky point of Kirkstone, the overhanging cliff of Hardknott,* the uniform mass of Fairfield and Rydal Head, with the far-extended mountains of Troutbeck and Kentmere, form as magnificent an amphitheatre, and as grand an assemblage of mountains, dells and charms, as ever the fancy of Poussin suggested or the genius of Rosa invented. The island is the centre of this amphitheatre, and in the opposite point, directly over the extremity of the lake, is Rydal Hall, sweetly seated for the enjoyment of these scenes and animating the whole in return. The immediate borders of the lake are adorned with villages and scattered cots. Calgarth Park† and Rayrigg grace its banks.

[Mr Cockin adds:]⁴⁴

The old mansion here is built much in the style of Levens and Sizergh. Some of the rooms have been elegantly finished; but having been a long time in the possession of farmers, who occupy but a part of it, it is much gone out of repair and has on the whole a melancholy appearance. This circumstance, in concurrence with the superstitious notions which have ever been common in country places, and the particulars mentioned below, have probably given rise to a report, which has long prevailed, that the house is haunted. And many are the stories of frightful visions and mischievous deeds, which the goblins of the place are said to have performed to terrify and distress the harmless neighbourhood. These fables are not yet entirely disbelieved. Spectres still are seen and there are two human skulls, which have lain in the window of a large room as long as can be remembered, whose history and reputed properties are too singular not to contribute something to this story of the haunted house and to let them pass over in this note.

It has been a popular tale in these parts, of immemorial standing, that these skulls formerly belonged to two poor old people who were unjustly executed for robbery; that, to perpetuate their innocence, some ghost brought them there, and that they are for that end indestructible and in effect immoveable. For it is said to what place soever they were taken, or however used, they were still presently seen again in their old dormitory, the window. As the report goes, they have been buried, powdered and dispersed in the wind and upon the lake several times, to no purpose as to their removal or destruction. So far says common fame. Certain it is human remains still exist. And it would be thought an impeachment

* Langdale Pikes, Wrynose and Hardknott are named as being in environs, and in the western canton of this amphitheatre, yet are in reality not seen from the island, being intercepted by a process of Furness Fells.

† Calgarth Park is now the property of Dr Watson, Lord Bishop of Landaff, who has built an elegant mansion thereon, which with the other improvements in that fine situation makes it one of the most elegant places of residence in this country.

of the taste and curiosity of the nymphs and swains of the neighbouring villages if they could not say they had once seen the skulls of Calgarth.

As a more rational account of the matter (though still lame and unsatisfactory), it is told by some that there formerly lived in the house a famous doctress who had two skeletons by her, for the usual purposes of her profession, and the skulls happening to meet with better preservation than the rest of the bones, they were accidentally honoured with singular notice. But be their origin what it may, their legend is too whimsical and improbable to deserve being recorded, otherwise than as an instance of the never-failing credulity of ignorance and superstition.

After enjoying these internal views from the bosom of the lake, I recommend sailing[45] down to Rawlinson's Nab. On the south side of it, a pretty bay opens for landing. In the course of the voyage, you should touch at the different islands in the way, where every object is varied by a change of features, in such a manner as renders them wholly new. The great island changes its appearance and, joined with the ferry points, cuts the lake in two. The house thereon becomes an important object. The ferry house, seen under the sycamore groves, has a fine effect and, the broken cliff over it, constitutes a most agreeable picture. The greatest beauty of shore, and the finest rural scenes in nature, are found by traversing the lake; and, viewing each in turn, they receive improvement from contrast. The western side is spread with enchanting sylvan scenes; the eastern waves with all the improved glory of rural magnificence.

Station IV[46]
Rawlinson's Nab is a peninsular rock, of a circular figure, swelling to a crown in the centre, covered with low wood; there are two of them, but it is from the crown of the interior nab you have the present surprising view of two fine sheets of water that bend different ways.

The view to the south is bounded on both sides by a bold and various shore. The hills are wooded and rough, but spotted in parts with small inclosures, and their tops burst into rocks of various shapes.

The view to the north is more beautiful: an extent of three miles of the lake is broken into by the bold promontory, the Storrs, and above that, Berkshire Island is charmingly placed. Banerigg and Orrest Head, rising inward from the shore in magnificent slopes, are seen from hence to great advantage. This beautiful scene is well contrasted on the opposite side by a ridge of hanging woods, spread over wild romantic grounds that shoot abruptly into bold and spirited projections.‡

Return to Bowness, and conclude the survey by taking Mr Young's general view of the lake, where at one glance you command all its

‡ As it commanded more of the mountains at the head of the lake, Mr Farrington has given the view from Gillhead.

striking beauties. No station can better answer the purpose, and it would be here an injustice done to the discoverer to deviate one tittle from his description.[47]

Station V[48]

Thus having viewed the most pleasing objects from these points, let me next conduct you to a spot where, at one glance, you command them all in fresh situations and all assuming a new appearance. For this purpose, you return to the village and, taking the bye-road to the turnpike, mount the hill without turning your head (if I was your guide, I would conduct you behind a small hill, that you might come at once upon the view) till you almost gain the top, when you will be struck with astonishment at the prospect spread at your feet, which, if not the most superlative view that nature can exhibit, she is more fertile in beauties than the reach of my imagination will allow me to conceive. It would be mere vanity to attempt to describe a scene which beggars all description; but that you may have some faint idea of the outlines of this wonderful picture, I will just give the particulars of which it consists.

The point on which you stand is the side of a very large ridge of hills that form the eastern boundary of the lake, and the situation high enough to look down upon all the objects; a circumstance of great importance, which painting cannot imitate. In landscapes, you are either on a level with the objects, or look up to them; the painter cannot give the declivity at your feet, which lessens the object as much in the perpendicular line, as in the horizontal one. You look down upon a noble winding valley of about 12 miles along, everywhere inclosed with grounds, which rise in a very bold and various manner—in some places bulging into mountains, abrupt, wild and uncultivated; in others breaking into rocks, craggy, pointed and irregular; here rising into hills covered with the noblest woods, presenting a gloomy brownness of shade, almost from the clouds to the reflection of the trees in the limpid water of the lake they so beautifully skirt; there waving in glorious slopes of cultivated inclosures, adorned in the sweetest manner with every object that can give variety to art or elegance to nature; trees, woods, villages, houses, farms, scattered with picturesque confusion and waving to the eye in the most romantic landscapes that nature can exhibit.

This valley, so beautifully inclosed, is floated by the lake, which spreads forth to the right and left, in one vast, but irregular expanse of transparent water; a more noble object can hardly be imagined. Its immediate shore is traced in every variety of line that fancy can imagine; sometimes contrasting the lake into the appearance of a noble winding river; at others retiring from it and opening into large bays, as if for navies to anchor in: promontories spread with woods, or scattered with trees and inclosures projecting into the water in the most picturesque style imaginable; rocky points breaking the shore, and rearing their bold heads above the water; in a word, a variety that amazes the beholder.

But what finishes the scene, with an elegance too delicious to be imagined, is this beautiful sheet of water being dotted with no less than ten islands distinctly comprehended by the eye, all of the most bewitching beauty. The large one presents a waving various line, which rises from the water in the most picturesque inequalities of surface: high land in one place, low in another, clumps of trees in this spot, scattered ones in that, adorned by a farmhouse on the water's edge, and backed with a little wood, vying in simple elegance with Baromean palaces; some of the smaller islets rising from the lake, like little hills of wood; some only scattered with trees and others of grass of the finest verdure; a more beautiful variety is nowhere to be seen.

Strain your imagination to command the idea of so noble an expanse of water thus gloriously environed, spotted with islands, more beautiful than would have issued from the happiest painter. Picture the mountains rearing their majestic heads with native sublimity, the vast rocks boldly projecting their terrible craggy points and, in the path of beauty, the variegated inclosures of the most charming verdure, hanging to the eye in every picturesque form that can grace landscape, with the most exquisite touches of *la belle nature*. If you raise your fancy to something infinitely beyond this assemblage of rural elegancies, you may have a faint notion of the unexampled beauties of this ravishing landscape.

If the sun shines, this view of Mr Young's can only be enjoyed early in the morning; as that on the opposite shore, behind the two oak trees, is, from a parity of circumstances, an afternoon prospect. These are the finest stations on the lake for pleasing the eye, but are by much too elevated for the purpose of the artist, who will find the picturesque points on the great island well suited for his intention of morning and evening landscape, having command of foreground, the objects well ascertained, grouped and disposed in the finest order of nature. A picture of the north end of the lake, taken from this island, will far exceed the fanciful production of the happiest pencil. This may be easily verified by the use of the convex reflecting glass.[49]

Rawlinson's Nab is a picturesque point, either for the eye or the pencil. You are there advanced a great way into the lake, in the midst of the finest scenes, and with a charming foreground.

From the low Cat Crag, which is a little to the south of the Nab, you have a view of the south end of the lake, and as far north as the great island. The ferry points, the Storrs, the Nab and the lesser islands, are distinctly viewed in a fine order. The house on the island is a good object; and the beauties of the western shore to the south of the Crag are only seen from thence.

To sum up the peculiar beauties of Windermere, its great variety of landscapes and enchanting views, after what Mr Young has said of it, is unnecessary. He allowed himself time to examine this lake and the lakes in Cumberland, and he describes each of them with much taste and judgement; and it is evident he gives the preference to Windermere.¶ Yet this ought not to prejudice the minds of those who have the tour to make, against such as prefer Derwentwater or Ullswater. The styles are all different, and therefore the sensations they excite will also be different; and the idea that gives pleasure or pain in the highest degree, will be the rule of comparative judgement. It will, however, perhaps be allowed by all that the greatest variety of fine landscape is found at this lake.*

These stations will furnish much amusement to those who visit them; and others may perhaps be occasionally found equally pleasing. And whoever is delighted with water expeditions and entertainments, such as rowing, sailing, fishing &c., may enjoy them here in the highest perfection.

The principal feeders of Windermere are the rivers Rothay and Brathay. They unite their streams at the western corner of the head of the lake, below Clappergate, at a place called the Three-foot Brander, and after a short course boldly enter the lake.

The fish of this lake are char, trout, perch, pike and eel. Of the great char there are two varieties, the case char and the gelt char; the latter is a fish that did not spawn the last season, and is on that account more delicious.

The greatest depth of the lake is, opposite to Ecclerigg Crag, 222 ft. The fall from Newby Bridge, where the current of the lake becomes visible, to the high water mark of the tide at Low Wood (distant 2 miles) is 105 ft. The bottom of the lake is therefore 117 ft below the high water mark of the sea.

In Bowness there is nothing so remarkable as some remains of painted glass, in the east window of the church, that were brought from the abbey of Furness.† From Bowness to Ambleside is 6 miles, along the side of the lake. The Low Wood Inn, about two miles short of Ambleside, will attract the tourist's notice. No other inn in his route has so fine a view of a lake,[50] and the natural beauties of which he is in quest. A small cannon is kept here to gratify the curious with those remarkable reverberations of sound, which follow a report of a gun &c. in these singular vales, and of which a general description is given in the subsequent lines:

¶ Mr Pennant compares it to the chief of the Scotch lakes, and concludes it to be here what Lomond is there. On the banks of Windermere have been lately built many elegant villas: by Mr Law, at Brathay; Miss Prichard, Croft Lodge, Clappersgate; Mr Harrison, above Ambleside; Mrs Taylor, Cottage, Ambleside; the Bishop of Landaff, Calgarth; Mrs Taylor, Bellfield, near Bowness; John Bolton esquire, Storrs; Mr Taylor, Townhead; Mr Dixon, Fell Foot ; Mr Machel, Newby Bridge &c. These objects, as works of art, most of which are done in styles suitable to their situations, give an air of consequence to the country and, with the surrounding natural beauties, have lately made this neighbourhood and particularly about Ambleside, a place of the greatest celebrity.

* Not one bulrush or swampy reed defiles the margin of this imperial lake. No lake has its border so well ascertained, and of such easy access. Not one, after Lomond, can boast of so a vast guard of mountains, with such variety and diversity of shore. In navigating the lake upwards from the great island, the extremity appears singularly noble; its parts great and picturesque. The view of the surrounding mountains, from Cove to Kirkstone, is astonishing

† "The perfect remains of this window show that it has contained very fine

colouring in its former state. The arms of France and England, quartered, are well preserved at the top of the window. The design is a Crucifixion, in figures as large as life. By the hands, feet and parts remaining, it seems to be of singular beauty. On the dexter side of the crucifixion is St George slaying the dragon; on the sinister, the virgin Mary—an uncouth assemblage. Beneath are the figures of a knight and his lady kneeling, before whom are a group of kneeling monks, over whose heads are wrote W. Hartley, Tho. Honton, and other names by the breaking of glass rendered not legible."

(Hutchinson's *Excursion*)

‡ (Killarney).

¶ This place is said to have some resemblance of Ferney, on the Lake of Geneva, the seat of the late celebrated Voltaire.

* *Amboglana* in the imperial *Notitia Dignitatum*; *Dictis* in Horsley.

—————————————The cannons roar
Bursts from the bosom of the hollow shore.
The dire explosion the whole concave fills,
And shakes the firm foundation of the hills,
Now pausing deep, now bellowing from afar,
Now rages near the elemental war;
Affrighted echo opens all her cells,
With gather'd strength the posting clamour swells,
Check'd or impell'd, and varying in its course,
It slumbers, now awakes with double force,
Searching the strait, the crooked hill and dale,
Sinks in the breeze, or rises in the gale;
Chorus of earth and sky! The mountains sing,
And heaven's own thunders thro' the vallies ring.‡ [51]

On top of an eminence, a little behind Rayrigg,¶ there is a fine view[52] of the northern extremity of the lake. As you proceed along the banks, every step has importance, and the prospect becomes more and more august, exhibiting much variety of Apennine grandeur. Langdale Pikes, that guard the pass into Borrowdale on this side the Yoak, and spiral Hill Bell; the overhanging crags of lofty Rainbarrow; the broken ridge of Redscrees, Fairfield, and Scrubby crag (on whose precipitous front the eagle builds his nest, secure from the envious shepherds of the vale) with a chaos of other nameless mountains, are all in sight.

Just at the head of Windermere, and a little short of Ambleside, turn down a bye-road to the left and see the vestige of a Roman station. It lies in a meadow, on a level with the lake, and, as supposed, was called the *Dictis*, where a part of the cohort *Nerviorum Dictentium* was stationed. It is placed near the meetings of all the roads from Penrith, Keswick, Ravenglass, Furness and Kendal, which it commanded, and was accessible only on one side.

Ambleside*

Here nothing at present is found of all that Camden mentions of this place. So swift is time in destroying the last remains of ancient magnificence! Roman coins and arms have been frequently found here; and, in forming the turnpike road through Rydal, an urn was lately taken up, which contained ashes and other Roman remains, and serves to prove that the tract of the ancient road laid that way.

Though the author has not mentioned the circumstance,[53] it is supposed that the natural beauties of this part of the country are equal in variety and perfection to any to be seen in this tour, and that the lover of landscape in viewing many an undescribed scene would be highly gratified and delighted. But it is judged best not to descend to particulars. Let the admirer of rural nature please himself in their discovery as well as examination.

In mountainous countries, cascades, waterfalls and cataracts are frequent, but only to be seen in high perfection when in full torrent, and that is in wet weather or soon after it. About a mile above Ambleside, there is, in a place called the Groves, a cascade that, though the season should be dry, merits a visit on account of its singular beauty and distinguished features.†

It is the most curious you will see in the course of the tour. The stream here, though the water be low, is much divided, and broken by a variety of pointed dark rocks; after this, collecting itself into one torrent, it is precipitated with a horrid rushing noise into a dark gulf, unfathomable to the eye; and then, after rising in foam, it is once more dashed with a thundering noise headlong down a steep craggy channel till it joins the Rothay below Ambleside. The parts of this cataract are noble. The deep dark hue of the rocks, in the gloomy bosom of a narrow glen, just visible by day, and the foaming water, tinged with a hue of green caught from the trees and shrubs that wave over the fall, render this scene highly awful and picturesque.

Also, if the tourist love mountainous prospects, he may meet with one, in about a three hour's ride from this place, that will not fail to please him.[54] It is on Low Pike, in Rydal Park, from whence be seen many of the lakes, as Rydal Water, Grasmere, Windermere, Blencow Tarn, Elterwater, Esthwaite Water and Coniston Water, also the Isle of Walney, Pile of Foudry, the whole of Duddon, Ulverston, Lancaster and Millthorp Sands; the mountain Ingleborough, and at an opening between two hills, the hideous rocks in Borrowdale. A further walk of about an hour will give a view of Skiddaw, Helvellyn, Ullswater, the Vale of St John and other parts of Cumberland. This mountainous excursion over, the following lines may not unaptly be introduced to the reader's notice:

> Descending now from Aether's pure domain,
> By fancy borne to range the nether plain.
> Behold all-winning novelty display'd
> Along the vale, the mountain, and the shade.
> The scenes but late diminutive, resume
> Their native grandeur, and their wonted bloom.
> The woods expand their umbrage o'er the deep,
> And with ambitious aim ascent the steep,
> Stage above stage, their vig'rous arms invade,
> The tallest cliffs, and wrap them in the shade.
> Each in its own pre-eminence regains
> The high dominion of the subject plains
> Smiling beneath, such smiles the people wear,
> Happy in some paternal monarch's care.‡

† This cascade is called Stock Gill Force.

‡ From the poem 'Killarney'.

From Ambleside to Keswick, 16 miles of excellent mountain road, furnishes much amusement to the traveller. If the season be rainy, or immediately after rain, all the possible variety of cascades, waterfalls and cataracts are seen in this ride; some precipitating themselves from immense heights, others leaping and bounding from rock to rock, in foaming torrents, hurling huge fragments of them to the vale, that make the mountains tremble to their fall. The hollow noise swells and dies upon the ear by turns. The scenes are astonishing, and the succession of them matchless.

At Rydal Hall are two cascades worthy of notice. One is a little above the house, to which Sir Michael le Fleming made a convenient path, that brings you upon it all at once. This is a mighty torrent tumbling headlong and uninterruptedly, from an immense height of rock, into the rocky basin below, shaking the mountain under you with its fall, and the air above with the rebound. It is a surprising scene. This gentleman's example, in opening a road to the fall, recommends itself strongly to others of this country, which abounds with so many noble objects of curiosity, and which all travellers of the least taste would visit with pleasure, could they do it with convenience and safety.

The other cascade is a small fall of water, seen through the window of the summer-house, in Sir Michael's orchard.¶ The first who brought this sweet scene to light is the elegant and learned editor of Mr Gray's letters. And as no one described these views better than Mr Mason, the reader shall have the account of it in his own words.[55]

Here nature has performed everything in little, that she usually executes in her larger scale; and, on that account, like the miniature painter, seems to have finished every part of it in a studied manner. Not a little fragment of a rock thrown into the basin, not a single item of brushwood that starts from its craggy sides, but has a picturesque meaning; and the little central current, dashing down a cleft of the darkest coloured stone, produces an effect of light and shadow beautiful beyond description. This little theatrical scene might be painted as large as the original, on a canvas not bigger than those usually dropped in the opera house.*

Rydal Hall† has a grand situation,[56] at the feet of stupendous mountains (opening to the south at the entrance of the vale, over a noble foreground), and commands a charming view of Windermere water.‡ The River Rothay winds through the vale, amidst lofty rocks and hanging woods, to join the lake. The road serpentizes upwards, round a bulging rock fringed with trees, and brings you soon in sight of

¶ No. 13 of the *Views of the Lakes* by Mr Farrington.

* There is a cascade at Nunnery, near Kirkoswald in Cumberland, much in the same style as this. The accompaniments are as beautiful, the basin larger and the perpendicular fall 18 ft. But it is only one of a series of romantic scenes which abound at Nunnery, and are equal if not superior in their kind to any we have found in our tour: nor can we forbear to recommend this interesting spot to the notice of every traveller of taste: it is situated about 10 miles from Penrith, on the right of the road to Carlisle.

† Sir Michael le Fleming lately made a new front to Rydal Hall in a good style, which gives it a very interesting appearance.

‡ The style of this landscape will be seen in No. 15 of Mr Farrington's views.

Rydal Water

A lake about a mile in length, spotted with little isles, and which communicated by a narrow channel with

Grasmere Water

The River Rothay is their common outlet. Mount Grasmere hill[57] and, from the top, have a view of as sweet a scene as travelled eye ever beheld.¶ Mr Gray's description of this peaceful, happy vale will raise a wish in every reader to see so primæval a place.

> The bosom of the mountains, spreading here into a broad basin, discover in the midst Grasmere water; its margin is hollowed into small bays, with bold eminences; some of rock, some of soft turf, that half conceal and vary the figure of the little lake they command: from the shore, a low promontory pushes itself far into the water, and on it stands a white village, with a parish church rising in the midst of it; hanging inclosures, cornfields and meadows, green as an emerald, with their trees and hedges and cattle, fill up the whole space from the edge of the water; and just opposite to you is a large farmhouse, at the bottom of a steep smooth lawn, embosomed in old woods which climb halfway up the mountains' sides, and discover above them, a broken line of crags that crown the scene. Not a single red tile, no gentleman's flaring house, breaks in upon the repose of this little unsuspected paradise; but all is peace, rusticity and happy poverty, in its neatest, most becoming attire.*

Mr Gray's description is taken from the road descending from Dunmail Raise. But the more advantageous station, to view this romantic vale from, is on the south end of the western side. Proceed from Ambleside to Clappersgate along the banks of the River Brathay, and at Scalewith Bridge ascend a steep hill called Loughrig, that leads to Grasmere, and a little behind its summit[58] you come in sight of the valley and lake, lying in the sweetest order. Observe a few steps leading to a soft green knoll, and from its crown you have the finest view of the vale, the lake and the environs. The island is near the centre, unless the water be very low. Its margin is graced with a few scattered trees and an embowered hut. The church stands at a small distance from the lake, on the side of the Rothay, its principal feeder. On each hand spread cultivated tracts, up the steep sides of surrounding mountains, guarded by Steel Fell and Seat Sandle which, advancing towards each other, close the view at Dunmail Raise. The broken head of Helme Crag has a fine effect, seen from this point. Descend the hill, leave the church on the right hand,

¶ A little to the left of the road is No. 5 of Mr Farrington's views.

* The whole of Mr Gray's journal is given in the Addenda, Article III.

and you will presently arrive at the great road between Ambleside and Keswick. Here you have Mr Gray's view, and will see the difference. Mr Gray has omitted the island in his description, which is a principal feature in this scene.

This vale of peace is about 4 miles in circumference and guarded at the upper end by Helme Crag, a broken pyramidal mountain that exhibits an immense mass of antediluvian ruins. After this the road ascends Dunmail Raise, where lie the historical stones that perpetuate the name and fall of the last king of Cumberland, defeated there by the Saxon monarch Edmund, who put out the eyes of the two sons of his adversary, and for his confederating with Leolin, king of Wales, first wasted his kingdom and then gave it to Malcolm, king of Scots, who held it in fee of Edmund, AD 944 or 945.[59] The stones are a heap, that have the appearance of a cairn or barrow. The wall that divides the counties is built over them; which proves their priority of time in that form.

From Dunmail Raise the road is an easy descent of 9 miles to Keswick, except on Castlerigg, which is somewhat quick. Leaving the vale of Grasmere behind, you soon come in sight of

Leathes Water

Called also Wythburn or Thirlemere. It begins at the foot of Helvellyn, and skirts its base for the space of 4 miles, encreased by a variety of pastoral torrents that pour their silver streams down the mountains' sides and then, warbling, join the lake. The range of mountains on the right are tremendously great. Helvellyn and Cachidecam are the chief; and, according to the Wythburn shepherds, much higher than Skiddaw. It is, however, certain that these mountains retain snow many weeks after Skiddaw; but that may be owing to the steepness of Skiddaw's northern side and shivery surface, that attracts more forcibly the solar rays, than the verdant front of Helvellyn, and so sooner loses its winter covering.

A thousand huge rocks hang on Helvellyn's brow, which have been once in motion and are now seemingly prepared to start anew. Many have already reached the lake, and are at rest. The road sweeps through them, along the naked margin of the lake. The opposite shore is beautified with a variety of crown-topped rocks, some rent, some wooded, others not, rising immediately from or hanging towards the water; and all set off with a background of verdant mountains, rising in the noblest pastoral style. Its singular beauty is its being almost intersected in the middle by two peninsulas, that are joined by a bridge, which serves for an easy communication among the shepherds that dwell on the opposite banks.

At the sixth mile-post, from the top of an eminence on the left, there is a good general view of the lake and vale; but the most picturesque point is from an eminence behind Dale Head House.[60] This end is beautifully decorated with two small islands, dressed with wood and charmingly placed. The lake terminates sweetly with a pyramidal rock, wooded to the top; and, opposite to it, a silver grey rock hanging over its base, towards the lake, has a fine effect.

The road, after this, leads through the narrow green vale of Legberthwaite, divided into small inclosures, peopled with a few cots and nobly terminated by the romantic castle-like rock of St John. Below this, the vale contracts into a deep craggy dell, through which Leathes Water rolls till it joins the Greta at New Bridge, under the foot of Threlkeld Fell, a gloomy mountain of dark dun rocks that shuts up the view of the wide spreading vale of St John.

The road now winds to the left, by Smalthwaite Bridge, and ascends Naddle Fell by Causeway Foot to Castlerigg. At the turn of the hill, and within about a mile of Keswick, you come at once in sight of its glorious vale, with all its noble environs and enchanting scenes which, when Mr Gray beheld, it almost determined him to return to Keswick again and repeat his tour.

"I left Keswick," says he, "and took the Ambleside road, in a gloomy morning, and about two miles (or rather about a mile) from the town, mounted an eminence called Castle rig and, the sun breaking out, discovered the most enchanting view I have yet seen, of the whole valley behind me; the two lakes, the river, the mountains in all their glory; so that I had almost a mind to have gone back again." This is certainly a most ravishing morning view, of the bird's-eye kind. For here we have, seen in all their beauty, a circuit of 20 miles, two lakes, Derwent and Bassenthwaite, and the river serpentizing between them, the town of Keswick and the church of Crosthwaite in the central points, an extensive fertile plain and all the stupendous mountains that surround this delicious spot.

The druid temple, delineated in Pennant's tour, lies about half a mile to the right, but will be more conveniently seen from the Penrith road. Descend to

Keswick†

This small neat town is at present renowned for nothing so much as the lake it stands near, and which is sometimes called, from the town, the lake of Keswick, but more properly the lake of Derwent; and I am inclined to think, and hope to make it appear, that the ancient name of Keswick is the Derwent Town, or the town of Derwentwater. But first of the lake itself.‡

† *Derventione* in Raven. Chor.

‡ Some agreeable lines descriptive of this lake, by Dr Dalton, may be seen in the Addenda, Article II.

Derwentwater

The whole extent of the lake is about 3 miles from north to south; the form is irregular, and its greatest breadth exceeds not a mile and a half. The best method of viewing this enchanting water is in a boat, and from the banks. Mr Gray viewed it from the banks only, and Mr Mason, after trying both, prefers Mr Gray's choice; and, where the pleasure of rowing and sailing is out of the question, it will in general be found the best, on account of the foreground, which the boat does not furnish. Every dimension of the lake, however, appears more extended from its bosom, than from its banks. I shall therefore point out the favourite stations round the lake, that have often been verified.

Station I[61]

Cockshut Hill is remarkable for a general view. It is covered with a motley mixture of young wood, has an easy ascent to the top, and from it the lake appears in great beauty. On the floor of a spacious amphitheatre of the most picturesque mountains imaginable, an elegant sheet of water is spread out before you, shining like a mirror and transparent as crystal, variegated with islands, adorned with wood or clothed with the sweetest verdure, that rise in the most pleasing forms above the watery plain. The effects all around are amazingly great; but no words can describe the surprising pleasure of this scene on a fine day, when the sun plays upon the bosom of the lake, and the surrounding mountains are illuminated by his refulgent rays, and their rocky broken summits invertedly reflected by the surface of the water.

Station II[62]

The next celebrated station is at a small distance, named Crow Park, which formerly contained a grove of oaks of immemorial growth, whose fall the bard of Loweswater thus bemoans, in humble plaintive numbers:[63]

> That ancient wood where beasts did safely rest,
> And where the crow long time had built her nest,
> Now falls a destin'd prey to savage hands,
> Being doom'd, alas! to visit distant lands.
> Ah! what avails thy boasted strength at last!
> That brav'd the rage of many a furious blast;
> When now the body's spent with many a wound,
> Loud groans its last, and thunders on the ground,
> Whilst hills, and dales, and woods, and rocks resound.

This now shadeless pasture is a gentle eminence, not too high, on the very margin of the lake, which it commands in all its extent, and looks full into the craggy pass of Borrowdale. Of this station, Mr Gray speaks thus:

October 4, I walked to Crow park, now a rough pasture, once a glade of ancient oaks, whose large roots still remain in the ground, but nothing has sprung from them. If one single tree had remained, this would have been an unparalleled spot; and Smith judged right when he took his print of the lake from hence, for it is a gentle eminence, not too high, on the very margin of the water, and commands it from end to end, looking full into the gorge of Borrowdale. I prefer it even to Cockshut hill, which lies beside it, and to which I walked in the afternoon; it is covered with young trees, both sown and planted, oak, spruce, Scotch fir, &c. all which thrive wonderfully. There is an easy ascent to the top, and the view is far preferable to that on Castle hill, because this is lower and nearer the lake; for I find all points that are much elevated, spoil the beauty of the valley, and make its parts, which are not large, look poor and diminutive.

Station III[64]

A third station on this side will be found by keeping along the line of shore, till Stable Hills be on the right and Wallow Crag directly over you on the left; then, without the gate, on the edge of the common, observe two huge fragments of ferruginous coloured rock, pitched into the side of the mountain by their descent. Here all that is great or pleasing on the lake, all that is grand or sublime in the environs, lies before you in a beautiful order and natural disposition.

Looking down upon the water, the four large islands appear distinctly over the peninsula of Stable Hills: Lords Island, richly dressed in wood; a little to the left, Vicar's Isle rises in beautiful and circular form; Rampsholme is catched in a line between that and St Herbert's Island, which traverses the lake in an oblique direction, and has a fine effect. These are the four most considerable islands on the lake. Under Foe Park, a round hill completely clothed in wood,¶ two small islets interrupt the line of shore, and charm the eye in the passage from Vicar's Isle to Rampsholme. Another islet, above St Herbert's Island, has a similar effect.

All idea of river or outlet is here excluded; but, over a neck of undulated land finely scattered with trees, distant water is just seen behind Lord's Island. The white church of Crosthwaite is here visible, under Skiddaw, which forms the strongest background. The opposite shore is bounded by a range of hills, down to the entrance of Newland Vale, where Cawsey Pike and Thornthwaite rise in alpine pride, outdone only by their supreme lord, Skiddaw. Their skirts descend in gentle slopes, and end in cultivated grounds. The whole of the western coast is beautiful beyond what words can express, and the north end exhibits what is most gentle and pleasing in landscape.

¶ As one province of the Guide is to point out the characteristic features and distinguished parts of this lake, in order to exhibit the best landscape picture to the artist, and to give the most pleasure and entertainment to the company who make the tour, the author has taken all possible care to secure these ends in his choice of stations.

Yet there is one impediment attends his descriptions, which will in part prevent their permanency, and that is the annual fall of timber and coppice wood and the frequent removal of the picturesque trees which takes place on the borders of the lakes. These accidents, however, as they cannot be prevented, must be allowed for by the candid traveller, where he finds the original differing in these respects from the account given of it in the book.

The fall of Crow Park, on Derwentwater, has long been regretted. And Mr Gray's beautiful description of Foe Park, above mentioned, is not now to be verified.

It is true that the painter, by the creative power of his pencil, can supply such deficiencies in the features of his landscape, but the plastic power of nature or the careful hand of industry, directed by taste and judgement, can only make up such losses to the visitors of the lakes.

Thus much was thought proper to be subjoined in this place, as an apology, once for all, for the casual differences of this kind that may be found between the descriptions given of these lakes in this manual, and their real appearance at any future time.

* I do not know that the height of this cataract has been ascertained, but when viewing it, the reader may like to have it recalled to his mind that Carver says the fall of Niagara does not exceed 140 ft.

† This scene is the subject of No. 2 of Mr Farrington's views.

The southern extremity of the lake is a violent contrast to all this. Falcon Crag, an immense rock, hangs over your head, and upwards a forest of broken pointed rocks, in a semicircular sweep towering inward, form the most horrid amphitheatre that ever eye beheld in the wild forms of convulsed nature. The immediate margin of the lake is, however, a sweet variegated shore of meadow and pasture, up to the foot of the rocks. Over a border of hedgerow trees, Lowdore House is seen under Hallowstone Crag, a sloping rock, whose back is covered with soft vegetation. Beyond it appear the awful craggy rocks that conceal the pass into Borrowdale, and at their feet a stripe of verdant meadow through which the Derwent serpentizes to the lake in silence.

The road is along Barrowside, on the margin of the lake, narrow yet safe. It soon enters a glade, through which the lake is sweetly seen by turns. In approaching the ruins of Gowdar Crag, which hangs towering forward, the mind recoils at the huge fragments of crags, piled up on both sides, which are seen through a thicket of rocks and wood. But there is nothing of the danger remaining that Mr Gray apprehended here, the road being carefully kept open.

Proceed by the bridge of one arch over Park Gill, and another over Barrow Beck. Here Gowdar Crag presents itself in all its terrible majesty of rock, trimmed with trees that hang from its numerous fissures. Above this is seen a towering grey rock rising majestically rude, and near it, Shuttenoer, a spiral rock not less in height, hanging more forward over its base. Betwixt these, an awful chasm is formed, through which the waters of Watanlath are hurled. This is the Niagara of the lake,[65] the renowned cataract of Lowdore.*

To see this, ascend to an opening in the grove, directly over the mill. It is the misfortune of this celebrated waterfall to fail entirely in a dry season. The wonderful scenes peculiar to this part continue to the gorge of Borrowdale† and higher; and Castle Crag may be seen in the centre of the amphitheatre, threatening to block up the pass it once defended. The village of Grange is under it, celebrated as well for its hospitality to Mr Gray as for its sweet romantic site. And to affirm that all that Mr Gray says of the young farmer at Grange is strictly applicable to the inhabitants of these mountainous regions in general is but common justice done to the memory of repeated favours:

—————————————Hail sacred flood!
May still thy hospitable swains be blest
In rural innocence; thy mountains still
Teem with the fleecy race; thy tuneful woods
For ever flourish: and thy vales look gay.
(Armstrong, *On Health*)[66]

On the summit of Castle Crag are the remains of a fort; and much freestone, both red and white, has been quarried out of the ruins.

Not long since, a lead pan with an iron bow was taken out of them, and two masses of smelted iron, which probably were from the bloomery at the foot of the Stake in Borrowdale. The fort has most likely been of Roman origin, to guard the pass and secure the treasure contained in the bosom of these mountains. The Saxons, and after them, the Furness monks, maintained this fort for the same purpose.

All Borrowdale was give to the monks of Furness, probably by one of the Derwent family, and Adam de Derwentwater gave them free ingress and egress through all his lands.‡ The Grange was the place where they laid up their grain and their tithe, and also the salt they made at the salt spring, of which works there are still some vestiges remaining below Grange. The length of the castellum from east to west is about 70 yds, from south to north about 40 yds.

‡ *Antiquities of Furness,* page 106.

Station IV[67]

From the top of Castle Crag in Borrowdale, there is a most astonishing view of the lake and vale of Keswick, spread out to the north in the most picturesque manner. Every bend of the river is distinctly seen, from the pass of Borrowdale till it joins the lake; the lake itself spotted with islands; the most extraordinary line of shore, varied with all the surprising accompaniments of rock and wood; the village of Grange at the foot of the crag, and the white houses of Keswick with Crosthwaite church at the lower end of the lake; behind these, much cultivation, with a beautiful mixture of villages, houses, cots and farms standing round the skirts of Skiddaw, which rises in the grandest manner from a verdant base, and closes this prospect in the noblest style of nature's true sublime. From the summit of this rock, the views are so singularly great and pleasing, that they ought never to be omitted. The ascent is by one of the narrow paths cut in the side of the mountain, for carrying down the slate that is quarried on its top.

The view to the north, or the vale of Keswick, is already described; that to the south lies in Borrowdale. The river is seen winding upward from the lake through the rugged pass, to where it divides and embraces a triangular vale, completely cut into inclosures of meadow, enamelled with the softest verdure, and fields waving with fruitful crops. This truly secreted spot is completely surrounded by the most horrid, romantic mountains that are in this region of wonders; and whoever omits this *coup d'oeil* hath probably seen nothing equal to it.

The views here, taken in the glass, when the sun shines, are amazingly fine. This picture is reversed from the summit of Latrig.

Borrowdale

Mr Gray was so much intimidated with the accounts of Borrowdale, that he proceeded no farther than Grange. But no such difficulties as he feared are now to be met with. The road into Borrowdale is improved since his time, at least as far as is necessary for anyone to proceed to see what is curious. It serpentizes through the pass above Grange; and though upon the edge of a precipice that hangs over the river it is, nevertheless, safe. This river brings no mixture of mud from the mountains of naked rock, and runs in a channel of slate and granite, as clear as crystal. The water of all the lakes in these parts is clear, but the Derwent only is pellucid. In it the smallest pebble is seen at a great depth, nearly as in the open air.

The rocky scenes in Borrowdale are most fantastic, and the entrance rugged. One rock elbows out and turns the road directly against another. Bowder Stone, on the right in the very pass, is a mountain of itself, and the road winds round its base.¶ Here rock riots over rock, and mountain intersecting mountain, form one grand semicircular sweep. Extensive woods deck their steep sides; trees grow from pointed rocks, and rocks appear like trees. Here the Derwent, rapid as the Rhone, rolls his crystal streams through all the labyrinth of embattled obstacles. Indeed, the scenes here are sublimely terrible, the assemblage of magnificent objects so stupendously great, and the arrangement so extraordinary curious, that they must excite the most sensible feelings of wonder and surprise, and at once impress the mind with reverential awe and admiration.

The most gigantic mountains that form the outline of this tremendous landscape, and inclose Borrowdale, are Eagle Crag, Glaramara, Bull Crag and Serjeant Crag. On the front of the first, the bird of Jove has his annual nest—or, in more poetical terms,[68]

Here his dread seat the royal bird hath made,
To awe th'inferior subjects of the shade,
Secure he built it for a length of days
Impervious, but to Phoebus' piercing rays;
His young he trains to eye the solar light,
And soar beyond the fam'd Icarian flight.*

—which the dalesmen are careful to rob, but not without hazard to the assailant, who is let down from the summit of this dreadful rock by a rope of 20 fathoms or more, and who is obliged to defend himself from the attacks of the parent bird during his descent. The devastation made on the fold in the breeding season, by one eyrie, is computed at a lamb a day, besides the carnage made on the *feræ natura*. Glaramara is a mountain of perpendicular rock, immense in height and much broken. It appears on the western canton, and outline of the picture. Bull Crag and Serjeant Crag are in the centre, and their rugged sides concealed with hanging woods.

The road continues good to Rosthwaite, the first village in this romantic region, where it divides.

¶ This loose stone is of prodigious bulk. It lies like a ship on its keel. Its length is 62 ft; its circumference 184. Its solidity is about 23,090 ft, and its weight about 1,771 tons.

* From the poem 'Killarney'.

That on the right leads to the wad mines and to Ravenglass; that on the left to Hawkshead. Amidst these tremendous scenes of rocks and mountains, there is a peculiar circumstance, of consolation to the traveller, that distinguishes this from other mountainous tracts where the hills are divided by bogs and mosses often difficult to pass, which is, that the mosses here are on the tops of the mountains, and a way over or round them is never very difficult to find.

The inhabitants of the dales are served with turf-fuel from these mosses, and the manner of procuring it is very singular: a man carries on his back a sledge to the top of the mountain and conducts it down the most awful descents, by placing himself before it to prevent its running again. For this purpose a narrow furrow is cut in the mountain's side, which serves for a road to direct the sledge and to pitch the conductor's heel in. A sledge holds one-half of what a horse can draw on good road.

The mountains here are separated by wooded glens, verdant dells and fertile vales, which, besides forming a pleasing contrast, relieve the imagination with delighted ideas, that the inhabitants of these rude regions are far removed from the want of the necessaries of life for themselves, their herds and flocks, during the exclusion months from the rest of the community by the winter snows. About Rosthwaite, in the centre of the dale, fields wave with crops and meadows are enamelled with flowery grass.

This little delightful Eden[69] is marked with every degree of industry by the laborious inhabitants, who partake of the character of the country they live in, for they are hospitable, civil and communicative, and readily and cheerfully give assistance to strangers who visit their regions. On missing a track I was directed to observe, I have been surprised by the dale-lander from the top of a rock, waving me back, and offering me a safe conduct through all the difficult parts, and who blushed at the mention of a reward. Such is the extensive influence of virtue in the minds of those that are least acquainted with society.†

The shepherds only are conversant in the traditional annals of the mountains, and with all the secrets of the mysterious reign of chaos and old night; and they only can give proper information concerning their arcana: for others who live almost within the shadow of these mountains are often ignorant of their names.

Return to Keswick by Grange, and if the sun shines in the evening the display of rocks on the opposite shore, from Castle Rock to Wallow Crag, is amazingly grand. The parts are the same as in the morning ride, but the dispositions are entirely new. The crystal surface of the lake reflecting waving woods and rocks, backed by the finest arrangement of lofty mountains intersecting and rising above each other in great variety of forms, is a scene not to be equalled elsewhere. The whole ride down the western side is pleasant, though the road is but indifferent.

† In parts so sequestered from the world, the vulgar language (as well as manners) may be supposed to continue very little altered from what it has been for many ages, and to be what was once generally used through the country. And in order a little to gratify the curiosity of the reader, in Article X of the Addenda may be seen a specimen of the common Cumberland dialect.

Stake Pass

Whoever chooses an alpine journey of a very extraordinary nature may return through Borrowdale to Ambleside, or Hawkshead. A guide will be necessary from Rosthwaite, over the Stake of Borrowdale (a steep mountain so called) to Langdale Chapel. This ride is the wildest that can be imagined, for the space of 8 miles.[70]

Every part of nature has something to recommend it to the observation of the susceptible and ingenious. A walk or ride on the summits of mountains will afford a species of ideas which, though often neither of the social or luxuriant kind, will nevertheless greatly affect and entertain. The large unvariegated features of these hills, their elevation and even their desolate appearance are all sources of the sublime. And, in a publication of this kind, a word or two respecting their nature and characteristic properties seems as requisite as on several other subjects which are here discussed at some length.

The mountains among which these lakes are situated are formed in general of two sorts of rock or stone. The most prevailing kind is a blue rag, and where it appears the pasturage which is found among it is generally inclined to be mossy, lingy and wet. These particulars, and a number of swampy patches or pits of turbary, give the face of these mountains a rather savage and depressing look; and the indisposition of their soils readily to imbibe the waters which fall in rains is the occasion of the number of temporary cataracts which channel their sides.

The other kind of hills consist of limestone: and though generally of inferior height, their surface is infinitely more pleasing. They are perfectly dry and the bent, or grass, which covers their glades is peculiarly fine. Where this is not found, the bare rocks take place and appear in every fantastic form, which may be supposed to have arisen from some violent concussion, to which the earth has heretofore been subject. But, the whiteness and neatness of these rocks take off every idea of horror that might be suggested by their bulk or form. From the nature of the soil and the number of communicating clefts in the rock underground, they become dry soon after the heaviest rains; and, though they discover no streams of water issuing from their sides, a number of the most pellucid ones imaginable are seen bubbling out among the inclosures round their bases.

On these accounts, the face of such hills always appear singularly lightsome and cheerful. And, on a fine summer day, there is little doubt but that the curious stranger would find a walk or ride on the summits (though consisting of nothing but stone and turf), attended with uncommon pleasure. If he be of a poetical turn, he will see some of the serenest haunts for the shepherd that ever fancy formed; if of a philosophic turn, he may be equally delighted with contemplating several evident signs of the Mosaic deluge, and of the once-soft slate of the calcarious matter which is now hardened into rock. But our limits will not permit us to pursue the subject.

The greatest quantity of limestone hills contained in this tour lie within the district bounded by Kendal, Witherslack, Kellet and Hutton Roof. And the most beautiful of them, as seen at a distance, are Farlton and Arnside knots, Witherslack Scar and Warton Crag. The two first have their highest parts, which are neatly rounded, covered in a great measure with small fragments of limestone (called 'shillow') which gives them at all times an uncommon and beautiful appearance. But at the latter end of the year, when the foliage of the copses on their sides, and the grass which is interspersed along their glades near their tops, have gained an olive hue, no objects of the kind can appear more elegantly coloured. Farlton Knot, especially at that time of year, as seen from Burton churchyard, exhibits a brightness and harmony of colouring which could little be expected to result from a mixture of grass, wood and stone.‡

Above the cultivated tract the dale narrows, but the skirts of the mountains are covered with the sweetest verdure and have once waved with aged wood. Many large roots still remain, with some scattered trees.

Just where the road begins to ascend the Stake are said to be the remains of a bloomery, close by the waterfall on the left; but no tradition relates at what time it was last worked. This I could never verify from any visible remains. The mineral was found in the mountain, and the wood used in smelting had covered their steep sides. The masses of iron found on Castle Crag were probably smelted here. Cataracts and waterfalls abound on all sides. A succession of waterfalls will meet you on the ascent up the Stake, and others will accompany you down the most dreadful descent in Langdale. The scenes on the Borrowdale side are in part sylvan and pastoral, on the side of Langdale entirely rocky.

The Stake exhibits a miniature of very bad alpine road across a mountain, just not perpendicular, and about five miles over. The road makes many traverses so close that at every flexture it seems almost to return into itself, and such as are advancing in different traverses appear to go different ways. In descending the Stake on the Langdale side, a cataract accompanies you on the left, with all the horrors of a precipice.

Langdale Pike, called Pike-a-Stickle and Steel Pike, is an inaccessible pyramidal rock and commands the whole. Here nature seems to have discharged all her useless load of matter and rock, when form was first impressed on chaos. Pavey Ark is a hanging rock 600 ft in height, and under it is Stickle Tarn, a large basin of water, formed in the bosom of the rock, and which pours down in a cataract at Mill Beck. Below this, White Gill Crag opens to the centre, a dreadful yawning fissure. Beyond Langdale Chapel, the vale becomes more pleasing, and the road is good to Ambleside or Hawkshead, by Scalewith Bridge.

‡ A travelling party desirous of being gratified with the pleasure of one of these rides.may have it in perfection by going upon Farlton Knot, from Burton, through Claythorp, or traversing the heights of Warton Crag; both of which mountains, besides the particulars here mentioned, afford very extensive views, including part of the ocean, of a country abounding with agreeable images of rural nature.

Further prospects of Derwentwater

Mr Gray was much pleased with an evening view under Crow Park. "In the evening," says he, "I walked alone down to the lake, by the side of Crow park, after sunset, and saw the solemn colouring of the night draw on, the last gleam of sunshine fading away on the hill tops, the deep serene of the waters, and the long shadows of the mountains thrown across them, till they nearly touched the hithermost shore. At a distance were heard the murmurs of many waterfalls not audible in day time; I wished for the moon, but she was dark to me and silent,

Hid in her vacant interlunar cave."[71]

Station V[72]

This view is seen to much greater advantage from the side of Swinside, a little before sunset, where the vale and both the lakes are in full view, with the whole extent of rocky shore at the upper, and the flextures of the lower lake. And, when the last beams of the sun rest on the purple summit of Skiddaw and the deep shade of Wythop's wooded brows is stretched over the lake, the effect is amazingly great.

Station VI[73]

From Swinside continue the walk by Foe Park. This is a sweet evening walk and, had the sun shone out, Mr Gray would have perceived his mistake in being here in the morning. "October 5," he writes, "I walked through the meadows and cornfields to the Derwent, and crossing it, went up How hill; it looks along Bassenthwaite water, and sees at the same time the course of the river, and part of the upper lake, with a full view of Skiddaw: then I took my way through Portinscale village to the park (Foe park), a hill so called, covered entirely with wood; it is all a mass of crumbling slate; passed round its foot, between the trees and the edge of the water, and came to a peninsula that juts out into the lake, and looks along it both ways; in front rises Wallow crag and Castle hill, the town, the road to Penrith, Skiddaw, and Saddle back. After dinner walked up Penrith road," &c.

Station VII[74]

Another select station for a morning view is on Latrig, a soft green hill that interposes between the town and Skiddaw. The ascent is by Monk's Hall, leaving Ormathwaite on the left and following the mountain road about due east till you approach the gate in the stone-wall inclosure; then slant the hill to the right, looking towards Keswick, till you gain the brow of the hill, which exhibits a fine terrace of verdant turf, as smooth as velvet. Below you rolls the Greta and, in its course, visits the town before it joins the Derwent, where it issues from the lake, and then their united streams are seen meandering through the vale till they meet the floods of Bassenthwaite, under the verdant skirts of Wythop Brows.

The prospect to the south is the reverse of that from Castle Crag. The view is full into the rocky jaws of Borrowdale, through which the Derwent is seen pouring his crystal stream and, after winding through some verdant meadows which skirt the rocky coast, joining the lake at Lowdore. The lake itself is seen in its full extent, on all sides, with variety of shore, and its bosom spotted with diversity of islands. Castle Crag, in Borrowdale, stands first of all the forest of embattled rocks, whose forked heads, reared to the sky, shine in the sun like spears of burnished steel. In the rear, Langdale Pike, advancing to the clouds his cone-like head, overlooks them all. What charms the eye, in wandering over the vale, is that not one straight line offends. The roads all serpentize round the mountains, and the hedges wave with the inclosures. Everything is thrown into some path of beauty, or agreeable line of nature.

But to describe every picturesque view that this region of landscape presents would be an endless labour. And, did language furnish expression to convey ideas of inexhaustible variety that is found in the many grand constituent objects of these magnificent scenes, the imagination would be fatigued with the detail, and description weakened by redundancy. It is more pleasing to speculative curiosity to discover of itself the differences among such scenes as approach the nearest in likeness, and the agreement between such as appear most discordant, than to be informed of them. This sport of fancy and exercise of taste, arising from self-information, has the greatest effect on the mind, and the province of the guide is chiefly to point out the station, and leave to the company the enjoyment of reflection and the pleasures of the imagination.

Return to the gate, and enter the inclosure. Proceed, as soon as you can, to the right, having the wall at some distance, till you arrive at the brink of a green precipice;[75] there you will be entertained with the noise of the rapid Greta (roaring through a craggy channel) that, in a run of two miles, exhibits an uncommon appearance, forming twelve or more of the finest bends and serpentine curves that ever fancy pencilled. The point for viewing this uncommon scene is directly above the bridge, which hangs gracefully over the river.

The town of Keswick appears nowhere to greater advantage than from this station. Helvellyn, in front, overlooks a vast range of varied hills whose rocky sides are rent with many fissures, the paths of so many rills and roaring cataracts, that echo through the vales and swell the general torrent. To the east, Cross Fell is discerned like a cloud of blue mist, hanging over the horizon. In the middle space, Mell Fell, a green pyramidal hill, is a singular figure. The eye wandering over Castlerigg will discover the druid temple on the southern side of the Penrith road.

Return to the path that leads down the ridge of the hill to the east and, arrived at the gate that opens into a cross road, descend to the right along the precipitous bank of a brawling brook, Glenderaterra Beck, that is heard tumbling from the mountains and concealed by the woods that hang on its steep banks. In the course of the descent, remark Threlkeld Pike, browned with storms and rent by a dreadful wedge-like rock, that tends to the centre. There are many pastoral cots and rural seats scattered round the cultivated skirts of this side of the mountains of Skiddaw and Saddleback, sweetly placed and picturesque. The northern side is less hospitable, being more precipitous and much concealed in shade. From the bridge, the road leads to Threlkeld and falls into the Penrith road, 4 miles from Keswick. The last-mentioned brook, Glenderaterra, divides Skiddaw from Saddleback, called here Threlkeld Fell.

From the front of Mr Wren's house,[76] the eye will be delighted with the vale of St John, sweetly spread out in rural beauty between two ridges of hills, Lothwaite and Naddle fells, which in appearance join together just behind the Castle rocks. These, in the centre point of view, have the show of magnificent ruins. A river is seen on both sides of the vale, lengthening its course in meanders till it meets Threlkeld water, or Glenderamackin Beck at New Bridge, where it takes the name of Greta. This picture is improved at the brow of the hill, on the western side of the house. Here the Greta is seen from the bridge, running under the hill where you stand, and on the right coming forth in a fine deep-channelled stream between steep wooded banks. In a field on the left, near the second mile-post, stands conspicuous the above-mentioned wide circus of rude stones; the awful monument of the barbarous superstition which enslaved the minds of ancient times. Mr Pennant had in his possession an excellent drawing of these druidical remains.

Station VIII[77]

Another station remains, and which ought to be an evening one, in the vicarage garden. Mr Gray took it in his glass from the horsing-block, and speaks of it thus:[78]

> From hence I got to the parsonage a little before sunset, and saw in my glass a picture, that if I could transmit it to you, and fix it in all the softness of its living colours, would fairly sell for a thousand pounds. This is the sweetest scene I can yet discover, in point of pastoral beauty; the rest are in a sublime style.

The leading parts of this picture are over a rich cultivated foreground, the town of Keswick seen under a hill divided by grass inclosures, its summits crowned with wood. More to the east, Castlerigg is sweetly laid out, and over it sweeps in curves the road to Ambleside. Behind that are seen the range of vast mountains, descending from Helvellyn. On the western side, the chaos of mountains heaped upon mountains, that secrete the vale of Newland, make their appearance, and over them Cawsey Pike presides. Leaving these, the eye meets a well-wooded hill, on the margin of the lake, shining in all the beauties of foliage, set off with every advantage of form. Next a noble expanse of water, broken just in the centre by a large island dressed in wood; another, cultivated and fringed with trees, and a third with a hut upon it, stripped of its ornamental trees by the unfeeling hand of avarice.¶

On the eastern side, a bold shore, steep and wooded to the water's edge, is perceived, and above these rise daring rocks in every horrid shape. Also, a strange mixture of wood and rock succeed one another to the southern extremity of the lake, where the grand pyramidal Castle Crag commands the whole. The western shore is indented with wooded promontories down to Foe Park, the hill first described, on the lower margin of the lake, and the mountains all around rise immediately from its edge, but those that form the outline to the south are very much broken and hence more picturesque. These parts of the scene, Mr Gray says, are the sweetest he ever saw, in point of pastoral beauty. But whoever takes this view from Ormathwaite, in a field on the western side of the house, will be convinced of Mr Gray's loss in want of information. For the very spot he stood upon there is in the centre of the foreground, and makes a principal object in the pastoral part of the picture he praises so highly.

Sailing round the lake opens a new province for landscape.[79] Mr Gray neglected it, and Mr Mason thought he judged well. Messrs Young and Pennant tried it, and admired it. Dr Brown prefers sailing, and advises landing on every promontory and anchoring in every bay.* The transparent beauty of the lake is only seen in the boat, and it is very surprising. The bottom resembles a mosaic pavement of party-coloured stone. The fragments of spar, at the depth of 7 yds, either shine like diamonds or glitter in diversity of colour; and such is the purity of the water that no mud or ooze defiles its bottom. Mr Pennant navigated the lake; and as his description is more compressed than any other and gives a distinct idea of its appearances, I shall here subjoin it:[80]

The views on every side are very different; here all the possible variety of Alpine scenery is exhibited, with the horror of precipice, broken crag, overhanging rock, or insulated pyramidal hills, contrasted with others, whose smooth and verdant sides, swelling into immense aerial heights, at once please and surprise the eye.

The two extremities of the lake afford most discordant prospects: the southern is a composition of all that is horrible: an immense chasm opens, whose entrance is divided by a rude conic hill, once topt with a castle, the habitation of the tyrant of the

¶ This third is Vicar's Island, which has since been purchased by a gentleman, who has built a large mansion and made some other improvements upon it.

* The whole of Dr Brown's descriptive letter is inserted in the Addenda, Article I.

rocks; beyond, a series of broken mountainous crags, now patched with snow, soar one above the other, overshadowing the dark winding deep of Borrowdale. In the recesses are lodged a variety of minerals &c.

But the opposite, or northern view, is in all respects a strong and beautiful contrast. Skiddaw shows its vast base and, bounding all that part of the vale, rises gently to a height that sinks the neighbouring hills; opens a pleasing front, smooth and verdant, smiling over the country like a gentle generous lord, while the fells of Borrowdale frown on it like a hardened tyrant.

Each boundary of the lake seems to take part with the extremities and emulate their appearance: the southern varies in rocks of different forms, from the tremendous precipice of Lady's Leap, the broken front of Falcon's Nest, to the more distant concave curvature of Lowdore, an extent of precipitous rock, with trees vegetating from their numerous fissures, and the foam of a cataract precipitating amidst.

The entrance to Borrowdale divides the scene, and the northern side alters into milder forms; a salt spring, once the property of the monks of Furness, trickles along the shore; hills (the resort of shepherds), with downy fronts and lofty summits, succeed, with wood clothing their bases to the water's edge.

Not far from hence the environs appear to the navigator of the lake to the greatest advantage, for, on every side, mountains close the prospects, and form an amphitheatre almost matchless.

The isles that decorate this water are finely disposed, and very distinct, rise with gentle and regular curvatures above the surface, consist of verdant turf, or are planted with various trees. The principal is Lord's Island, above five acres, where the Ratcliff family had some time its residence and, from this lake, took the title of Derwentwater.

St Herbert's Isle was noted for the residence of that saint, the bosom friend of St Cuthbert, who wished and obtained his desire of departing this life on the same day, hour and minute with that holy man.†

The water of Derwentwater is subject to violent agitations, and often without any apparent cause, as was the case this day; the weather was calm, yet the waves ran a great height and the boat was tossed violently, with what is called bottom wind.

† In the register of Bishop Appleby, in the year 1374, there is an indulgence of 40 days to every of the inhabitants of the parish of Crosthwaite that should attend the vicar of St Herbert's Island on the 13th of April yearly, and there to celebrate mass in memory of St Herbert. (Nicholson's *Cumberland*, page 86)

Dr Brown recommends, as a conclusion of the tour of this lake, that it be viewed by moonlight. He says, "A walk by still moonlight (at which time the distant waterfalls are heard in all the variety of sound) among these enchanting dales opens a scene of such delicate beauty, repose and solemnity as exceeds all description."[81]

An expedition of this kind depends much on the choice of time
in making the tour. It is better a little before, than after the full moon.
If the evening be still, the voices of the waterfalls are re-echoed from
every rock and cavern, in a manner truly singular and pleasing. The
setting sun tips the mountain's top with the softest refulgence; and the
rising moon with her silver rays just continues in vision the glories of
its base. The surface of the lake, that in the day reflects the azure sky,
the deep green woods or hoar-coloured rocks, is now a sable mirror,
studded with the reflected gems of the starry heavens, a plain on which
are pencilled by the moon the fair outlines and shadows of the hills
behind which she labours. All now is in faint light, grave shade or solemn
darkness, which apparently increases the vastness of the objects and
enwraps them in a solemn horror, that strikes the mind of the beholder
with reverential awe and pleasing melancholy.

Here the reader's mind may be fitly prepared for perusal of the following
beautiful night-piece of Dr Brown:[82]

> Now sunk the Sun, now twilight sunk, and night
> Rode in her zenith; not a passing breeze
> Sigh'd to the grove, which in the midnight air
> Stood motionless, and in the peaceful floods
> Inverted hung, for now the billow slept
> Along the shore, nor heav'd the deep, but spread
> A shining mirror to the moon's pale orb,
> Which dim and waning, o'er the shadowy cliffs,
> The solemn woods, and spiry mountains' tops,
> Her glimmering faintness threw: now every eye,
> Oppress'd with toil, was drown'd in deep repose,
> Save that the unseen shepherd in his watch,
> Prop'd on his crook, stood list'ning by the fold,
> And gaz'd the starry vault, and pendant moon;
> Nor voice, nor sound broke on the deep serene,
> But the soft murmur of swift-gushing rills,
>
> Forth issuing from the mountain's distant steep,
> (Unheard till now, and now scarce heard) proclaim'd
> All things at rest, and imag'd the still voice
> Of quiet whisp'ring in the ear of night.‡

‡ Preserved to us by Mr Cumberland in
the dedication of his 'Ode to the Sun'.

The characteristic of this lake is that it retains its form viewed from
any point, and never assumes the appearance of a river. The following
sketch[83] of the appearance of this amphitheatre in a hard frost appeared
in the *Cumberland Pacquet*, February 10, 1784:

Derwent lake has been frozen over for several days, and quantities of timber have been drawn across it by horses. The appearance of this celebrated piece of water and the surrounding mountains is described by numbers who have seen it as the most delightful of any prospect that can be conceived. The four islands have been visited by crowds of people, who agree that the whole scene is at present more awfully grand and enchanting than in the height of summer. The summits and sides of the mountains, at present clad with snow, the icicles hanging from the different cliffs and the glassy surface of the lake, all these glittering in the sun fill the eye with such an assemblage of natural magnificence and beauty as beggars all description.¶

The fish here are trout, perch, pike and eel.

Bassenthwaite Water

Having seen the glory of Keswick, the beauties of the lake, and the wonders of the environs, there remains a pleasant ride to Ouse Bridge, in order to visit the lake of Bassenthwaite. Messrs Gray and Pennant took the ride, but did not see the beauties of the lake, either for want of time or proper information.

Mr Pennant says,
> Pass along the vale of Keswick and keep above Bassenthwaite water, at a small cultivated distance from it: this lake is a fine expanse of four miles in length, bounded on one side by high hills, wooded in many places to their bottoms; on the other side by fields and the skirts of Skiddaw. From Mr Spedding's, of Armathwaite, at the low extremity of the lake, you have a fine view of the whole.[84]

Mr Gray allowed himself more time for particulars. "October 6," he says:

> went in a chaise, 8 miles, along the east side of Bassenthwaite water to Ouse bridge; it runs directly along the foot of Skiddaw. Opposite to Wythop brows, clothed to the top with wood, a very beautiful view opens down to the lake, which is narrower and longer than that of Keswick, less broken into bays and without islands; at the foot of it, a few paces from the brink, gently sloping upwards, stands Armathwaite, in a thick grove of Scotch firs, commanding a noble view directly up the lake. At a small distance behind this, a ridge of cultivated hills, on which, according to the Keswick proverb, the sun always shines; the inhabitants here, on the contrary, call the vale of Derwentwater, the devil's chamberpot, and pronounce the name of Skiddaw fell, which terminates here, with a

¶ The following passage may be worth reading here, taken from a description of the curiosities in the Peak of Derbyshire in the *London Magazine* for October 1778:

Long has been the contention between gentlemen of Derbyshire and Cumberland, respecting Dovedale and Keswick, each claiming the superiority of natural beauties, and Dr Brown has been thought by many to carry the dispute in favour of Keswick. I have carefully surveyed both, without being a native of either country; and if I might presume to be any judge of the matter, I should compare Dovedale to the soft and delicate maiden, and Keswick to the bold and sturdy Briton.

sort of terror and aversion. Armathwaite house is a modern fabric, not large, and built of dark red stone.

But the singular beauties of this lake have not before been noticed, viz the grand sinuosity of three noble bays.

Station I[85]

From Armathwaite, the lower bay is in full display; a fine expanse of water, spreading itself both ways behind a circular peninsula (Castle How) that swells in the middle and is crowned with wood. In former times it has been surrounded with water, by the lake on one side, and the assistance of a brook that descends from Embleton, on the other. The accessible parts have been defended by trenches, one above another. The upper part must have been occupied with building, as the vestiges of the ruins are visible; and, like other such places in this region, they were probably secured by the first inhabitants, as places of difficult access and of easy defence.

From the bottom of the bay, some waving inclosures rise to the side of a green hill, and some scattered houses are seen at the upper end of a fine slope of inclosures. The banks of the lake are fringed with trees, and under them the crystal water is caught in a pleasing manner. At the north-west corner, the Derwent issues from the lake, and is spanned by a handsome stone bridge of three arches. The whole western boundary is the noble range of wooded hills called Wythop Brows.

On the eastern shore, the lake retires behind a peninsula that rushes far into the water, and on its extreme point a solitary oak, waving to every wind, is most picturesque. This is Scareness. The coast upward is a fine cultivated tract to the skirts of Skiddaw. Far to the south, Wallow Crag, with all the range of rock and broken craggy mountains in Borrowdale, are seen in fine perspective; and on their outline, the spiral point of Langdale Pike appears blue as glass. The deep green woods of Foe Park and the golden front of Swinside form a pleasing termination.

Station II[86]

Return to the road by Scareness, and descend from the house to the oak tree on the extremity of the promontory. The lake is here narrowest, but immediately spreading itself on both hands, forms two semicircular bays. That on the right is a mile across; the bay on the left is smaller; the shore on both sides is finely variegated with low wood and scattered bushes, as is more especially the peninsula itself. The upper bay is perfectly circular, and finely wooded. In front Wythop Brows rise swift from the water's edge. The extremity of some inclosures are picturesquely seen just over the wood, with part of a cottage. The village of Wythop lies behind it, in an aerial site. A grass inclosure, scooped in the bosom of the hanging wood, and under it a cot on the very brink of the lake, stands sweetly.

The views downward are fine; the banks high and woody to the bridge, of which two arches are in sight. Behind it a white house is charmingly placed. More to the right, at the head of a gentle slope, in the very centre of view, stands Armathwaite, winged with groves; and behind it, at a small distance, are deep hanging woods, and over them, spreading far to the right and left, a great reach of cultivated grounds. This termination is rich and pleasing to the eye.

The view to the south is, on the upper lake, much softened by distance. In the afternoon, if the sun shine, the appearance of the silver-grey rocks, glistening through the green woods that hang on their fissures, is most elegant. Behind, an appendix of Skiddaw rises in rude form; and over it, this chief of mountains frowns in alpine majesty. This view is also well seen from the house of Scareness.

Station III[87]

The next remarkable promontory is Bradness, a round green hill that, spreading itself into the lake, forms a bay, with Bowness to the south. The best general view of the lake is from the crown of this hill, behind the farmhouse. Here you look over three bays finely formed. Nothing can be imagined more elegant than the sinuosity of this side, contrasted with the steep shore and lofty woods of the opposite. The view upwards is not less charming, being indented and wooded to the water's edge.

If these views are taken, beginning with Bradness, then from Scareness, take the road to Bassenthwaite Halls (a few houses so called) and, from the road on the north side of the village, called Rakes, you have a very fine view of a rich cultivated tract, stretching along the banks of the lake and spreading itself upwards to the skirts of Skiddaw. The elevation is such that every object is seen completely and every beauty distinctly marked. The lake appears in its full magnitude, shaded by a bold wooded shore on the west and graced by a sweet spreading vale on the east, that terminates in a bold style under the surrounding mountains. The sloping ground to the bridge is charming, and the far-extended vales of Embleton and Isel lie in fine perspective. The River Derwent has his winding course through the latter.

Antiquities

Caer-mot is about two miles further to the north, on the great road to Old Carlisle and Wigton. It is a green high-crowned hill and on its skirt, just by the road side, are the manifest vestiges of a square encampment, inclosed with a double foss, extending from east to west 120 paces, and from south to north 100 paces. It is subdivided into several cantonments, and the road from Keswick to Old Carlisle has crossed it at right angles. Part of the agger is visible[88] where it issues from the north side of the camp, till where it falls in with the line of the present road. It is distant about 10 miles from Keswick and as much from Old Carlisle, and is about 2 miles west of Ireby.

Camden proposes Ireby for the *Arbeia* of the Romans, where the *Bercarii Tigrinensis* were garrisoned, but advances nothing in favour of his opinion. The situation is such as the Romans never made choice of for a camp or garrison, and there remain no vestiges of either. By its being in a deep glen, among surrounding hills, where there is no pass to guard, or country to protect, a body of men would be of no use.

On the northern extremity of the said hill of Caer-mot are the remains of a beacon, and near it the vestiges of a square encampment, inclosed with a foss and rampart of 60 ft by 70. This camp is in full view of *Blatumbulgii* (Bowness) and *Olenacum* (Old Carlisle); and, commanding the whole extent of the Solway Firth, would receive the first notice from any frontier station where the Caledonians might make an attempt to cross the firth, or had actually broken in upon the province; and notice of this might be communicated by the beacon on Caer-mot to the garrison at Keswick by the watch on Castle Crag, in Borrowdale. The garrison at Keswick would have the care of the beacon on the top of Skiddaw, the mountain being of the easiest access on that side. By this means, the alarm would soon become general, and the invaders be either terrified into flight, or else the whole country quickly in arms to oppose them.

Whether these camps are the *Arbeia*, I pretend not to say, but that they were of use to the Romans is evident; and what the Britons thought of them, is recorded in the name they have conferred on the hill where they are situated.

The larger camp has no advantage of site, and is but ill supplied with water. The ground is of a spongy nature, and retains wet long, and therefore could only be occupied in the summer months. They seem to have the same relation to Old Carlisle and Keswick, as the camp at Whitbarrow has to Old Penrith and Keswick.

From Caer-mot descend to Ouse Bridge, and return to Keswick up the western side of the lake. Every lover of landscape should take this ride in the afternoon; and if the sun shine it is exceedingly pleasant. The road branches off from the great road to Cockermouth a little below the bridge, and leads through the wood, and round Castle How. In some places it rises above the lake a considerable height, and the water is agreeably seen at intervals through a screen of low wood that decks its banks. Then the road descends to the level of the water, and presents you with a variety of surprising views in different styles, that show themselves in an agreeable succession as the eye wanders in amazement along the lake.

Station IV[89]

At Beck Wythop, the lake spreads out to a great expanse of water, and its outlet is concealed by Castle How. The immediate shore is lined with rocks, that range along banks completely dressed in low wood, and over them Wythop Brows rise almost perpendicular. The opposite shore is much variegated, and deeply embayed by the bold promontories of Scareness, Bowness and Bradness.

Just opposite to you, a little removed from the margin of the lake and under a range of wood, see the solitary church of Bassenthwaite. Its background is gloomy Ullock, a descendant hill of parent Skiddaw, robed in purple heath, trimmed with soft verdure. The whole cultivated tract between the mountains and the lake is seen here in all its beauty, and Skiddaw appears nowhere of such majestic height as from this point, being seemingly magnified by the accompaniments of the lesser hills that surround its base.

Over the northern extremity of this expanse of water, the ground rises in an easy slope, and in the point of beauty Armathwaite is seated, queen of the lake, on which she smiles in graceful beauty. On each hand are hanging woods. The space between displays much cultivation, and is divided by inclosures, waving up the farms seen under the skirts of Caermot, the crown-topped hill that closes this scene in the sweetest and most elegant manner possible. If the sun shine, you may be entertained here for hours with a pleasing variety of landscapes.

All the views up the lake are in a style great and sublime. They are seen in the bosom of the lake, softened by reflection, but to the glass is reserved the finished picture in the truest colouring, and most just perspective. As you come out of the wood, at the gate leading to the open space, there is a magnificent bird's-eye view of Keswick, in the centre of a grand amphitheatre of mountains. Proceeding along the banks of the lake, the road leads through Thornthwaite and Portinscale to Keswick.

On taking leave of Bassenthwaite Water[90] we may observe that it was the first lake that was honoured with one of those amusements* called regattas; this was on the 24th of August, 1780. Another was exhibited on the 1st of August, 1781 (when the swimming sweepstakes were introduced); and the last on the 4th of September, 1782. This species of entertainment was begun on Derwentwater, on the 28th of August, 1781, and continued there once in every year till 1791.

As the permanent beauties of this matchless vale became more known and frequented, this amusement was laid aside: it resembled too much the busy scenes from which the opulent wish to retire to the enjoyment of rural delight: nor could it long be thought necessary to employ the assistance of art, in that way, to heighten the most exalted charms of nature.

Next, a morning ride up the vale of Newland, to

Buttermere

This ride remains hitherto unnoticed, though one of the most pleasing and surprising in the environs of Keswick. Company who visit the vale of Keswick, and view its lake from Castlerigg, Latrig, Swinside and the vicarage, imagine inaccessible mountains only remain beyond the

* That the reader who has not been present at one of these rural fetes may form some idea of their nature and effects, we subjoin from the *Cumberland Pacquet* the following description of the regatta exhibited on Derwentwater, the 6th of September, 1782. But it will be allowed, by all who have had an opportunity of seeing it, that every representation, in the absence of the beauties that surround the scene, must fall infinitely short of the romantic grandeur it labours to hold up to the imagination.

At 8 o'clock in the morning, a vast concourse of ladies and gentlemen appeared on the side of the Derwent lake, where a number of marquees extending about 400 yds were erected for their accommodation. At 12, such of the company as

line of this amazing tract. But whoever takes a ride up Newland vale†
will be agreeably surprised with some of the finest solemn pastoral
scenes they have yet beheld. Here present themselves an arrangement
of vast mountains, entirely new, both in form and colouring of rock;
large hollow craters scooped in their bosoms, once the seeming seats of
raging liquid fire, though at present overflowing with the purest water,
that foams down the craggy brows; other woods ornament their base,
and other lakes, clear as the Derwent, lie at their feet. The softer part of
these scenes are verdant hills patched with wood, spotted with rock and
pastured with herds and flocks.

Newlands

The ride is along Swinside; and, having turned the brow of the hill and
passed the first houses through which the road leads, observe at the gate
on the right a view down a narrow vale, which is pleasing in a high degree.

The road continues winding through a glade, along the side of a
rapid brook that tumbles down a stony channel with water as clear as
crystal. At the hedgerow tree under Rawling End (a brawny mountain)
turn, and have a new and pleasant view of the vale of Keswick. The road
has then a gentle ascent, and the rivulet is heard murmuring below. At
the upper end of the cultivated part of the vale, a green pyramidal hill,
divided into waving inclosures, looks down the vale upon Keswick &c.
The verdant hills on each side terminate in rude and awful mountains
that tower to the skies in a variety of grotesque forms, and on their
murky furrowed sides hang many a torrent.

Above Keskadale, the last houses in Newland, no traces of human
industry appear. All is naked solitude and simple nature. The vale now
becomes a dell, and the road a path. The lower parts are pastured with a
motley herd; the middle tract is assumed by the flocks; the upper regions
(to man inaccessible) are abandoned to the birds of Jove. Here untamed
nature holds her reign in solemn silence, amidst the gloom and grandeur
of dreary solitude.

And here Mr Cockin believes the following exclamation of young Edwin
may be properly recalled to the reader's remembrance:[91]

Hail, awful scenes, that calm the troubled breast,
And woo the weary to profound repose,
Can passion's wildest uproar lay to rest,
And whisper comfort to the man of woes!
Here innocence may wander safe from foes,
And contemplation soar on seraph wings;
O solitude, the man who thee foregoes,
When lucre lures him, or ambition stings,
Shall never know the source whence real grandeur springs.‡

were invited by Mr Pocklington passed
over in boats to the island which bears
his name and, on their landing, were
saluted by a discharge of his artillery.
This might properly be called the
opening of the Regatta; for as soon as
the echo of this discharge had ceased,
a signal gun was fired and five boats,
which lay upon their oars (on that part
of the water which runs nearest the
town of Keswick) instantly pushed off
the shore and began the race.

A view from any of the attendant
boats (of which there were several)
presented a scene which exceeds all
description. The sides of the hoary
mountains were clad with spectators
and the glassy surface of the lake was
variegated with a number of pleasure
barges; which, tricked out in all the
gayest colours and glittering in the
rays of a meridian sun, gave a new
appearance to the celebrated beauties
of this matchless vale.

The contending boats passed
Pocklington's Island, and rounding
St Herbert's and Rampsholme edged
down by the outside of Lord's Island,
describing in the race almost a perfect
circle and, during the greater part of it,
in full view of the company.

About 3 o'clock, preparations
were made for the sham-attack
on Pocklington's Island. The fleet
(consisting of several barges armed
with small cannon and muskets)
retired out of view behind Friar Crag,
to prepare for action: previous to
which, a flag of truce was sent to
the governor, with a summons to
surrender upon honourable terms.
A defiance was returned; soon after
which the fleet was seen advancing
with great spirit before the batteries,
and instantly forming in a curved line,
a terrible cannonade began on both
sides, accompanied with a dreadful
discharge of musketry.

This continued for some time
and, being echoed from hill to hill
in an amazing variety of sounds,

65

Buttermere

filled the ear with whatever could produce astonishment and awe. All nature seemed to be in an uproar, which impressed on the awakened imagination the most lively ideas of the 'war of elements' and 'crush of worlds.'

After a severe conflict, the enemies were driven from the attack in great disorder. A feu-de-joye was then fired in the fort and oft repeated by the responsive echoes. The fleet after a little delay formed again and, practising a variety of beautiful manoeuvres, renewed the attack. Uproar again sprang up, and the deep-toned echoes of the mountains again joined in the solemn chorus, which was heard to the distance of 10 leagues to leeward, through the eastern opening of the vast amphitheatre, as far as Appleby.

The garrison at length capitulated, and the entertainments of the water being finished (towards the evening) the company moved to Keswick; to which place, from the water's edge, a range of lamps were fixed, very happily disposed, and a number of fireworks were played off.

An assembly room (which has been built for the purpose) next received the ladies and gentlemen, and a dance concluded this annual festivity; a chain of amusement which we may venture to assert, no other spot can possibly furnish, and which want only to be more universally known to render this a place of more general resort than any other in the kingdom.

To those whom nature's works alone can charm, this spot will at all times be viewed with rapture and astonishment; but no breast, however unsusceptible of pleasure, can be indifferent to that display of every beauty which decks the ancient vale of Keswick on a Regatta-day.

The morning sun beaming on the blue and yellow mountains' sides produces effects of light and shade the most charming that ever a son of Apelles imagined.

In approaching the head of Newland Hawse, on the left a mountain of purple-coloured rock presents a thousand gaping chasms, excavated by torrents that fall into a basin formed in the bosom of the mountain, and from thence precipitating themselves over a wall of rock, become a brook below. In front is a vast rocky mountain, the barrier of the dell, that opposes itself to all further access. Among the variety of waterfalls that distinguish this awful boundary of rock, one catches the eye, at a distance that exceeds the boasted Lowdore in height of rock and unity of fall, whilst the beholder is free of all anxiety of mind in the approach. Not one pebble or grain of sand offends; but all is nature, in her sweetest trim of verdant turf, spread out to please her votaries.

Whoever would enjoy, with ease and safety, alpine views and pastoral scenes in the sublime style may have them in this morning ride.

The road, or rather track, becomes now less agreeable than it was for a few roods, not from any difficulty there is in turning the mountain turf into good road, at a small expense, but from the inattention of the dalesmen, who habituate themselves to tread in the track made by their flocks and wish for nothing better. It will not be labour lost to walk a few roods here and see a new creation of mountains, as unlike those left behind, as the Andes are to the Alps. The contrast is really striking, and appears at once on the summit of the hill. On the right, at the head of a deep green hill, a naked furrowed mountain, of an orange hue, has a strange appearance amongst its verdant neighbours, and sinks, by his height, even Skiddaw itself.

Descend the track on the left, and you soon have in sight the highest possible contrast in nature. Four spiral towering mountains, dark, dun and gloomy at noon-day, rise immediately from the western extremity of the deep narrow dell, and hang over Buttermere. The more southern is by the dalesmen, from its form, called Hayrick; the more pyramidal, High Crag; the third, High Stile; and the fourth, from its ferruginous colour, Red Pike. Between the second and third there is a large crater that, from the parched colour of the conical mountains in whose bosom it is formed, appears to have been the focus of a volcano in some distant period of time, when the cones were produced by explosion. At present it is the reservoir of water, that feeds the roaring cataract you see in the descent to Buttermere. Here all is barrenness, solitude and silence, only interrupted by the murmurs of a rill that runs unseen in the bottom of a deep dell.

There is one curious spectacle, often seen by the shepherd on the tops of these mountains, which the traveller may never chance to see, but which is so happily delineated in the following stanza that he may the less regret it. What I mean is the effects of mists, which frequently involve every object round in the bases of these eminences, and which in the district of pointed hills just described, must be experienced in the greatest perfection:

> And oft the craggy cliff he lov'd to climb,
> When all in mist the world below was lost;
> What dreadful pleasure! there to stand sublime,
> Like shipwreck'd mariner on desert coast,
> And view th'enormous waste of vapour, tost
> In billows length'ning to th'horizon round,
> Now scoop'd in gulps, with mountains now embos'd;
> And hear the voice of mirth and song rebound,
> Flock, herds, and water-falls along the hoar profound!¶

The smooth verdant sides of the vast hills on the right have many furrows engraven in their sides by the winter rains; and the sable mountains in front present all the horrors of cloven rock, broken cliff and mountain streams tumbling headlong.

Buttermere village

Some traces of industry, obtruding themselves at the foot of the glen, disturb the solemn solitude with which the eye and mind have been entertained, and point out your return to society; for now you approach the village of Buttermere, which is situated between the lakes and consists of 16 houses. The chapel here is very small, the stipend not large, for though twice augmented with the queen's bounty, it exceeds not £20 per annum. This is one of the cures Mr Pennant mentions;[92] but the perquisites of the clog-shoes, harden-sark, whittle-gate and goose-gate have no better support than in some ancient and probably idle tale. The life of the inhabitants is purely pastoral. A few hands are employed in the slate quarries; the women spin woollen yarn and drink tea. Above the village, you have a view of the upper lake, 2 miles in length and short of one in breadth. It is terminated on the western side by the ferruginous mountain already mentioned. A stripe of cultivated ground adorns the eastern shore.

A group of houses, called Gatesgarth, is seated on the southern extremity, under the most extraordinary amphitheatre of mountainous rocks that ever eye beheld. Here we see Honister Crag rise to an immense height, flanked by two conic mountains, Fleetwith to the eastern and Scarf on the western side; a hundred mountain torrents form never-failing cataracts that thunder and foam down the centre of the rock and form the lake below. Here the rocky scenes and mountain landscapes are diversified and contrasted with all that aggrandizes the object in most sublime style, and constitutes a picture the most enchanting of any in these parts.

† Here, in a hill called Gold Scope, are the remains of a famous ancient copper mine, which exhibit some curious excavations, called the Pen Holes. One shaft, reaching from the top of the hill to the bottom (into which, if a large stone be let fall, it occasions a most tremendous noise) is met by a level passage, cut quite through the mountain, along which a stream of water (from Bank Beck) was conveyed to turn a draining wheel at its meeting with the shaft.

These mines were wrought in Henry 8th's time, and some of the succeeding reigns. But the metal yielding a considerable quantity of gold, they came to be considered as royal mines and occasioned a dispute between the crown and the Duke of Somerset, then lord of the manor, and a discontinuance of the works. In 1757, Mr Gilbert and company drained them to the very bottom, at the expense of about £100, but did not find the metal such, or so plentiful, as to encourage them to proceed on at so prodigious a depth. [Wm Cockin]

‡ From Beattie's *Minstrel*, Bk the 2nd. [Wm Cockin]

¶ *Minstrel*, Bk the 1st. [Wm Cockin]

Mr Gray's account of Barrowside and his relation of Borrowdale are hyperboles—the sport of fancy he was pleased to indulge himself in. A person that has crossed the Alps or Apennines[93] will meet here only miniatures of the huge rocks and precipices, the vast hills and snow-topped mountains he saw there. And though he may observe much similarity in the style, there is none in the danger. Skiddaw, Helvellyn and Cachidecam are but dwarfs, when compared with Mont Maudite[94] above the Lake of Geneva and the guardian mountains of the Rhone.

If the roads in some places be narrow and difficult, they are at least safe. No villainous *banditti* haunt the mountains; innocent people live in the dells. Every cottager is narrative of all he knows; and mountain virtue and pastoral hospitality are found at every farm. This constitutes a pleasing difference betwixt travelling here and on the Continent, where every innholder is an extortioner, and *voiturin* an imposing rogue.

The space betwixt the lakes is not a mile, and consists of pasture and meadow ground. The lower lake is called

Cromack Water*

Soon opens after you leave the village, and pass through an oaken grove. A fine expanse of water sweeps away to the right under a rocky promontory, Randon Knot or Buttermere Hawse. The road then serpentizes round the rock and under a rugged, pyramidal, craggy mountain. From the crest of this rock, the whole extent of the lake is discovered. On the western side the mountains rise immediately from the water's edge, bold and abrupt. Just in front, between Blea Crag and Mellbreak (two spiral hills) the hoarse resounding noise of a waterfall is heard across the lake, concealed within the bosom of the cliff, through which it has forced its way, and when viewed from the foot of the fall is a most astonishing phenomenon.

This lake is beautified with three small isles. One of rock lies just before you. The whole eastern shore is diversified with bays, the banks with scattered trees and a few inclosures, terminated by a hanging wood. At the foot of the lake, a high-crowned hill pushes forward, fringed with trees and sweetly laid out with inclosures; and above it, on a cultivated slope, is the chapel of Loweswater, surrounded with scattered farms. Behind all, Low Fell raises its verdant front, a sweet contrast to his murky neighbours, and a pleasing termination, either as seen from the top of this rock or from the bosom of the lake.

The chain of pyramidal mountains on each side of this narrow vale are extremely picturesque. They rise from distinct bases, and swell into the most grotesque forms of serrated or broken rocks.

These lakes are of a much greater depth than Derwentwater, and this may be the only reason why they have char, and some others have not. The char, in the summer months, retire to the deeps, probably to avoid

* This lake abounds with the finest char and red trout, and contains also some pike and perch.

the heat. The water here is clear, but not so transparent as the lake of Derwent. The outlet is at the north-east corner, by the River Cocker, over which is a handsome stone bridge of four arches. This lake is 4 miles in length, and in some places almost half a mile over.

Loweswater

Proceed from the bridge by High Cross to Loweswater.

View I[95]

Having passed through a gate that leads to the common, the lake spreads out before you, a mile in length, and of an equal breadth of about a quarter of a mile. The extremities are rivals in beauty of hanging woods, little groves and waving inclosures, with farms seated in the sweetest points of view. The south end is overlooked by lofty Mellbreak, at whose foot a white house within some grass inclosures, under a few trees, stands in the point of beauty. The eastern shore is open and indented with small bays; but the opposite side is more pleasing.

Carling Knot presents a broad pyramidal front of swift ascent, covered with soft vegetation and spotted with many aged solitary thorns. On each side the outlines wave upwards in the finest manner, terminating in a cone of grey rocks patched with verdure.

This lake, in opposition to all the others, has its course from north to south, and under Mellbreak falls into Cromack Water. It is of no great depth, and without char; but it abounds with pike and perch, and has some trout.

View II[96]

An evening view of both lakes is from the side of Mellbreak, at the gate, under a coppice of oaks, in the road to Ennerdale. Nothing exceeds in composition the parts of this landscape. They are all great, and lie in fine order of perspective. If the view be taken from the round knoll at the lower end of the lake, the appearance of the mountains that bound it is astonishing. You have Mellbreak on the right and Grasmere on the left, and betwixt them a stupendous amphitheatre of mountains, whose tops are all broken and dissimilar, and of different hues, and their bases skirted with wood or clothed with verdure. In the centre point of this amphitheatre is a huge pyramidal broken rock, that seems with its figure to change place, as you move across the foreground, and gives much variety to the scenes and alters the picture at every pace.

In short, the picturesque views in this district are many; some mixed, others purely sublime, but all surprise and please. The genius of the greatest adepts in landscape might here improve in taste and judgement; and the most enthusiastic ardour for pastoral poetry and painting will here find an inexhaustible source of scenes and images.

† An account of a ride from Keswick to Ennerdale has been communicated by a friend of the publishers and is inserted in the Addenda, Article IX.

‡ An account of this inundation is given in the *Philosophical Transactions* for the year 1750, No. 494. [Wm Cockin]

When the roads to Ennerdale and Wastwater are improved, they may be taken in this morning ride.†

View III[97]

From the bridge at the foot of the lake, ascend the road to Brackenthwaite. At the ale-house, Scalehill, take a guide to the top of the rock above Mr Bertie's woods and have an entirely new view of Cromack Water. The River Cocker is seen winding through a beautiful and rich cultivated vale, spreading far to the north, variegated with woods, groves and hanging grounds in every pleasing variety.

The most singular object in this vale of Lorton and Brackenthwaite is a high-crowned topped rock that divides the vale, and raises a broken craggy head over hanging woods that skirt the sloping sides, which are cut into waving inclosures and varied with groves and patches of coppice wood. To the west a part of Loweswater is seen, under a fringe of trees at High Cross. Behind you, awful Grasmire (the Skiddaw of the vale) frowns in all the majesty of furrowed rock, cut almost perpendicularly to the centre by the waterfalls of ages. The swell of a cataract is here heard, but entirely concealed within the gloomy recess of a rocky dell formed by the rival mountains, Grasmire and Whiteside. At their feet lie the mighty ruins, brought down from the mountains by the memorable waterspout that deluged all the vale in September, 1760.‡

I do not know whether an account of the effects of the storm has been published; but the following description of a similar one which happened in St John's vale, given as the most authentic that has yet appeared, by a native of the place, may here merit a perusal.[98]

In the evening of 22nd of August, 1749, that day having been much hotter than was ever known in these parts, a strange and frightful noise was heard in the air, which continued for some time to the great surprise of the inhabitants, sounding over them like a strong wind, though they could not perceive it. This was succeeded by the most terrible claps of thunder and incessant flashes of lightning breaking over their heads. At the same time the clouds poured down whole torrents of water on the mountains to the east, which in a very little time swelled the channels of their rivulets and brooks, so as to overflow every bank and overwhelm almost every obstacle in their way. In a moment they deluged the whole valley below, and covered with stones, earth and sand many acres of fine cultivated ground.

Several thousands of huge fragments of broken rocks were driven by the impetuosity of these dreadful cataracts into the fields below, and such was their bulk, that some of them were more than ten horses could move, and one fairly measured 19 yards in circumference.

A corn-mill, dwelling-house and stable, all under one roof, lay in the tract of one of these currents, and the mill from the one end, and the stable from the other, were both swept away, leaving the little habitation standing in the middle, rent open at both ends, with the miller, who was very old and infirm, in bed, and who was ignorant of the matter till he arose the next morning to behold nothing but ruin and desolation. His mill was no more! and instead of seeing green ground in the vale below, all was covered with large stones and rubbish, 4 yards deep, and among which one of the millstones was irrecoverably lost. The old channel of the stream too was entirely choked up, and a new one cut open on the other side of the building, through the middle of a large rock, 4 yards wide and 9 deep.

Something similar to this happened at several other places in the neighbourhood, for the space of 2 miles along Legberthwaite and Fornside, but happily through the providence of the Almighty no person's life was lost.

After this, the mountains become humble hills, and terminate the sweet vale that stretches from the feet of Black Crag and Carling Knot, and spreads itself into a country watered by the Cocker.

The ride down this vale is pleasant. All the scenes are smiling, rich and rural. Every dale-lander appears to be a man of taste, and every village, house and cot is placed in the choicest site, and decorated in the neatest manner and style of natural elegance. Not one formal avenue, or straight-lined hedge or square fish-pond offends the eye in all this charming vale. The variety of situation gives diversity of views, and a succession of pleasing objects creates the desire of seeing.

The back view is under a wooded hill, near the fifth mile-post, and is fine. Here return up the great road to Keswick.¶

Towards Penrith
From Keswick to Penrith, 17 miles of very good road through an open wild country.

Antiquities
Upon Hutton Moor and on the north side of the great road may be traced the path of the Roman way that leads from Old Penrith, or Plumpton Wall, in a line almost due west to Keswick. Upon the moor are the traces of a large encampment that the road traverses. And a little beyond the eighth mile-post, on the left at Whitbarrow, are strong vestiges of a square encampment. The Roman road beyond that is met with in the inclosed fields of Whitbarrow, and is known by the farmers by the opposition they meet in ploughing across it. After that it is found

¶ While staying at Keswick it may be worth while to see two museums kept there. They contain a great variety of fossils and other natural curiosities of the country, several pieces of antiquity and many other articles.

entirely on the common called Greystock Low Moor; and lately they have formed a new road on the agger of it.

It proceeds in a right line to Greystock town, where it makes a flexure to the left, and continues in a line to Blencow; it is then found in a ploughed field, about 200 yds to the north of Little Blencow, pointing at Coachgate; from thence it passes on the north side of Kellbarrow and through Cowclose, and was discovered in making the new turnpike road from Penrith to Cockermouth, which it crossed near the toll gate. From thence it stretches over Whitrigg in a right line, is visible on the edge of the wood at Fairbank and in the lane called Low Street. From thence it points through inclosed land to the south end of the station called Plumpton Wall and Old Penrith. It crosses the brook Petteral at Topinholme.

In the year 1772 near Little Blencow, in removing a heap of stones, two urns were taken up, about 2½ ft high, made of very coarse earth and crusted on both sides with a brown clay, the tops remarkably wide and covered with a red flat stone. Besides ashes and bones, each urn had a small cup within it, of a fine clay, in the shape of a teacup. One was pierced in the centre of the bottom part. The place where they were taken up is called Loddon How, within 20 yds of the road between Penrith and Skelton, about 200 yds from the Roman road and 4 miles from the station.

Also, on the banks of the Petteral, a few roods[99] from the south corner of the station, a curious altar was lately found. It was 3 ft 4 ins in height and near 16 ins square. It had been thrown down from the upper ground, and the corners broken off in the fall. The front had been filled with an inscription, the letters short and square, but not one word remains legible. On the right-hand side is the *patera*, with a handle, and underneath the *secespita*. On the opposite side is the *ampula*, and from its lip a serpent or viper descends in waves. The back part is rude, as if intended to stand against a wall. The emblems are in excellent preservation.*

The castrum is 168 paces from south to north, by 110 within the foss, which was also surrounded with a stone-wall. The stones have been removed to the fence-wall on the roadside and, being in Plumpton, is called Plumpton Wall.

The station is a vast heap of ruins, of stone building. The walls are of great thickness and cemented. The town has surrounded the station, except on the side of the Petteral. But whether the station took its name from the river, as being upon its banks, and was called the Petriana, or whether the station gave name to the river (which is perhaps the least probable) let him who can determine.

The station is 12¾ miles from Carlisle, 5¼ from Penrith, about 7 from Brougham Castle, and about 18 from Keswick, where an intermediate station must have been between Ambleside and Moresby, having Caer-mot between it and Old Carlisle, and Papcastle between it and Moresby. The summer station would be on Castle Hill, and the winter station on the area of the present town of Keswick, or on some

* This curious altar, after being some time in the possession of the late Dr James of Arthuret, was removed into the valuable collection of antiquities at Netherby.

convenient place betwixt the conflux of the rivers Greta and Derwent. And it is more probable that the *Derventione* of the Chorographia was here than at Papcastle, which comes better in for the *Pampocalio* of the same Chorographia.[100]

A station here would be an efficacious check on any body of the enemy that might cross the estuaries above or below Boulness, and pass the watch there, and the garrisons at Old Carlisle, Ellenborough, Papcastle and Moresby; for it was impossible for any body of men to proceed to the south but by Borrowdale or Dunmail raise, and a garrison at Keswick commanded both these passes.

The watch at Caer-mot would give the alarm to that on Castle Crag in the pass of Borrowdale, and the sentinel on Castle Head, that overlooks Keswick, would communicate the same to the garrison there; so it is apparently impossible that any body of men could pass that way unnoticed or unmolested. But if they attempted a route on the northern side of Skiddaw and over Hutton Moor to Patterdale, the watch at Caer-mot was in sight both of Old Carlisle and Keswick, and the garrison of the latter might either pursue or give notice to Whitbarrow and Ambleside, to meet them in the pass at the head of Patterdale, called Kirkston, which is so steep, narrow and crowded with rocks, that a few veteran troops would easily stop the career of a tumultuous crowd. If they made good the pass, and turned to the east before the Romans arrived, they would in that case be harassed in the rear till they arrived at Kendal, where the watchmen from Watercrook would be ready to receive them, and then they would be attacked in front and rear. That the Romans have had engagements at Kirkston Pass is evident from the Roman arms that were lately found in the adjoining moss and the many heaps of stones collected thereabouts, which have the appearance of barrows.

These are the only passes amongst the mountains that a body of Caledonians could attempt in their way to the south, and these could not be secured without a station at Keswick, and that could not be more advantageously placed than where the town now stands, on the meeting of the roads from the surrounding stations, all being about an equal distance from it, and at such a distance as rendered a station there necessary, and the several castellums on Castle Crag, and Castle Hill and Castlet, useful in giving notice in order to guard these important posts.

That no vestige is now visible of a station ever being there, nor any notice taken of it by Camden and Horsley,[101] nor even a traditional record of its existence, are seeming difficulties, which put the negative on what has been advanced. But this may only prove that no care was taken to preserve the memory of such remains, and that the town occupies the whole area of the station and that the station had been placed within the site of the town, probably in the lower part, facing the pass of the Greta. In the wheel of the Greta, in a meadow peninsulated by the river just below the town and called Goats Field, there are vestiges of a foss, but too imperfect to draw a conclusion from in favour of the station.

The ground round the town is very fertile, and has been long enough cultivated to destroy any remains of it, and what have been accidentally discovered, may be gone into oblivion; and no change happening in the town itself to occasion new discoveries, farther proofs may still be wanting.

If Camden visited Keswick, he was satisfied with the then present state of the "little town which king Edward I made a market". The face of the country only drew his attention. That Horsley never visited these parts is evident, from his mistaken account of the road from Plumpton Wall to Keswick, which he says passed through Greystock Park. This, had he but seen the face of the country, he could never have imagined. His mistake, and Camden's silence, gave occasion to a regular survey of the said road; and, finding the military roads from Papcastle, Ellenborough, Moresby, Ambleside and Plumpton all to coincide at Keswick, for this and the other reasons already assigned it appeared evident that a station must be somewhere near.

The Castle Hill, above Keswick, is a faithful record of the existence of a station in this country. Here was the seat of the ancient lords of the manor of Derwentwater, probably raised on the ruins of the Roman fortress: but after the heiress of that family was married to Ratcliff's, the family seat was removed into Northumberland and the castle went to ruins; and with the stones thereof the Ratcliffs built a house of pleasure in one of the islands in Derwentwater.† The name Castle Hill, being more ancient than the last erection, is still retained. At Ambleside, when I enquired for the Roman station a few years ago, no person could inform me of it, till one considering my description answered, It is the castle. The station at Plumpton is called by the same name; and at Kendal, the castellum that overlooks the station is also called the Castlesteads.

So here the Castle Hill was probably the place of the summer station; but being a fruitful tract, and much ploughed, I have not been able to trace any appearance of a foss, or vallum, and therefore the whole must rest upon the necessity, or at least on the expediency, of a station here. Since the above was written, an urn, with other remains, were turned up by the plough in a field below the town, and said to be Roman.

† Nicholson's *History of Cumberland*, page 86.

Ullswater

Those that do not choose to go as far as Penrith may, near the eighth mile-post, turn off to the right (leaving Mell Fell, a round green hill, on the left) to Matterdale, and proceed to Gowbarrow Park, which will bring them upon Ullswater, about the middle part of it, where it is seen to great advantage. But here it must be observed that some of the principal beauties of the lake, and the sweetest pastoral scenes, are entirely lost by this route. Dunmallet, the greatest ornament of the lake, with the whole of the first great bend, cannot here be seen and much of the dignity of the lake is thereby lost.

The lower reach of the lake

It is therefore better to ride to the gate on the right that leads to Dacre, and over Dacre Common, to the foot of Dunmallet.[102] By this course, every part of the lake will be viewed to the greatest advantage. Mr Gray's choice of visiting this lake was from Penrith, up the vale of Emont. "A grey autumnal day," he writes,

> went to see Ullswater, 5 miles distant; soon left Keswick road, and turned to the left, through shady lanes, along the vale of Emont, which runs rapidly on near the way, rippling over the stones; to the right, Dalemain, a large fabric of pale red stone, with nine windows in front, and seven on the side. Further on, Hutton St John, a castle-like old mansion of Mr Huddlestone. Approach Dunmallet, a fine pointed hill covered with wood. Began to mount the hill and with some toil gained the summit.
>
> From hence, saw the lake opening directly at my feet, majestic in calmness, clear and smooth as a blue mirror, with winding shores and low points of land covered with green inclosures, white farmhouses looking out among the trees and cattle feeding. The water is almost everywhere bordered with cultivated lands, gently sloping upwards, from a mile to a quarter of a mile in breadth, till they reach the feet of the mountains, which rise very rude and awful, with their broken tops, on each hand. Directly in front, at better than three miles distance, Place Fell, one of the bravest among them, pushes its bold breast into the midst of the lake, and forces it to alter its course, forming first a large bay to the left, and then bending to the right.
>
> Descended Dunmallet by a side avenue, only not perpendicular and came to Barton Bridge, over the Emont. Then walked through a path in the wood, round the bottom of the hill, came forth where the Emont issues out of the lake and continued my way along the western shore, close to the water and generally on a level with it; it is 9 miles long, and at the widest under a mile in breadth. After extending itself 3 ½ miles in a line to the south-west, it turns at the foot of Place Fell almost due west, and is here not twice the breadth of the Thames at London. It is soon again interrupted by the root of Helvellyn, a lofty and very rugged mountain, and spreading again, turns off to the south-east and is lost among the deep recesses of hills. To this second turning I pursued my way about 4 miles along its borders, beyond a village scattered among trees and called Watermillock.

Here Mr Gray leaves us and the greatest part of the lake unseen, and its most picturesque parts undescribed.[103] For the last bend of the lake is spotted with rocky isles, deeply indented with wooded promontories on one side and rocks on the other, from which result many a truly pleasing picture.

Antiquities

Before you quit the top of Dunmallet, observe the vestiges of its former importance in the remains of a Roman fort. An area of 110 paces by 37, surrounded with a foss, is yet visible, and stones of the rampart still peep through the grass. The well, that supplied the guard kept here, was but lately filled with stones. This fort must have been of great consequence in guarding the lake and commanding the pass, and in maintaining a connection between the garrisons of Ambleside and Brougham, it being 5 or 6 miles distance from the latter, and 19 from the former. There are also strong vestiges of a square fort on Soulby Fell, which communicates with this and the camp at Whitbarrow.

The middle reach of the lake

Opposite to Watermillock, a cataract descends down the front of Swarth Fell in Martindale Forest. At Skelling Nab, a bold promontory, the lake is contracted to a span, but it soon spreads itself again both ways, forming a variety of sweet bays and promontories. After a reach of 3 miles, it winds with a grand sweep round the smooth breast of Place Fell and, making a turn directly south, advances with equal breadth towards Patterdale. The western shore is various.

Drawing near the second bend, the mountains strangely intersect each other. Behind many wooded hills rises Stonecross Pike and, over all, steep Helvellyn shows his sovereign head. On the western side, Yew Crag, a noble pile of rock, fronts Place Fell, where its streams tumble in a cataract to the lake. Gowbarrow Park opens with a grand amphitheatre of shining rock, the floor of which is spread with soft green pasture, once shaded with ancient oaks, to which many decayed roots bear witness, Scattered thorns, trees and bushes vary the ground, which is pastured with flocks, herds of cattle and fallow deer. The road winds along the margin of the lake, and at every turn presents the finest scenes that can be imagined.

The upper reach of the lake

At the upper end of Gowbarrow Park, the last bend of the lake, which is by much the finest, opens, scattered with small rocky islands. The shores are bold, rocky, wooded and much embayed. Pass Newbridge, and the road winds up a steep rock, having the lake underneath you on the left. From the top,[104] you have a view under the trees, both up and down the lake. Martindale Fell, a naked grey rock on the opposite shore, rises abruptly from the water to an alpine height, and with an astonishing effect. The rock you stand on hangs over the lake, which seems blue and unfathomable to the eye. An island in the middle space has a beautiful appearance. This is the most romantic, striking and terrible situation upon the lake, especially if the wind blows the surges of water against the rock below you. The shores on both sides upwards are very pleasing, and the little decorating isles are scattered in the most exquisite taste, and delightful order. The ride along the banks, since the repair of the road, is charming.

The upper end terminates in sweet meadows, surrounded to the right by towering rocky hills, broken and wooded. Martindale Fell is the opposite boundary, skirted here with hanging inclosures, cots and farms. The principal feeders of this lake are Grysdale Beck, on the western corner, and Goldrill Beck, which descends from Kirkston Fell. They enter it in a freer manner than the feeder of Derwent does, and make a much finer appearance at their junction.

From the bridge in Patterdale,‡ Goldrill Beck serpentizes sweetly through the meadows, and falls easily into the lake about the middle of the vale. Glencairn Beck, descending from Helvellyn, joins the lake at the bridge which unites the counties of Westmorland and Cumberland.

There is from the top of the rock, above the inn,[105] a very charming view of the last bend of the lake, which constitutes one of the finest landscapes on it and takes in just enough for a delightful picture. The nearest foreground is a fall of inclosures. A rocky wooded mountain that hangs over Patterdale House (called Martindale Fell) is in a proper point of distance to the right. Steep rocks, and shaggy woods hanging from their sides, are on the left. Gowbarrow Park rises in a fine style from the water edge for the background, and a noble reach of water, beautifully spotted with rocky isles, charmingly disposed, with perpetual change of rocky shore, fill the middle space of this beautiful picture.

The lake is of a depth sufficient for breeding char, and abounds with a variety of other fish. Trout of 30 lb weight and upwards, are said to be taken in it.

The water of the lake is very clear, but has nothing of the transparency of Derwent, and is inferior to Buttermere and Cromack Water also in this respect. The stones in the bottom, and along the shores, are coated with mud.

Other men's views of Ullswater

Mr Gray viewed this lake in the same manner as that at Keswick, proceeding along its banks and facing the mountains, judging that the idea of magnitude and magnificence were thereby increased, and the whole set off with every advantage of foreground. But this lake viewed from any height, except Dunmallet, also loses much of its dignity as a lake, from the number of its flexures and jutting out of promontories; it nevertheless retains the appearance of a magnificent river ingulfed in rocks.

The bold winding hills, the intersecting mountains, the pyramidal cliffs, the bulging, broken, rugged rocks, the hanging woods and the tumbling, roaring cataracts, are parts of the sublime scenes presented in this surprising vale. The cultivated spots wave upward from the water in beautiful slopes, intersected by hedges, decorated with trees, in the most

‡ After crossing the bridge in Patterdale and ascending the side of Martindale Fell to a certain height, in the view across the head of the lake the mountains assume more pointed and alpine forms than any we have seen in this country. No. 12 of Mr Farrington's views represents this subject.

pleasing manner; mansions, cottages and farms, placed in the sweetest situations, are the rural parts and altogether form the most delightful and charming scenes. The accompaniments of this lake are disposed in the most picturesque order, bending round its margins and spreading upwards in craggy rocks and mountains, irregular in outline; yet they are certainly much inferior in sublimity and horrible grandeur to the environs of Keswick and the dreadful rocks of Borrowdale.

But in this opinion we have Mr Cumberland against us, who, having visited the other lakes in dark unfavourable weather, when nothing could be seen besides weeping rocks, flooded roads and watery plains, darkened by sable clouds that hovered over them and concealed their variegated shores, entertained an unfavourable idea of them; and, being more fortunate in a fine day in that part of the tour where he visited Ullswater, he attuned his lyre in honour of this enchanting lake and sung its charms not only in preference to Windermere, Grasmere and the vale of Keswick, but he also raises it above the pride of Lomond and the marvellous Killarney.

Our bard, in the sweet ode alluded to, represents himself upon the banks of the lake of Ullswater, bemoaning the hardness of his fate in being deprived of a fine day for this view, when the sun, beaming forth, blessed him with a full display of all the beauties of this enchanting lake. In gratitude for so special a favour, in a true poetic rapture, he dedicates this ode to the God of Day, and commemorates his partiality to the lake of Patterdale in the following harmonious numbers:

> Me turbid skies and threat'ning clouds await,
> Emblems, alas! of my ignoble fate.
> But see! the embattled vapours break,
> Disperse and fly,
> Posting like couriers down the sky;
> The grey rock glitters in the glassy lake—
> And now the mountain tops are seen
> Frowning amidst the blue serene;
> The variegated groves appear,
> Deck'd in the colours of the waning year;
> And as new beauties they unfold,
> Dip their skirts in beaming gold.
> Thee, savage Wyburn, now I hail,
> Delicious Grasmere's calm retreat,
> And stately Windermere I greet,
> And Keswick's sweet fantastic vale—
> But let her naiads yield to thee,
> And lowly bend the subject knee,
> Imperial lake of Patrick's dale!
> For neither Scottish Lomond's pride,
> Nor smooth Killarney's silver tide,

Nor aught that learned Poussin drew,
Or dashing Rosa flung upon my view,
Shall shake thy sovereign undisturbed right,
Great scene of wonder and sublime delight!

Hail to thy beams, O Sun! for this display,
What, glorious orb, can I repay?
—The thanks of an unprostituted muse.¶

¶ 'Ode to the Sun', page 18. The whole
of this ode is inserted in the Addenda,
Article IV.

* *Excursion to the Lakes*, page 65.

The navigators of this lake find much amusement by discharging guns, or small cannon, at certain stations. The effect is indeed truly curious, for the report is reverberated from rock to rock, promontory, cavern and hill, with every variety of sound; now dying away upon the ear, and again returning like peals of thunder, and thus re-echoed seven times distinctly.

This effect is thus described by Mr Hutchinson:[106]

Whilst we sat to regale, the barge put off from shore to a station where the finest echoes were to be obtained from the surrounding mountains. This vessel was provided with six brass cannon mounted on swivels; on discharging one of these pieces, the report was echoed from the opposite rocks, where by reverberation it seemed to roll from cliff to cliff, and return through every cave and valley, till the decreasing tumult gradually died away upon the ear.

The instant it had ceased, the sound of every distant waterfall was heard, but for an instant only, for the momentary stillness was interrupted by the returning echo on the hills behind; where the report was repeated like a peal of thunder bursting over our heads, continuing for several seconds, flying from haunt to haunt till once more the sound gradually declined; again the voice of the waterfalls possessed the interval till, to the right, the more distant thunder arose upon some other mountain, and seemed to take its way up every winding dell and creek, sometimes behind, on this side or on that, in wondrous speed running its dreadful course; when the echo reached the mountains within the line and channel of the breeze, it was heard at once on the right and left at the extremities of the lake. In this manner was the report of every discharge re-echoed seven times distinctly.*

Opposite to Watermillock is one of these stations.[107] The higher end of the lake is 14 miles from Penrith and 10 from Ambleside, of good turnpike road, save only at Styboar Crag where it is cut into the rock that awfully overhangs it, and is too narrow.

Above Goldrill Bridge, the vale becomes narrow and poor, the mountains steep, naked and rocky. Much blue slate of an excellent kind is excavated out of their bowels. The ascent from the lake to the top of

Kirkston is easy, and there are many waterfalls from the mountains on both sides. From the top of Kirkston to Ambleside the descent is quick. Some remarkable stones near the gorge of the pass are called Highcross. After what we have seen, the only lake that remains to be visited in this tour is

Haweswater

This is a pleasant morning ride from Penrith; or it may be taken in the way to Shap, or from Shap and return to Kendal. There is also a road from Pooley Bridge over the mountain to Bampton vale, a beautiful secreted valley.

Ascending the road from Pooley Bridge to the south, from the brow of the common you have a grand general view of Ullswater, with all its winding shore and accompaniments of woods, rocks, mountains, bays and promontories, to the entrance of Patterdale. To the north-east you look down on Pooley Bridge, and the winding of the river guides the eye to a beautiful valley, much ornamented with plantations, in the midst of which Dalemain is seated, queen of the vale of Emont.

Turning south, proceed by White Raise, a large cairn of stones, and near it are the remains of a small circus, ten stones of which are still erect. A little further on are the vestiges of a larger one, of 22 paces by 25. All the stones except the pillar are removed. It stands on the south side of the circus, and the place is called Moor Dovack. Here the vale of Bampton opens sweetly to the view, ascending to the south and spreading upwards in variety of dale-land beauty. At the bridge the road turns to the right, and soon brings you upon Haweswater.

Mr Young is the first that says anything in favour of this sweet but unfrequented lake.

> The approach to the lake is very picturesque: you pass between two high ridges of mountains, the banks finely spread with inclosures; upon the right, two small beautiful hills, one of them covered with wood; they are most pleasantly elegant. The lake is a small one, above 3 miles long, half a mile over in places and a quarter in others; almost divided in the middle by a promontory of inclosures, joined only by a strait, so that it consists of two sheets of water.
>
> The upper end of it is fine, quite inclosed with bold, steep craggy rocks and mountains; and in the centre of the end, a few little inclosures at their feet, waving upward in a very beautiful manner. The south side of the lake is a noble ridge of mountains, very bold and prominent down to the water's edge. They bulge out in the centre of a fine, bold, pendant, broad head that is venerably magnificent: and the view of the first sheet of the lake, losing itself in the second, among hills, rocks, woods &c. is picturesque.

The opposite shore consists of inclosures, rising one above another, and crowned with craggy rocks.†

† *Six Months' Tour,* Vol. 3, page 168.

The narrowest part, by report, is 50 fathoms deep,[108] and a man may throw a stone across it. Thwaite Force or fall is a fine cataract on the right, and opposite to it the first sheet of water is lost among the rocks and wood in a beautiful manner. Bleakhow Crag, a ruinous rock, and over it Castle Crag, a staring shattered rock, have a formidable appearance; and above all is seen Kidstow Pike, on whose summit the clouds weep into a crater of rock that is never empty. On the eastern side, a front of prominent rock bulges out into a solemn naked mass, and a waving cataract descends the furrowed side of a soft green hill. The contrast is fine. At Bleakhow Crag there is a pleasing back view.

Above the chapel, all is hopeless waste and desolation. The little vale contracts into a glen, strewed with the precipitated ruins of mouldering mountains and the destruction of perpetual waterfalls.

Kendal is 14 miles from the chapel, and whoever chooses an alpine ride may proceed to it up this vale. From the chapel to the top of the mountains is 3 miles, and the descent into Long Sleddale is as much more. In approaching the mountain, Harter Fell scowls forward in all the terrific grandeur of hanging rock. As you advance, a yawning chasm appears to divide it upwards from the base, and within it is heard the hoarse noise of ingulfed waters. The tumult of cataracts and waterfalls on all sides adds much to the solemnity of these tremendous scenes. The path soon becomes winding, steep and narrow, and is the only possible one across the mountain. The noise of a cataract on the left accompanies you during the ascent. On the summit of the mountain you soon come in sight of Long Sleddale, Lancaster Sands &c., and in the course of your descent you will presently be accompanied by a cataract on the right. The road traverses the mountain as on the other side, but is much better made and wider, on account of the slate taken from the sides of these mountains and carried to Kendal, &c. The waterfalls on the right are extremely curious.

You enter Long Sleddale between two shattered rocky mountains. That on the left, Crowbarrow, is not less terrible to look up at, when under it, than any rock in Barrowside or Borrowdale, and it has covered a much larger space with ruins. Here is every possible variety of waterfalls and cataracts; the most remarkable of which is on the left. Over a most tremendous wall of rock, a mountain torrent in one unbroken sheet leaps headlong 100 yds and more. The whole vale is narrow; the hills rise swift on each hand; their brows are wooded; their feet covered with grass or cultivated, and their summits broken. The road along the vale is tolerable, and joins the great road at Watchgate, about 4 miles from Kendal.

Haweswater may be taken the first in the morning, and then cross the mountains by the road to Pooley Bridge for Ullswater, and return in the evening to

Penrith‡

‡ *Bereda*, Rav. Chor; *Vereda*, Anton. Iter.

So much is already said of this town, that little remains now to be added here. The situation is pleasant, and open to the south. It is tolerably well built, and rather a genteel than a trading town. The town's people are polite and civil, and the inns commodious and well served.

Saving the few resident families, the life of this town is its being a thoroughfare. For, although seated in the midst of a rich and fruitful country, few manufacturers have been induced to fix here. Before the interest of the sister kingdoms became one, Penrith was a place of uncertain tranquillity and too precarious for the repose of trade and manual industry, being better circumstanced for a place of arms and military exercise. Yet since this happy change of circumstances, no more than one branch of tanning and a small manufacture of checks have taken place. This must be owing either to want of attention in people of property or of industry of the inhabitants. The latter is not to be supposed, for the spirit of agriculture, introduced by the gentlemen of the environs, is in as flourishing a way amongst the farmers of this neighbourhood as in other parts of the kingdom. The superfluities of the market are bought up for Kendal, where much of that produce is wanting which superabounds here.

The most remarkable objects at Penrith are the beacon, on the summit of the hill above the town, and the awful remains of the royal fortress on the crest of the rising ground that commands the town. It is supposed to be an erection of Henry VI out of the ruins of a more ancient structure called Mayburgh, but this is not very probable, since stones are easier quarried here than they could be got there. But as popular records have generally some fact to rest upon and some truth in the bottom, so some facings and other principal stones taken from Mayburgh might give rise to the tradition. There might also have been a stronghold here in the time of the Romans. At present the buildings are ruins in the last stage. One stone arched vault only remains, that from its situation appears to have been the keep, now no longer terrible, since the border service ceased and a mutual intercourse of trade and alliance happily took the place of national reprisals and family feuds.

The antiquity of this town is supposed to be found in its name being of British derivation, from *Pen* and *Rhudd*, signifying in that language a 'red head or hill'; and such is the colour of the hill above the town, and the ground and stones round it. But with respect to situation, it may well be derived from *Pen*, 'the head', and *Ryn*, 'a promontory', and so be referred to the beacon hill. It might however be judged a more honourable etymon to derive the name from *Pen* and *Rhydd*, of *Rhyddaw*, 'to make free', and that, on account of special service or fidelity to the Roman government, the Britons of this town were emancipated from the abject slavery which the nation in general were subjected to by their tyrannical masters. This, in their own language, might be *Penrhydd* and pronounced by the Britons, as by the Welsh at this day, 'Penrith'.[109]

However this may be, it has been the happiness of this town to remain a royal franchise through all the ages of feudal servitude, at least ever since the reign of Edward I, without the incumbrance of a charter, and it is now peaceably governed by the steward of the honours and a free jury. The honours of both town and castle belong to the Duke of Portland.

In the churchyard are some sepulchral monuments, which have long been the subject of antiquarian speculation, not yet decided. Thus much is evident, that the pillars alluded to are of one stone, formed like the ancient spears; the shafts round, for about 7 ft high; above that, they appear to be square, and to have terminated in a point. They are about 10 ft high, stand parallel to the church, distant from each other 15 ft. The space between is inclosed with circular stones, by some conjectured to represent boars.

There remains visible, on the upper part of the pillars, some ornamental work, but no inscription or figures appear at present, and the stones are so much fretted by time that it rests upon mere conjecture to affirm there ever were any. They probably mark the tomb of some great man, or family, before the custom was introduced of interring within churches; and are most likely British or, if not, must be Saxon.

The environs of Penrith

There are many pleasing rides in the environs of Penrith; most of them lead to curious remains of ancient monuments, or to modern rural improvements. In Whinfield Park are the Countess Pillar, the White Hart tree and the Three Brothers' tree. The first particular is a filial tribute of Ann, Countess Dowager of Pembroke, to the memory of her pious mother, Mary, Countess Dowager of Cumberland; and the trees are the remains of large, aged oaks that have long outlived their own strength. One of them is upwards of 9 yds in circumference. Brougham castle is an awful ruin, the *Brovoniacum* of the Romans, and since that the bulwark of Westmorland on that side and the pride of its earls for many descents. In the roof of a gallery is a stone with a Roman sepulchral inscription, much defaced. At Little Salkeld is the largest druidical circle in the northern parts.

Near Eamont Bridge is Arthur's round table, and at a small distance from it is Mayburgh, both of remote antiquity and doubtful use. The first may be presumed to have been a place of public exhibition for martial exercises, and the latter has the circumstances of a British fort; but the rude pillar inclines some to believe it the remains of a druid temple. It is entirely formed of loose stones and pebbles, collected from the adjacent rivers and fields. That the height has once been great may be collected from the vast breadth of the base, increased by the fall of stones from the top. It incloses an area of 80 yds or more, and near the middle stands a red stone, upwards of 3 yds high. The entrance is on the eastern side, and opens to a sweet view of Brougham House, to which the rude pillar when whitened (and of this Mr Brougham is very careful) is a fine obelisk.

If the name of this very extraordinary monument was *Breingwin*, then Mr Pennant, from Rowland,[110] has pointed out its use, viz "a supreme consistry of druidical administration, as the British name imports". But if the present name be a Saxon corruption of the ancient name, which probably was Mysirion, by the Saxons pronounced Maybirion or Maybir, and to bring it still nearer to their own language, Mayburgh, then this conjecture being admitted, it will signify a place of study and contemplation.¶ Such places the druids had, and were the public schools destined for the colloquial instruction of pupils in mysteries of religion and the arcana of civil government. Druidical remains are frequent in the neighbourhood, and many of them similar, but Mayburgh is such a huge and singular construction, that it must have been designed for some extraordinary use.

¶ *Mona Antiqua*, page 84.

From the beacon the views are many, all extensive and vast.[111] The eye is in the centre of a plain, inclosed with a circle of stupendous mountains of various forms. The plain is adorned with many ancient towns, and more ancient castles, stations and castellums, where the Roman eagle long displayed her wings; but which are now possessed by a happier people, who enjoy with freedom all the refinements of liberal taste and flourishing industry.

Shap

Haweswater may be conveniently visited from Penrith, returning from it by the ruins of Shap (or Heppe) Abbey to Shap. The remains of this ancient structure are inconsiderable, yet picturesque. A square tower, with piked windows, is the chief part of the ruins and does honour to the reign of King John, when it was built for canons of the Praemonstratensian Order, that had been first placed at Preston Patrick, near Kendal, by Thomas, son of Gospatrick.

This abbey was dedicated by the first founder to St Mary Magdalene, and he endowed it with a large portion of his lands in Preston, near Kendal. His son translated it to Magdalene Vale, near Shap, and further endowed it with the lands of Karl or Karlwath. Robert de Vetripont (Vipont), first Lord of Westmorland, confirmed the preceding grants and added to that of Matilda his mother, and Ivo his brother, the tithes of all his mills and of the game killed in all his lands in Westmorland. This grant is dated on Saturday, April 24, in the 13th of King John.

From this sequestered spot, continue the route to the village of Shap, a proper place for refreshment, before you face Shap Fells, a dreary, melancholy tract of 12 miles.

[Mr Cockin adds here:] This elevated tract being near the centre of
Westmorland, and where we may suppose its Genius is most likely to sit
enthroned, it may afford the reader a seasonable amusement to peruse in
this place a little ode addressed to that imaginary being by a late elegant
bard,[112] when on one of his visits to his native country:

Ode
To the Genius of Westmorland
Hail, hidden Power of these wild groves,
These uncouth rocks and mountains grey;
Where oft, as fades the closing day,
The family of fancy roves.

In what lone cave, what secret cell,
Coeval with the birth of time,
Wrapt in high cares, and thought sublime,
In awful silence dost thou dwell!

Oft in the depth of winter's reign,
As blew the dark winds o'er the dale,
Moaning along the distant gale,
Has fancy heard thy voice complain.

Oft in the dark wood's lonely way,
Swift has she seen thee glancing by;
Or down the summer evening sky,
Sporting in clouds of gilded day.

I caught from thee the sacred fire,
That glow'd within my youthful breast;-
Those thoughts too high to be express'd,
Genius, if thou didst once inspire.

O! pleas'd, accept this votive lay,
That in my native shade retir'd,
And once, once more by thee inspir'd,
In gratitude I pay.*

* Langhorne's *Effusions of Friendship
and Fancy*, Vol. 1, Let. 25. [Wm Cockin]

On the east side of the road, soon after you leave the village, observe a
double range of huge granites, pitched in the ground and at some distance
from each other, leading to circles of small stones, and increasing the space
between the rows as they approach the circles, where the avenue is about 27
paces wide. They are supposed to have run quite through the village, and
terminated in a point. It has long embarrassed the antiquaries what to call
this very uncommon monument of ancient date. Mr Pennant has given

a plausible explanation of it from Olaus Magnus, and supposes the row of granites to be the recording stones of a Danish victory obtained on the spot, and the stony circles to be grateful tributes to the memory of consanguineous heroes slain in the action.

There is at a small distance to the east from these stones a spring called Shap Spa, in smell and taste like that of Harrowgate, and much frequented by the people of the country for scorbutic complaints and eruptions of the skin. Leaving this gloomy region of black moors and shapeless mountains behind you, you approach a charming vale, which Mr Young in his elegant manner describes thus:[113]

> After crossing this dreary tract, the first appearance of a good country is most exquisitely fine. About 3 miles from Kendal, you at once look down from off this desolate country upon one of the finest landscapes in the world—a noble range of fertile inclosures, richly enamelled with the most beautiful verdure—and, coming to the brow of the hill, have a most elegant picturesque view of a variegated tract of waving inclosures, spreading over the hills and hanging to the eye in the most picturesque and pleasing manner that fancy can conceive. Three hills in particular are overlooked, cut into inclosures in a charming style, of themselves forming a most elegant landscape and worthy the imitation of those who would give the embellishments of art to the simplicity of nature.

The station from whence this description is taken[114] is about midway between the third and fourth mile-stone on the top of a rock, on the east side of the old road, called Stone Crag, which cannot be mistaken. The three hills referred to in the description are on the near ground of the landscape. There are many beautiful hills and knolls scattered about the valley, some cultivated, others covered with wood or shining in the softest verdure. But the most remarkable one for picturesque form is an oval green hill crowned with the ruins of a castle; it divides the valley and overlooks a town hanging on the side of a steep mountain. This is

Kendal†

The approach to it from the north is pleasant. A noble river, the Kent, is discovered flowing briskly through fertile fields and visiting the town in its whole length. It is crossed by a handsome bridge, where three great roads coincide, from Sedbergh, Kirkby Stephen and Penrith. The main street leading from the bridge slopes upwards to the centre of the town, and contracts itself into an inconvenient passage‡ where it joins another principal street, which falls with a gentle declivity both ways, and is a mile in length and of spacious breadth. Was an area for a marketplace opened at the incidence of these two streets, it would be a noble improvement.

† *Concangium* in the imperial *Notitia.*

‡ This passage is now widened, and a new street has been opened from near the centre of the town to the riverside, which has much improved the road through it for carriages.

The entrance from the south is by another bridge, which makes a short awkward turn into the suburbs, but after that the street opens well and the town has a cheerful appearance. The principal inns are genteel, commodious and plentifully served. Here is a workhouse for the poor which for neatness and economy exceeds most of the kind in the kingdom.

The objects most worthy of notice here are the manufactories. The chief of these are of Kendal cottons (a coarse woollen cloth), of linseys, toilonets, kerseymeres, callicoes,[115] and of knit worsted stockings. Also a considerable tannery is carried on in this town. The lesser manufactures are of fish hooks, of waste silk (which is received from London and, after scouring, combing and spinning, is returned), of ivory combs and of wool cards, in which branch considerable improvements have been made by the curious machines invented here for that purpose. There are other articles of industry well worth seeing, as the mills for scouring, fulling and frizing cloth, for cutting and rasping dying wood, &c.

But what is most to the credit of this place is that, notwithstanding many inconveniences which this town has laboured under, the manufactures have all along continued to flourish, and have of late years been greatly increased by the spirit and industry of the inhabitants. These manufactures are particularly noticed so early as the reign of King Richard II and Henry IV, when special laws were enacted for the better regulation of Kendal cloths, &c.¶

About a mile and a half from Kendal, on the road to Ulverston, is Scout Scar, a high rock, on which is a terrace of about a mile in length, facing the west, from which there is a most extensive and surprising view, which you come upon all at once as you approach the top, and is equal, if not superior, to most of the views in this romantic country.[116]

When William the Conqueror gave the barony of Kendal to Ivo de Taillebois, the inhabitants of the town were villein tenants of the baronial lord; but one of his successors emancipated them, and confirmed their burgages to them by charter. Queen Elizabeth, in the 18th year of her reign, erected it into a corporation, by the name of aldermen and burgesses, and afterwards King Charles I incorporated it with a mayor, 12 aldermen and 20 capital burgesses.

Mr Gray's description of this town is injurious to it; but his account of the church and castle is worth transcribing.[117]

Near the end of the town stands a handsome house of Colonel Wilson's,*[118] and adjoining to it the church, a very large Gothic fabric with a square tower; it has no particular ornaments, but double aisles and at the east end four chapels, or choirs.

Mr Gray's account then proceeds to the inside of the church,† which he describes with his usual accuracy and ease. Speaking of the four chapels or choirs, he says,

¶ At Mr Todhunter's Museum in Kendal may be seen a large collection of fossils and other articles of natural history, mostly of this country, as well as various articles of antiquity, ancient armour, coins, medals, sculpture, carvings in wood and various other curiosities well worth the attention of tourists.

A quarry of marble has lately been discovered near this town, which produces quite a new variety. It is of different colours, beautifully variegated, and takes the highest polish. When inlaid in statuary marble it has the best effect, and is equal, if not superior, to any imported from Greece or Italy. Chimneypieces and other ornamental works are made of it, and of the common limestone of the country, which also polishes very fine, in a good style, by Mr Francis Webster in Kendal, who has erected a mill for sawing and polishing the same.

* This is called Abbot Hall, and is now the property of Christopher Wilson esquire.

† [Mr C. adds:] The following epitaph, composed for himself by Mr Ravlph Tirer, vicar of Kendal (who died in 1627), and placed in the chancel, may be worth the reader's perusal on account of its quaintness and yet uncommon historical precision.

London bredd me, Westminster fedd me,
Cambridge sped me, my sister wed me,
Study taught me, Liuing sought me,
Learning brought me, Kendall caught me,
Labour pressed me, Sickness distressed me,
Death oppressed me, & Graue
    possessed me,
God first gave me, Christ did saue me,
Earth did crave me, & Heauen would
    haue me.

[Wm Cockin]

‡ In the reign of King Edward II, Richard Bellingham married Margaret, daughter and heiress of Gilbert Burnshead, of Burnshead, Knight, near Kendal.

there is one of the Parrs, another of the Stricklands, the third is the proper choir of the church, and the fourth of the Bellinghams, a family now extinct. The Bellinghams came into Westmorland before the reign of Henry VII, and were seated at Burneside.‡ In the reign of Henry VIII, Alan Bellingham purchased of the king the 20th part of a knight's fee in Helsington, parcel of the possession of Henry, Duke of Richmond and Sir John Lumley (Lord Lumley) which his father, Thomas Bellingham, had farmed of the crown; he was succeeded by his son, James Bellingham, who erected the tomb in the Bellinghams' chapel. There is an altar tomb of one of them (viz Alan Bellingham) dated 1577, with a flat brass arms and quarterings; and in the window their arms alone: argent, a hunting horn sable, strung gules.

In the Stricklands' chapel are several modern monuments, and another old altar tomb not belonging to the family: on the side of it, a fess dancette between ten billets deincourt. This tomb is probably of Sir Ralph D'Aincourt, who in the reign of King John married Helen, daughter of Anselm de Furness, whose daughter and sole heiress, Elizabeth D'Aincourt, was married to William, son and heir of Sir Robert de Strickland, of Great Strickland, knighted in the 23rd year of Henry III. The son and heir was Walter de Strickland, who lived in the reign of Edward I, was possessed of the fortunes of Anselm de Furness and D'Aincourt in Westmorland, and erected the above tomb to the memory of his grandfather, Ralph D'Aincourt. The descendants of the said Walter de Strickland have lived at Sizergh, in the neighbourhood, ever since, and this chapel is the family burial place.

In Parrs' chapel is a third altar tomb, in the corner—no figure or inscription, but on the side, cut in stone, an escutcheon of Ross of Kendal: three water budgets, quartering Parr, two bars in a border engrailed; 2dly, an escutcheon, vaire, a fess for Marmion; 3dly, an escutcheon, three chevronels braced, and a chief which I take for Fitzhugh; at the foot is an escutcheon surrounded with the garter, bearing Ross and Parr quarterly, quartering the other two before mentioned. I have no books to look in and therefore cannot say whether this is Lord Parr of Kendal, Queen Catharine's father, or her brother the Marquis of Northampton. Perhaps it is a cenotaph for the latter, who was buried at Warwick, 1571.

The castle he describes thus:

The remains of the castle are seated on a fine hill, on the side of the river opposite to the town; almost the whole inclosure wall remains, with four towers, two square and two round, but their upper parts and embattlements are demolished: it is of rough stone and cement, without any ornament of arms, round, inclosing a court of the like form and surrounded by a moat; nor ever could it have been larger than it is, for there are no traces of outworks. There is a good view of the town and river, with a fertile open valley through which it winds.

Had Mr Gray ascended from the end of Stramongate bridge to the castle, which was the only way to it when in its glory and is the easiest at present, he would have observed a square area that had been fortified with a deep moat, and connected with the castle by a drawbridge, where was probably the base court. The stones are now entirely removed, and the ground levelled, "and laughing Ceres reassumes the land".

The present structure was undoubtedly raised by the first barons of Kendal and probably on the ruins of a Roman station, this being the most eligible site in the country for a summer encampment and at a small distance from Watercrook. There are still some remains of a dark red freestone, used in facings and in the doors and windows, and have been brought from the environs of Penrith, more probably by the Romans, than by either the Saxon or Norman lords. Fame says this castle held out against Oliver Cromwell, and was battered from the Castlelaw Hill, but this is not so probable as that its present ruinous state is owing to the jealousy of that usurper.

The environs of Kendal

There is a most pleasant morning ride of 5 miles down the east side of the river. Watercrook is one mile distant, on the right, close by the side of the Kent. This is the *Concangium* of the Romans, where a body of the *vigilatores* (or watchmen) kept guard, and was the intermediate station betwixt the *Dictis* at Ambleside and the garrison at Overborough. The line of the foss may be still traced, though much defaced by the plough. Altars, coins and inscribed stones have been found here. And in the wall of the barn, on the very area of the station, is still legible the inscription preserved by Mr Horsley¶ to the memory of two freed men, with an imprecation against anyone who should contaminate their sepulchre and a fine to the fiscal. There is also an altar without an inscription, and a Silenus without a head. At a small distance is a pyramidal knoll, crowned with a single tree, called Sattury, where probably something dedicated to the god Saturn has stood.

Pass through the village of Natland and on the crest of a green hill on the left, called Helm, are the vestiges of a castellum called Castlesteads, which, during the residence of the watchmen at Watercrook, corresponded (by smoke in the day and flame in the night) with the garrison at Lancaster, by the beacon on Warton Crag. There is a house at a distance to the north, called Watch House, where Roman coins have been found.

¶ Horsley, *Britannia*, page 300.

* Near this place are large works for the manufactory of gunpowder.

* Near this place are large works for the manufactory of gunpowder.

† The Earl of Suffolk. The gardens belonging to this seat are rather curious, in the old style, and said to have been planned by the gardener of James II, who resided here with Colonel Graham during some part of the troubles of his royal master.

‡ Sizergh Hall is a venerable old building, in a pleasant situation, formed like the rest in ancient times for a place of defence. The tower is a square building, defended by two square turrets and battlements. One of them is over the great entrance, and as a guard-room capable of containing ten or a dozen men with embrasures. The winding staircase terminates in a turret, which defends the other entrance. (Burn's *Westmorland*)

¶ An obelisk was erected on top of this hill by a subscription of the inhabitants of Kendal in 1788, which seen from almost every part of the vale is a handsome object, and being the centenary of the revolution in 1688 has this inscription:

Sacred to Liberty.
THIS OBELISK
WAS ERECTED IN THE YEAR 1788,
IN MEMORY OF
THE REVOLUTION IN 1688.

* *Coccium* in Rav. Chor. On the edge of the mountain about a mile and a half to the north of this town is a natural curiosity called Claythrop Clints or Curwenwood Kins, which many tourists would probably like to see. It consists of a large plain of naked limestone rock, a little inclined to the horizon, which has evidently once been one continued calcarious mass, in a

Proceed through Sedgwick* and fall in with the course of the river at Force Bridge, and from the crown of it have a very singular romantic view of the river both ways, working its passage in a narrow, deep channel of rocks, hanging over it in a variety of forms, and streaming a thousand rills into the flood. The rocks in the bottom are strangely excavated into deep holes of various shapes which, when the river is low, remain full of water and from their depth are black as ink. The bridge is one bold arch, supported by the opposite rocks, of unknown antiquity. A mantle of ivy veils its ancient front, and gives it a most venerable appearance.

If you ride down the west side of the river from the bridge as far as the forge, to see the waterfall of the whole river, let it be remembered that the stream is much impaired in beauty since the forge was erected. And if, from the end of the uppermost house, you look up between the trees in the midst of the channel, you will see the whole body of the river issuing from a sable cavern and tumbling over a rock, of height just sufficient to convert it into a froth as white as snow, and behind it the arch of the bridge is partly caught in a disposition that forms a very uncommon assemblage of picturesque beauties. This is seen in the highest perfection when the stream is full. Return to the bridge, and ride down the east side of the river to Levens Park. In order to ride through the park, you must be favoured with a key from Levens Hall.

Here is one of the sweetest spots that fancy can imagine. The woods, the rocks, the river and the grounds are rivals in beauty of style and variety of contrast. The bends of the river, the bulging of the rocks over it, under which in some places it retires in haste and again breaks out in a calm and spreading stream, are matchless beauties. The ground in some places is bold, and hangs abruptly over the river, or falls into gentle slopes and easy plains. All is variety, with pleasing transition. Thickets cover the brows; ancient thorns and more ancient oaks are scattered over the plain; and clumps and solitary beech trees of enormous size that equal, if not surpass, anything the Chiltern hills can boast. The park is well stocked with fallow deer. The side of the Kent is famous for petrifying springs, that incrust vegetable bodies, such as moss, leaves of trees, &c. There is one on the park, called the Dropping Well.

At a small distance is Hincaster, where the Romans had a camp. Within the park is Kirkshead, mentioned by Camden as a place frequented by the Romans, yet nothing of late belonging to that people has been discovered at either place. Levens Hall was the seat of a family of that name for many ages; then of Redman, for several descents; afterwards it came to Bellingham, and Alan—or his son James—Bellingham gave it the present form in the reign of Queen Elizabeth; and in taste of carvings in wood attempted to outdo his contemporary, Walter Strickland esquire of Sizergh. After Bellingham it came to Colonel Graham, and from his daughter by marriage[119] to the ancestor of the late noble possessor.†

Return by Levens Bridge to Kendal, 5 miles. Have a new view of the valley and the east side of the Kent. At the park gate have a charming view of Sizergh,[120] showing itself to the morning sun and appearing to advantage from an elevated site under a bold and wooded background. The tower was built in the reign of Henry III, or Edward I, by Sir William Strickland, who had married Elizabeth, the general heiress of Ralph D'Aincourt. This is evident from an escutcheon cut in stone on the west side of the tower, and hung cornerwise: D'Aincourt quartering Strickland, three scallop shells; the crest, on a close helmet, a full-topped holly-bush. The same are the arms of the family at this time, and this has been their chief residence ever since.‡

Before you leave Kendal, visit the Castlelaw Hill. This is an artificial mount, that overlooks the town and faces the castle, and surpasses it in antiquity, being one of those hills called laws, where in ancient times distributive justice was administered. From its present appearance, it seems to have been converted to different purposes, but though well situated as a watch upon the castle, it could never be a proper place to batter it from, as has been reported.¶

From Kendal to Lancaster

To Lancaster by Burton-in-Kendal* is 22 miles. Observe on the left, before you reach Burton, Farlton Knot,† a beautiful naked limestone mountain said to resemble much in form the rock of Gibraltar.

Between Burton and Lancaster, see Dunald Mill Hole,‡ a subterraneous cavern with a brook running through it, and many curious petrifactions, in style and kind like those in Derbyshire.

Lancaster

Finis chartæque viæque.[121]

state of softness like that of mud at the bottom of a pond. It is now deeply rent with a number of fissures, of 6, 8 or 10 inches wide, just in the form of those which take place in clay or mud that is dried in the sun. It also exhibits such channels in its surface as can only be accounted for by supposing them formed by the ebbing of copious waters (probably those of the deluge) before the matter was become hard. It is 500 or 600 yards in length, and about 200 in breadth.

There are several other limestone plains of the same kind in the neighbourhood, but this is the most remarkable and extensive. In the crevices of the rock, the botanist may meet with the belladonna or *solanum lethale* (the deadly nightshade) and some other curious plants. [Wm Cockin]

† By a trigonometrical process, the height of the monument was found to be 594 ft above the level of the turnpike.

‡ This place is particularly described in Article VI of the following Addenda.

A Table of the Height of Mountains and Lakes

Seen in this Tour, and of Others in Different Parts of the World,
All Taken from the Level of the Sea in the North of England,
Taken by Mr John Dalton

Mountains[122]

	Yards
Scafell, north point, east of Wastwater	1080
Helvellyn	1070
Skiddaw	1060
Bowfell (Langdale)	1030
Rydalhead	1030
Grasmire, north-east of Crummock Lake	955
Red Pike, near Buttermere	950
Kentmere High Street	912
Coniston Old Man	860
Whernside, near Dent	825
Hillbell, north-west of Kendal	812
Carrock, west pike, Colbeck	744
Knoutberry Hill, near Dent	728
Goatscar, summit of the road from Haweswater to Kendal	663
Pendale Hill, Lancashire	548
Whinfell Beacon, north-east of Kendal	500
Rivington Pike, between Bolton and Chorley, Lancashire	400
Benson Knot, near Kendal	366
Penrith Beacon	340
Kendal Fell, north-west summit	216
Town of Kendal	46

Lakes

	Yards
Haweswater	238
Leathes Water, Wythburn [Thirlmere]	182
Ullswater	106
Crummock Water	91
Derwentwater	76
Bassenthwaite water	70
Esthwaite Water	66
Grasmere Water	60
Rydal Water	52
Windermere Water	36

In Scotland

From Pennant's Tour, 1769

	Yards
Ben Lomond	1080
Benevish	1450

Ben-y-bourd still higher, which, with Laghin-y-gair and Benewewish, are never without snow.

In other parts

By M. T. Bouritt

Summit of Dole, the highest mountain of Jura	1800
Valley of Chamonix, in Savoy	1121
Ridge de Brevin, a glacier in the valley of Chamonix	2949
Valley of Mountainvert, in Savoy	1865
Abbey of Sixt, in Savoy	797
Summit of Grenier	2782
Summit of Grenarion	2958
Summit of Buet	3315
Mont Blanc	5081
Mount Ætna	4000
Lake of Geneva, at the lower passage of the Rhone	398
Lake of Neuchatel	456

By different authors

Highest part of the Table, at the Cape of Good Hope	1153
Pike Rucia in the island of Madeira	1689
Pike of Tenerife	4399
The same, according to Dr Heberden	5132
Summit of Cotopaxis in South America, according to Don Antono de Ulloa	6643
Corambour, under the equator	6000
Chimboraco	6440
Petchinca	4860
Carason	4940

From this survey of mountains it appears that Scafell is the highest in England, yet below the point of permanent snow. It has been observed by the French academicians that amongst the Cordilleras, in the province of Quito, Petchinca and Carason are the highest accessible mountains, and that all of greater heights are vested with eternal snow.

On the glaciers, snow is permanent at a much inferior height; and, where the sun's rays fall more obliquely, less height is found the boundary between temporary and eternal snow. But no mountain in England touches the zone of barrenness that intervenes between this region and the limits of vegetation. Sheep pasture the summits of Snowden, Helvellyn and Skiddaw, and barrenness only prevails where rock and precipice are invincible obstacles to vegetation.

Roads from Lancaster to the Lakes

Miles

	Lancaster
3	Hest Bank
9	Over Lancaster Sands to Carter House
2	Cartmel or Flookburgh
2	Holker Gate
3	Over Ulverston Sands to Carter House
1	Ulverston
12	Dalton, Furness Abbey, and back to Ulverston
4	Penny Bridge
2	Lowick Bridge
Or, 5	From Ulverston to Lowick Bridge
2½	Through Nibthwaite to Coniston waterfoot
6	Coniston waterhead
3	Hawkshead
5	Ambleside
Or, 4	From Hawkshead to the ferry on Windermere Water
1	Bowness across Windermere Water
6	Ambleside
2	Rydal
2	Grasmere
2½	Dunmail Raise stones
3½	Dalehead
4¾	Castlerigg
1	Keswick
3	Lowdore waterfall
1	Grange
1	Bowdar Stone, Castle Hill
2½	Rosthwaite
2½	Seathwaite
9	Keswick
8	Down Bassenthwaite Water by Bowness, Bradness and Scareness, to Armathwaite
9	Up the other side of the lake to Keswick
5	Keskadale
3	Buttermere
6	Down Cromack Water to Lorton
7½	Keswick
4	Threlkeld
6	Whitbarrow
1	Penruddock
6¾	Penrith

5	Dunmallet, at the foot of Ullswater, and Pooley Bridge
9	Watermillock, Gowbarrow Park, Airey Bridge to the head of Ullswater
9	Ambleside
Or, 14	From the head of Ullswater to Penrith
10½	By Lowther, Askham and Bampton, to Haweswater
15	Through Long Sleddale to Kendal
Or, 5	From Haweswater to Shap, by Ross and Shap Abbey
7	Hawes foot
8	Kendal
10	Down the east side of Kent to Levens Park, and return to Kendal by Sizergh
11	Burton-in-Kendal
11	Lancaster

Addenda

It having been judged that the principal detached pieces which have appeared on the subject of the Lakes by esteemed writers, if collected together, might accommodate the reader and contribute to the chief purport of this manual, they are here subjoined, along with some other connected articles and similar descriptions which relate to the same country.

Article I

Dr Brown's Letter[123]

Describing the Vale and Lake of Keswick

In my way to the north from Hagley, I passed through Dovedale; and, to say the truth, I was disappointed in it. When I came to Buxton, I visited another two of their romantic scenes; but these are inferior to Dovedale. They are but poor miniatures of Keswick, which exceeds them more in grandeur than I can give you to imagine—and more, if possible, in beauty than in grandeur.

Instead of the narrow slip of valley which is seen at Dovedale, you have at Keswick a vast amphitheatre, in circumference above 20 miles. Instead of a meagre rivulet, a noble living lake 10 miles round, of an oblong form adorned with a variety of wooded islands. The rocks indeed of Dovedale are finely wild, pointed and irregular; but the hills are both little and unanimated, and the margin of the brook is poorly edged with weeds, morass and brushwood.

But at Keswick, you will on one side of the lake see a rich and beautiful landscape of cultivated fields, rising to the eye in fine inequalities, with noble groves of oak happily dispersed and climbing the adjacent hills, shade above shade, in the most various and picturesque forms. On the opposite shore you will find rocks and cliffs of stupendous height, hanging broken over the lake in horrible grandeur, some of them a thousand feet high, the woods climbing up their steep and shaggy sides, where mortal foot never yet approached. On these dreadful heights, the eagles build their nests, a variety of waterfalls are seen pouring from the summits and tumbling in vast sheets from rock to rock in rude and terrible magnificence, while on all sides of this immense amphitheatre the lofty mountains rise round, piercing the clouds in shapes as spiry and fantastic as the very rocks of Dovedale.

To this I must add the frequent and bold projection of the cliffs into the lake, forming noble bays and promontories; in other parts they finely retire from it and often open in abrupt chasms or cliffs, through which at hand you see rich and cultivated vales, and beyond these, at various distances, mountain rising over maintain, among which new prospects present themselves in mist, till the eye is lost in agreeable perplexity:

> Where active fancy travels beyond sense,
> And pictures things unseen————

Were I to analyse the two places into their constituent principles, I should tell you that the full perfection of Keswick consists of three circumstances—*beauty*, *horror* and *immensity*—united, the second of which is alone found in Dovedale. Of beauty it hath little, nature having left it almost a desert: neither its small extent, nor the diminutive and lifeless form of the hills, admit magnificence.

But to give you a complete idea of these three perfections, as they are joined in Keswick, would require the united powers of Claude, Salvator and Poussin. The first should throw his delicate sunshine over the cultivated vales, the scattered cots, the groves, the lake and wooded islands. The second should dash out the horrors of the rugged cliffs, the steeps, the hanging woods and foaming waterfalls; while the grand pencil of Poussin should crown the whole with the majesty of the impending mountains.

So much for what I would call the *permanent* beauties of this astonishing scene. Were I not afraid of being tiresome, I could now dwell as long on its varying or *accidental* beauties. I would sail round the lake, anchor in every bay and land you on every promontory and island. I would point out the perpetual change of prospects: the woods, rocks, cliffs and mountains, by turns vanishing or rising into view, now gaining on the sight, hanging over our heads in their full dimensions, beautifully dreadful, and now by a change of situation assuming new romantic shapes, retiring and lessening on the eye and insensibly losing themselves in an azure mist. I would remark the contrast of light and shade produced by the morning and evening sun—the one gilding the western, and the other the eastern side of this immense amphitheatre—while the vast shadow projected by the mountains buries the opposite part in a deep and purple gloom, which the eye can hardly penetrate.

The natural variety of colouring which the several objects produce is no less wonderful and pleasing, the ruling tints in the valley being those of azure, green and gold, yet ever various, arising from an intermixture of the lake, the woods, the grass and cornfields; these are finely contrasted by the grey rocks and cliffs, and the whole heightened by the yellow streams of light, the purple hues and misty azure of the mountains.

Sometimes a serene air and clear sky disclose the tops of the highest hills; at others, you see the clouds involving their summits, resting on their sides or descending to their base, and rolling among the valleys, as in a vast furnace. When the winds are high, they roar among the cliffs and caverns like a peal of thunder; then too the clouds are seen in vast bodies, sweeping along the hills in gloomy greatness, while the lake joins the tumult and tosses like a sea. But in calm weather, the whole scene becomes new, the lake is a perfect mirror and the landscape in all its beauty—islands, field, woods, rocks and mountains—is seen inverted and floating on its surface.

I will now carry you to the top of a cliff where, if you dare approach the ridge, a new scene of astonishment presents itself, where the valley, lake and islands seem lying at your feet, where this expanse of water appears diminished to a little pool amidst the vast immeasurable objects that surround it: for here the summits of more distant hills appear beyond those you had already seen; and, rising behind each other in successive ranges, and azure groups of craggy and broken steeps, form an immense and awful picture, which can only be expressed by the image of a tempestuous sea of mountains.

Let me now conduct you down again to the valley, and conclude with one circumstance more, which is that a walk by still moonlight (at which time the distant waterfalls are heard in all their variety of sound) among these enchanting dales opens a scene of such delicate beauty, repose and solemnity as exceeds all description.

Article II

Extract from Dr Dalton's
Descriptive Poem[124]

Enumerating the Beauties of the Vale of Keswick*

* First printed in 1775—see Pearch's
Collection of Poems, Vol. 1.

——————————To Nature's pride,
Sweet Keswick's vale, the muse will guide,
The muse who trod th' enchanted ground,
Who sail'd the wond'rous lake around,
With you will haste once more to hail
The beauteous brook of Borrowdale.

From savage parent, gentle stream!
Be thou the muse's favourite theme:—
O soft insinuating glide
Silent along the meadow's side,
Smooth o'er the sandy bottom pass,
Resplendent all through fluid glass,
Unless upon thy yielding breast
Their painted heads the lilies rest,
To where in deep capacious bed,
The widely liquid lake is spread.

Let other streams rejoice to roar
Down the rough rocks of dread Lowdore,
Rush raving on with boist'rous sweep,
And foaming rent the 'frighted deep,
Thy gentle genius shrinks away
From such a rude unequal fray;
Through thine own native dale, where rise
Tremendous rocks amid the skies,
Thy waves with patience slowly wind,
Till they the smoothest channel find,
Soften the horrors of the scene,
And through confusion flow serene.

Horrors like these at first alarm,
But soon with savage grandeur charm,
And raise to noblest thoughts the mind;
Thus by thy fall, Lowdore, reclin'd,
The craggy cliff, impendant wood,

Whole shadows mix o'er half the flood,
The gloomy clouds with solemn sail,
Scarce lifted by the languid gale,
O'er the capp'd hill, and dark'ned vale:—
The rav'ning kite, and bird of Jove,
Which round the aerial ocean rove,
And, floating on the billowy sky,
With full expanded pinions fly,
Then fluttering on their belating prey,
Thence with death-dooming eye survey.—
Channels by rocky torrents torn,
Rocks to the lake in thunders borne,
Or such as o'er our heads appear
Suspended in their mid-career,
To start again at his command,
Who rules fire, water, air and land,
I view with wonder and delight,
A pleasing, though an awful sight:
For, seen with them, the verdant isles
Soften with more delicious smiles,
More tempting twine their op'ning bowers,
More lively glow the purple flowers.
More smoothly slopes the border gay,
In fairer circles bends the bay,
And last, to fix our wand'ring eyes,
Thy roofs, O Keswick, brighter rise,
The lake, and lofty hills between,
Where giant Skiddaw shuts the scene.

Article III

Mr Gray's Journal

In a letter to Dr Wharton, October 18th, 1769
Published in the memoirs of his life
By Mr Mason[125]

I hope you got safe and well home, after that troublesome night.† I long to hear you say so. For me, I have continued well, being so favoured by the weather that my walks have never once been hindered till yesterday (that is a fortnight and three or four days, and a journey of more than 300 miles). I am now at Aston for two days. Tomorrow I go to Cambridge. Mason is not here, but Mr Alderson received me. According to my promise, I send you the first sheet of my journal, to be continued without end.

Sep. 30. A mile and a half from Brough, where we parted, on a hill lay a great army‡ encamped: to the left opened a fine valley, with green meadows and hedgerows, a gentleman's house peeping forth from a grove of old trees. On a nearer approach appeared myriads of cattle and horses in the road itself and in all the fields round me, a brisk stream hurrying across the way, thousands of clean healthy people in their best party-coloured apparel—farmers and their families, esquires and their daughters, hastening up from the dales and down the fells from every quarter, glittering in the sun, and pressing forward to join the throng— while the dark hills, on whose tops the mists were yet hanging, served as a contrast to this gay and moving scene, which continued for near 2 miles more along the road, and the crowd (coming towards it) reached as far as Appleby.

On the ascent of the hill above Appleby, the thick hanging wood and the long reaches of the Eden—clear, rapid and full as ever, winding below, with views of the castle and town—gave much employment to the mirror,¶[126] but now the sun was wanting and the sky overcast. Oats and barley cut everywhere, but not carried in. Passed Kirkby Thore, Sir William Dalston's house at Acorn Bank, Winfield Park, Harthorn Oaks, Countess Pillar, Brougham Castle, Mr Brougham's large new house, crossed the Eden and the Emont with its green vale, and dined at 3 o'clock with Mrs Buchanan, at Penrith, on trout and partridge.

In the afternoon walked up Beacon Hill, a mile to the top, and could see Ullswater through an opening in the bosom of that cluster of broken mountains, which the doctor well remembers, Winfield and Lowther parks &c. and the craggy tops of an hundred nameless hills: these lie to the west

† Dr Wharton, who had intended to accompany Mr Gray to Keswick, was seized at Brough with a violent fit of his asthma, which obliged him to return home. This was the reason Mr Gray undertook to write the following journal of his tour for his friend's amusement. He sent it under different covers; I give it here in continuation. It may not be amiss however to hint to the reader that if he expects to find elaborate and nicely turned periods in his narration, he will be greatly disappointed. When Mr Gray described places, he aimed only to be exact, clear and intelligible; to convey peculiar not general ideas, and to paint by the eye, not the fancy. There have been many accounts of the Westmorland and Cumberland lakes, both before and since this was written, and all of them better calculated to please readers who are fond of what they call fine writing; yet those who can content themselves with an elegant simplicity of narrative will, I flatter myself, find this to their taste; they will perceive it written with a view rather to inform than surprise; and, if they make it their companion when they take the same tour, it will enhance their opinion of its intrinsic excellence—in this way I tried it myself, before I resolved to print it.

‡ There is a great fair for cattle kept on the hill near Brough on this and the preceding day.

¶ Mr Gray carried usually with him on these tours a plano-convex mirror of about 4 ins diameter, on a black foil, and bound up like a pocket-book. A glass of this sort is perhaps the best and most convenient substitute for a camera obscura, of anything that has hitherto been invented, and may be had of any optician.

and south. To the north, a great extent of black and dreary plains. To the east, Cross Fell, just visible through mists and vapour hovering round it.

Oct. 1.   A grey autumnal day, the air perfectly calm and mild, went to see Ullswater, 5 miles distant. Soon left the Keswick road and turned to the left through shady lanes along the vale of Emont, which runs rapidly on near the way, rippling over the stones: to the right is Dalemain, a large fabric of pale red stone, with nine windows in the front and seven on the side, built by Mr Hazel; behind it a fine lawn surrounded by woods, and a long rocky eminence rising over them. A clear brisk rivulet runs by the house to join the Emont, whose course is in sight and at a small distance. Further on appears Hutton St John, a castle-like old mansion of Mr Huddleston.

Approached Dunmallet, a fine pointed hill, covered with wood planted by old Mr Hazel before mentioned, who lives always at home and delights in planting. Walked over a spongy meadow or two, and began to mount the hill through a broad straight green alley among the trees, and with some toil gained the summit. From hence saw the lake open directly at my feet, majestic in its calmness, clear and smooth as a blue mirror, with winding shores and low points of land covered with green inclosures, white farmhouses looking out among the trees and cattle feeding. The water is almost everywhere bordered with cultivated lands, gently sloping upwards from a mile to a quarter of a mile in breadth till they reach the feet of the mountains which rise very rude and awful with their broken tops on each hand. Directly in front at better than 3 miles distance, Place Fell, one of the bravest among them, pushes its bold broad breast into the midst of the lake and forces it to alter its course, forming first a large bay to the left and then bending to the right.

I descended Dunmallet again by a side avenue, that was only not perpendicular, and came to Barton Bridge over the Emont; then, walking through a path in the wood round the bottom of the hill, came forth where the Emont issues out of the lake and continued my way along its western shore, close to the water and generally on a level with it. Saw a cormorant flying over it and fishing.

The figure of the lake nothing resembles that laid down in our maps. It is 9 miles long and at widest under a mile in breadth. After extending itself 3½ miles in a line to south-west, it turns at the foot of Place Fell almost due west and is here not twice the breadth of the Thames at London. It is soon again interrupted by the root of Helvelyn, a lofty and very rugged mountain, and spreading again turns to the south-east and is lost among the deep recesses of the hills. To this second turning I pursued my way about 4 miles along its border, beyond a village scattered among trees and called Watermillock, in a pleasant grave day, perfectly calm and warm, but without a gleam of sunshine; then the sky seeming to thicken and the valley to grow more desolate, and the evening drawing on, I returned by the way I came, to Penrith.

Oct. 2.	I set out at 10 for Keswick, by the road we went in 1767;[127] saw Greystock town and castle to the right, which lie about 3 miles from Ullswater over the fells; passed through Penruddock and Threlkeld at the foot of Saddleback, whose furrowed sides were gilt by the noon-day sun, whilst its brow appeared of a sad purple, from the shadow of the clouds as they sailed slowly by it. The broad and green valleys of the Gardies and Lowside, with a swift stream glittering among the cottages and meadows, lay to the left, and the much finer, but narrower valley of St John opening into it; Hill Top—the large though low mansion of the Gasgarth's, now a farmhouse, seated on an eminence among woods under a steep fell—was what appeared the most conspicuous, and beside it a great rock, like some ancient tower nodding to its fall. Passed by the side of Skiddaw and its cub, called Latrigg, and saw from an eminence at 2 miles' distance the vale of Elysium[128] in all its verdure, the sun playing on the bottom of the lake and lighting up all the mountains with its lustre. Dined by 2 o'clock at the Queen's Head, and then straggled out alone to the parsonage, where I saw the sun set in all its glory.

Oct. 3.	A heavenly day; rose at 7, and walked out under the conduct of my landlord to Borrowdale. The grass was covered with a hoar frost, which soon melted and exhaled in a thin bluish smoke; crossed the meadows obliquely, catching a diversity of views among the hills, over the lake and islands, and changing prospect at every ten paces. Left Cockshut (which we formerly mounted) and Castle Hill, a loftier and more rugged hill behind me, and drew near the foot of Wallow Crag, whose bare and rocky brow, cut perpendicularly down above 400 ft (as I guess, though the people call it much more) awfully overlooks the way. Our path here tends to the left—and the ground gently rising, and covered with a glade of scattered trees and bushes on the very margin of the water—opens both ways the most delicious view that my eyes ever beheld.

Opposite, the thick woods of Lord Egremont, and Newland valley, with green and smiling fields embosomed in the dark cliffs; to the left, the jaws of Borrowdale with that turbulent chaos of mountain behind mountain, rolled in confusion; beneath you, and stretching far away to the right, the shining purity of the lake reflecting rocks, woods, fields and inverted tops of hills, just ruffled by the breeze, enough to show it is alive, with the white buildings of Keswick, Crosthwaite church and Skiddaw, for a background at a distance. Behind you, the magnificent heights of Wallow Crag: here the glass played its part divinely. The place is called Carf-close-reeds; and I choose to set down these barbarous names that anybody may enquire on the place and easily find the particular station that I mean.

This scene continues to Barrowgate—and a little farther, passing a brook called Barrow Beck, we entered Borrowdale. The crags named Lowdore Banks begin now to impend terribly over the way, and more terribly when you hear that three years since an immense mass of rock tumbled at once from the brow, barred all access to the dale (for this is the only road) till they could work their way through it. Luckily no one was passing by at the time of this fall, but down the side of the mountain and far into the lake lie dispersed the huge fragments of this ruin, in all shapes and in all directions.

Something farther we turned aside into a coppice ascending a little in front of Lowdore waterfall: the height appeared to be about 200 ft, the quantity of water not great, though (these three days excepted) it hath rained daily for near two months before; but then the stream was nobly broken, leaping from rock to rock and foaming with fury. On one side a towering crag, that spired up to equal, if not overtop the neighbouring cliffs (this lay all in shade and darkness); on the other hand, a rounder, broader, projecting hill shagged with wood and illuminated by the sun, which glanced sideways on the upper part of the cataract. The force of the water, wearing a deep channel in the ground, hurries away to join the lake.

We descended again, and passed the stream over a rude bridge. Soon after we came under Gowdar Crag, a hill more formidable to the eye and to the apprehension than that of Lowdore, the rocks at top deep-cloven perpendicularly by the rains, hanging loose and nodding forwards, seen just starting from their base in shivers. The whole way down, and the road on both sides, is strewed with piles of the fragments, strangely thrown across each other and of a dreadful bulk. The place reminds me of those passes in the Alps, where the guides tell you to move with speed, and say nothing, lest the agitation of the air should loosen the snows above and bring down a mass that would overwhelm a caravan. I took their counsel here and hastened on in silence.

Non ragioniam di lor, ma guarda e passa.[129]

The hills here are clothed all up their steep sides with oak, ash, birch, holly &c. Some of it has been cut forty years ago, some within these eight years; yet all is sprung again, green, flourishing and tall for its age, in a place where no soil appears but the staring rock, and where a man could scarce stand upright. Here we met a civil young farmer overseeing his reapers (for it is now oat harvest) who conducted us to a neat white house in the village of Grange, which is built on a rising ground in the midst of a valley; round it the mountains form an awful amphitheatre, and through it obliquely runs the Derwent, clear as glass and showing under its bridge every trout that passes.

Beside the village rises a round eminence of a rock covered entirely with old trees and over that more proudly towers Castle Crag, invested also with wood on its sides and bearing on its naked top some traces of a fort, said to be Roman. By the side of this hill, which almost blocks up the way, the valley turns to the left and contracts its dimensions till there is hardly any road but the rocky bed of the river. The wood of the mountains increases, and their summits grow loftier to the eye and of more fantastic forms—among them appear Eagle's Cliff, Dove's Nest, Whitedale Pike &c., celebrated names in the annals of Keswick.

The dale opens about 4 miles higher, till you come to Seathwaite, where lies the way, mounting the hill to the right, that leads to the wad-mines; all farther access is here barred to prying mortals, only there is a little path winding over the fells and for some weeks in the year passable to the dalesmen; but the mountains know well that these innocent people will not reveal the mysteries of their ancient kingdom, "the reign of *Chaos* and *Old Night*"[130]—only I learned that this dreadful road, divided again, leads one branch to Ravenglass and the other to Hawkshead.

For me, I went no farther than the farmer's (better than 4 miles from Keswick) at Grange; his mother and he brought us butter that Siserah would have jumped at, though not in a lordly dish,[131] bowls of milk, thin oaten cakes and ale, and we had carried a cold tongue thither with us. Our farmer was himself the man that last year plundered the eagles' eyrie: all the dale are up in arms on such an occasion, for they lose abundance of lambs yearly, not to mention hares, partridges, grouse &c. He was let down from the cliff, in ropes, to the shelf of the rock on which the nest was built, the people above shouting and hallooing to fright the old birds, which flew screaming around, but did not dare to attack him.

He brought off the eaglet (for there is rarely more than one) and an addled egg. The nest was roundish and more than a yard over, made of twigs twisted together. Seldom a year passes, but they take the brood or eggs, and sometimes they shoot one, sometimes the other, parent; but the survivor has always found a mate (probably in Ireland) and they breed near the old place. By his description I learn that this species is the Erne,[132] the vulture of Abicilla of Linnaeus in his last edition (but in yours *Falco Albicilla*), so consult him and Pennant about it.

We returned leisurely home the way we came, but saw a new landscape: the features indeed were the same in part, but many new ones were disclosed by the mid-day sun, and the tints were entirely changed. Take notice this was the best, or perhaps the only day for going up Skiddaw, but I thought it better employed: it was perfectly serene, and hot as midsummer.

In the evening, I walked alone down to the lake by the side of Crow Park after sunset and saw the solemn colouring of the night draw on, the last gleam of sunshine fading away on the hill tops, the deep serene of the waters and the long shadows of the mountains thrown across them, till they nearly touched the hithermost shore. At a distance were heard the murmurs of many waterfalls, not audible in the daytime; I wished for the moon, but she was dark to me and silent,

Hid in her vacant interlunar cave.[133]

Oct. 4. I walked to Crow Park—now a rough pasture, once a glade of ancient oaks, whose large roods still remain in the ground, but nothing has sprung from them.[134] If one single tree had remained, this would have been an unparalleled spot; and Smith judged right when he took his print of the lake from hence, for it is a gentle eminence, not too high, on the very margin of the water, and commanding it from end to end, looking full into the gorge of Borrowdale. I prefer it even to Cockshut Hill, which lies beside it and to which I walked in the afternoon; it is covered with young trees, both sown and planted, oak, spruce, Scotch fir &c., all which thrive wonderfully.

There is an easy ascent to the top, and the view far preferable to that on Castle Hill (which you remember), because this is lower and nearer the lake; for I find all points that are much elevated spoil the beauty of the valley, and make its parts, which are not large, look poor and diminutive. [Mr West adds: The picturesque point is always thus low in all prospects— a truth which, though the landscape painter knows, he cannot always observe[135] since the patron who employs him to take a view of his place usually carries him to some elevation for that purpose, in order I suppose, that he may have more of him for his money.]* While I was here, a little shower fell, red clouds came marching up the hills from the east, and part of a bright rainbow seemed to rise along the side of Castle Hill.

From hence I got to the parsonage a little before sunset, and saw in my glass a picture, that if I could transmit to you and fix it in all the softness of its living colours, would fairly sell for a thousand pounds. This is the sweetest scene I can yet discover in point of pastoral beauty; the rest are in a sublimer style.

Oct. 5. I walked through the meadows and cornfields to the Derwent and, crossing it, went up How Hill. It looks along Bassenthwaite Water and sees at the same time the course of the river and a part of the upper lake, with a full view of Skiddaw. Then I took my way through Portinscale village to the Park, a hill so called, covered entirely with wood; it is a mass of crumbling slate. Passed round its foot, between trees and the edge of the water, and came to a peninsula that juts out into the lake and looks along it both ways; in front rises Wallow Crag and Castle Hill, the town, the road to Penrith, Skiddaw and Saddleback. Returning, met a brisk and cold north-eastern blast, that ruffled all the surface of the lake and made it rise in little waves that broke at the foot of the wood.

After dinner walked up the Penrith road 2 miles or more and, turning into a cornfield to the right called Castlerigg, saw a druid circle of large stones, 108 ft in diameter, the biggest not 8 ft high, but most of them still erect; they are 50 in number.† The valley of St John appeared in sight, and the summits of Cachidecam (called, by Camden, Casticand) and Helvellyn, said to be as high as Skiddaw and to rise from a much higher base.

* Yet, when I say this, I would not be thought to mean that a drawing should be made from the lowest point possible—as for instance in this very view, from the lake itself—for then a foreground would be wanting. On this account, when I sailed on Derwentwater, I did not receive so much pleasure from the superb amphitheatre of mountains round me as when, like Mr Gray, I traversed its margin, and therefore think he did not lose much by not taking boat.

† See this piece of antiquity more fully described, with a plate annexed, by Mr Pennant, in his second tour to Scotland (1772), page 38.

Oct. 6.   Went in a chaise 8 miles along the east side of Bassenthwaite Water to Ouse Bridge, the road in some part made and very good, the rest slippery and dangerous cart road or narrow rugged lanes, but no precipices; it runs directly along the foot of Skiddaw. Opposite to Wythop Brows, clothed up to the top with wood, a very beautiful view opens down to the lake, which is narrower and longer than that of Keswick, less broken into bays and without islands.‡ At the foot of it, a few paces from the brink, gently sloping upwards, stands Armathwaite, in a thick grove of Scotch firs, commanding a noble view directly up the lake.

At a small distance behind the house is a large extent of wood, and still behind this a ridge of cultivated hills, on which, according to the Keswick proverb, *the sun always shines*. The inhabitants here, on the contrary, call the vale of Derwentwater *the devil's chamberpot*, and pronounce the name of Skiddaw Fell, which terminates here, with a sort of terror and aversion. Armathwaite House is a modern fabric, not large and built of dark red stone, belonging to Mr Spedding, whose grandfather was steward to old Sir James Lowther and bought this estate of the Highmores.

The sky was overcast, and the wind cool; so, after dining at a public house which stands here near the bridge (that crosses the Derwent just where it issues from the lake) and sauntering a little by the waterside, I came home again. The turnpike is finished from Cockermouth hither, 5 miles, and is carrying on to Penrith. Several little showers to day. A man came in who said there was snow on Cross Fell this morning.

Oct. 7.   I walked in the morning to Crow Park, and in the evening up Penrith road. The clouds came rolling up the mountains all round, very dark, yet the moon shone at intervals. It as too damp to go towards the lake. Tomorrow I mean to bid farewell to Keswick.

Botany might be studied here to great advantage at another season, because of the great variety of soils and elevations, all lying within a small compass. I observed nothing but several curious lichens, and plenty of gale or Dutch myrtle, perfuming the borders of the lake. This year the wad mine had been opened, which is done once in five years; it is taken out in lumps, sometimes as big as a man's fist, and will undergo no preparation by fire, not being fusible; when it is pure, soft, black and loose-grained, it is worth sometimes 30s. a lb.

There are no char ever taken in these lakes, but plenty in Buttermere Water, which lies a little way north of Borrowdale, about Martinmas, which are potted here. They sow chiefly oats and bigg here, which are now cutting and still on the ground; the rains have done much hurt; yet observe, the soil is so thin and light, that no day has passed in which I could not walk out with ease; and you know I am no lover of dirt. Fell mutton is now in season for about six weeks; it grows fat on the mountains, and nearly resembles venison. Excellent pike and perch, here called *bass*; trout is now out of season; partridge in great plenty.

‡ It is somewhat extraordinary that Mr Gray omitted to mention the islands on Derwentwater, one of which—I think they call it Vicar's Island—makes a principal object in the scene. See Smith's view of Derwentwater.

Oct. 8.   I left Keswick and took the Ambleside road, in a gloomy morning; about two miles (rather a mile) from the town, mounted an eminence called Castlerigg and, the sun breaking out, discovered the most enchanting view I have yet seen of the whole valley behind me, the two lakes, the river, the mountains, all in their glory; so that I had almost a mind to have gone back again.

The road is in some few parts not completed, yet good country road, through sound but narrow and stony lanes, very safe in broad daylight. This is the case about Causeway Foot and among Naddle Fells to Langthwaite. The vale you go in has little breadth, the mountains are vast and rocky, the fields little and poor, and the inhabitants are now making hay and see not the sun by two hours in the day so long as at Keswick.

Come to the foot of Helvellyn, along which runs an excellent road, looking down from a little height on Leathes Water (called also Thirlmere or Wythburn Water) and soon descending on its margin. The lake looks black from its depth and from the gloom of the vast crags that scowl over it, though really clear as glass. It is narrow and about 3 miles long, resembling a river in its course; little shining torrents hurrying down the rocks to join it, but not a bush to overshadow them or cover their march; all is rock and loose stones up to the very brow, which lies so near your way that not above half the height of Helvellyn can be seen.

Next I passed the little chapel of Wythburn, out of which the Sunday congregation were then issuing. Soon after, a beck near Dunmail Raise, where I entered Westmorland a second time and now began to see Helm Crag, distinguished from its rugged neighbours not so much by its height as by the strange broken outline of its top, like some gigantic building demolished, and the stones that composed it flung across each other in wild confusion.

Just beyond it, opens one of the sweetest landscapes that art ever attempted to imitate. The bosom of the mountains, spreading here into a broad basin, discovers in the midst Grasmere Water; its margin is hollowed into small bays, with bold eminences—some of rock, some of turf—that half-conceal and vary the figure of the little lake they command; from the shore, a low promontory pushes itself far into the water, and on it stands a white village with the parish church rising in the midst of it; hanging inclosures, cornfields and meadows, green as an emerald, with their trees and hedges and cattle, fill up the whole space from the edge of the water; and just opposite to you is a large farmhouse at the bottom of a deep smooth lawn, embosomed in old woods, which climb halfway up the mountains' sides, and discover above them a broken line of crags that crown the scene. Not a single red tile, no gentleman's flaring house, or garden walls, break in upon the repose of this little unsuspected paradise; but all is peace, rusticity and happy poverty, in its neatest, most becoming attire.

The road here winds over Grasmere hill, whose rocks soon conceal the water from your sight; yet it is continued along behind them and, contracting itself to a river, communicates with Rydal Water—another small lake, but of inferior size and beauty: it seems shallow too, for large patches of reeds appear pretty far within. Into this vale the road descends. On the opposite banks large and ancient woods mount up the hill; and just to the left of our way stands Rydal Hall, the family seat of Sir Michael le Fleming, a large old-fashioned fabric, rounded with wood. Sir Michael is now on his travels, and all this timber far and wide belongs to him. Near the house rises a huge crag, called Rydal Head, which is said to command a full view of Windermere, and I doubt it not; for within a mile that lake is visible even from the road. As to going up the crag, one might as well go up Skiddaw.

I now reached Ambleside, 16 miles from Keswick, meaning to lie there; but, on looking into the best bedchamber, dark and damp as a cellar,¶ grew delicate, gave up Windermere in despair and resolved I would go on to Kendal directly, 14 miles farther.* The road in general fine turnpike, but some parts (about 3 miles in all) not made, yet without danger.

For this determination, I was unexpectedly well rewarded: for the afternoon was fine, and the road for the space of full 5 miles ran along the side of Windermere, with delicious views across it and almost from one end to the other. It is 10 miles in length and at most a mile over, resembling the course of some vast and magnificent river—but no flat marshy grounds, no other beds or patches of scrubby plantations on its banks.

At the head, two valleys open among the mountains: one that by which we came down, the other Langdale, in which Wrynose and Hardknot, two great mountains, rise above the rest. From thence the fells visibly sink and soften along its sides; sometimes they run into it (but with a gentle declivity) in their own dark and natural complexion; oftener they are green and cultivated, with farms interspersed and round eminences, on the border covered with trees. Towards the south it seemed to break into large bays, with several islands, and a wider extend of cultivation. The way rises continually, till at a place called Orrest Head it turns south-east, losing sight of the water.

Passed by Ings Chapel and Stavely; but I can say no farther for, the dusk of the evening coming on, I entered Kendal almost in the dark and could distinguish only a shadow of the castle on a hill, and tenter grounds spread far and wide around the town, which I mistook for houses. My inn promised sadly, having two wooden galleries, like Scotland, in front of it; it was indeed an old, ill-contrived house, but kept by civil sensible people; so I stayed two nights with them, and fared and slept very comfortably.

¶ The inn at Ambleside has been greatly improved since Mr Gray's time, and is now as commodious as any in the country.

* By not staying a little at Ambleside, Mr Gray lost the sight of two magnificent cascades: the one not half a mile behind the inn, the other down Rydal Crag, where Sir Michael le Fleming is now making a pathway to the top of it. These, when I saw them, were in full torrent; whereas Lowdore waterfall, which I visited in the evening of the very same day, was almost without a stream. Hence I conclude that this distinguished feature in the vale of Keswick is, like most of the northern rivers, only in high beauty during bad weather.

But his greatest loss was in not seeing a small waterfall visible only through the window of a ruined summer-house in Sir Michael's orchard. Here nature has performed every thing in little that she usually executes on her larger scale; and on that account, like the miniature painter, seems to have finished every part of it in a studied manner; not a little fragment of a rock thrown into the basin, not a single stem of brushwood that starts from its craggy sides, but has its picturesque meaning; and the little central stream dashing down a cleft of the darkest coloured stone, produced an effect of light and shadow beautiful beyond description. This little theatrical scene might be painted as large as the original, on a canvas not bigger than those usually dropped in the opera house.

† The accounts of things given by hasty travellers are generally inaccurate and often injudicious. As to the principal streets in Kendal, they are neither three in number, nor nearly parallel. They are but two: one about a mile in length, and another about half a mile. These streets contain indeed not many elegant houses; they are however on the whole as open and well-built as in most other towns. As to the bad rough cast our author speaks of, judges of rough cast have always supposed this country no way deficient in the materials or in the manner of laying it on.

Oct. 9. The air mild as summer, all corn off the ground and the skylarks singing aloud (by the way, I saw not one at Keswick, perhaps because the place abounds in birds of prey). I went up the castle hill; the town chiefly consists of three nearly parallel streets, almost a mile long; except these, all the other houses seem as if they had been dancing a country dance, and were out: there they stand back to back, corner to corner, some uphill, some down, without intent or meaning. Along by their side runs a fine brisk stream, over which there are three stone bridges: the buildings (a few comfortable houses excepted) are mean,[136] of stone and covered with a bad rough cast.†

Near the end of the town stands a handsome house of Colonel Wilson's and, adjoining to it, the church, a very large Gothic fabric with a square tower; it has no particular ornaments, but double aisles and at the east end four chapels, or choirs: one of the Parrs, another of the Stricklands, the third is the proper choir of the church, and the fourth of the Bellinghams, a family now extinct. There is an altar tomb of one of them dated 1577, with a flat brass arms and quarterings, and in the window their arms alone: argent, a hunting horn sable, strung gules.

In the Stricklands' chapel several monuments, and another old altar tomb not belonging to the family: on the side of it a fess dancette between ten billets deincourt. In the Parrs' chapel is a third altar tomb in the corner, no figure or inscription, but on the side cut an escutcheon of Ross of Kendal (three water buckets) quartering Parr (two bars in a bordure engrailed). 2dly, an escutcheon vaire, a fess for marmion; 3dly, an escutcheon, three chevronels braced, and a chief (which I take for Fitzhugh); at the foot is an escutcheon, surrounded with the garter, bearing Ross and Parr quarterly, quartering the other two before mentioned. I have no books to look in, therefore cannot say whether this is the Lord Parr of Kendal, Queen Catharine's father, or her brother the Marquis of Northampton; perhaps it is a cenotaph for the latter, who was buried at Warwick in 1571.

The remains of the castle are seated on a fine hill on the side of the river opposite the town. Almost the whole inclosure of the walls remains, with four towers—two square and two round—but their upper parts or embattlements are demolished. It is of rough stone and cement, without any ornament or arms, round, inclosing a court of like form and surrounded by a moat; nor could it ever have been larger than it is, for there are no traces of outworks. There is a good view of the town and river, with a fertile open valley through which it winds.

After dinner, I went along the Millthorp turnpike 4 miles to see the falls, or force, of the River Kent, came to Sizergh (pronounced Siser) and turned down a lane to the left. This seat of the Stricklands, an old Catholic family,[137] is an ancient hall house with a very large tower, embattled; the rest of the buildings added to it are of a later date, but all is white and seen to advantage on a background of old trees; there is a small park also well wooded.

Opposite to this, turning to the left, I soon came to the river; it works its way in a narrow and deep, rocky channel, overhung with trees. The calmness and brightness of the evening, the roar of the waters and the thumping of huge hammers at an iron-forge not far distant, made it a singular walk, but as to the falls (for there are two) they are not 4 ft high. I went on down to the forge and saw the demons at work by the light of their own fires; the iron is brought in pigs to Millthorp by sea from Scotland, &c. and is here beat into bars and plates. Two miles farther, at Levens, is the seat of Lord Suffolk, where he sometimes passes the summer; it was a favourite place of his late Countess; but this I did not see.

Oct. 10.   I proceeded by Burton to Lancaster, 22 miles: very good country, well inclosed and wooded, with some common interspersed. Passed at the foot of Farlton Knot, a high fell. Four miles north of Lancaster, on a rising ground called Bolton (pronounced Bouton), we had a full view of Cartmell Sands, with here and there a passenger riding over them (it being low water), the points of Furness shooting far into the sea, and lofty mountains partly covered with clouds extending north of them. Lancaster also appeared very conspicuous and fine, for its most distinguished features, the castle and church, mounted on a green eminence, were all that could be seen. Woe is me! When I got thither, it was the second day of the fair; the inn in the principal street was a great old gloomy house, full of people, but I found tolerable quarters and even slept two nights in peace.

   In a fine afternoon I ascended the castle hill. It takes up the higher top of the eminence on which it stands and is irregularly round, encompassed with a deep moat. In front, towards the town, is a magnificent gothic gateway, lofty and huge; the overhanging battlements are supported by a triple range of corbels, the intervals pierced through and showing the day from above. On its top rise light watch-towers of small height. It opens below with a grand pointed arch; over this is a wrought tabernacle, doubtless once containing its founder's figure; one side a shield of France semi-quartered with England; on the other, the same, with a label ermine for John of Gaunt, Duke of Lancaster.

   This opens to a court within, which I did not much care to enter, being the county gaol and full of prisoners, both criminals and debtors. From this gateway the walls continue and join it to a vast square tower of great height, the lower part at least of remote antiquity; for it has small round-headed lights, with plain short pillars on each side of them. There is a third tower, also square, and of less dimensions. This is all the castle.

   Near it, and but a little lower, stands the church, a large and plain Gothic fabric. The high square tower at the west end has been rebuilt of late years, but nearly in the same style. There are no ornaments of arms &c. anywhere to be seen; within it is lightsome and spacious, but not one monument of antiquity or piece of painted glass is left. From the churchyard there is an extensive sea view (for now the tide had almost covered the sands and filled the river) and besides the greatest part of Furness, I could distinguish Peel Castle on the Isle of Foudry, which lies off its southern extremity.

The town is built on the slope and, at the foot of the castle hill, more than twice the bigness of Aukland,[138] with many new buildings of neat white stone, but a little disorderly in their position, and *ad libitum* like Kendal. Many also extend below, on the quays by the riverside, where a number of ships were moored, some of them three-masted vessels, decked out with their colours in honour of the fair. Here is a good bridge of four arches over the Lune, that runs, when the tide is out, in two streams divided by a bed of gravel, which is not covered but in spring tides; below the town, it widens to near the breadth of the Thames at London, and meets the sea at 5 or 6 miles distance to the south-west.

Oct. 11.   I crossed the river and walked over a peninsula 3 miles to the village of Poulton, which stands on the beach. An old fisherman mending his nets (while I enquired about the danger of passing those sands) told me, in his dialect, a moving story[139] how a brother of the trade—a cockler, as he styled him—driving a little cart with two daughters (women grown) in it, and his wife on horseback following, set out one day to cross the seven-mile sands, as they had been frequently used to do (for nobody in the village knew them better than the old man did). When they were about half-way over, a thick fog rose, and as they advanced they found the water much deeper than they expected.

The old man was puzzled; he stopped, and said he would go a little way to find some mark he was acquainted with. They stayed a while for him, but in vain; they called aloud, but no reply; at last the young women pressed the mother to think where they were, and go on. She would not leave the place; she wandered about forlorn and amazed; she would not quit her horse and get into the cart with them. They determined after much time wasted to turn back and give themselves up to the guidance of their horses. The old woman was soon washed off and perished; the poor girls clung close to their cart, and the horse, sometimes wading and sometimes swimming, brought them back to land alive, but senseless with terror and distress, and unable for many days to give any account of themselves. The bodies of their parents were found the next ebb, that of the father a very few paces distant from the spot where he had left them.

In the afternoon, I wandered about the town and by the quay, till it grew dark.

Oct. 12.   I set out for Settle by a fine turnpike road, 29 miles, through a rich and beautiful country, diversified with frequent villages and churches—very unequal ground and on the left the River Lune winding in a deep valley, its hanging banks clothed with fine woods, through which you catch long reaches of the water as the road winds about a considerable height above it. In the soft picturesque part of the way, I passed the part belonging to the Hon. Mr Clifford, a Catholic. The grounds between him and the river are indeed charming.¶ The house is ordinary, and park nothing but a rocky fell scattered over with ancient hawthorns.

Next I came to Hornby, a little town on the River Wenning, over which a handsome bridge is now built; the castle, in a lordly situation, attracted me, so I walked up the hill to it. It first presents itself as a large white ordinary sashed gentleman's house, and behind it rises the ancient keep, built by Edward Stanley, Lord Monteagle. He died about 1529, in King Henry VIII's time. It is now only a shell; the rafters are laid within it as flooring. I went up a winding stone staircase in one corner to the leads, and at the angle is a single hexagon watch-tower, rising some feet higher, fitted up in the taste of a modern summer-house, with sash windows in gilt frames, a stucco cupola and on the top a vast gilt eagle, built by Mr Charteris, the present possessor. He is the second son of the Earl of Wemyss, brother to the Lord Elcho and grandson to Colonel Charteris, whose name he bears.

From the leads of the tower there is a fine view of the country round, and much of the wood near the castle. Ingleborough, which I had seen before distinctly at Lancaster to the north-east, was now completely wrapped in clouds, all but the summit, which might have easily been mistaken for a long black cloud too, fraught with an approaching storm. Now our road began to gradually to mount towards the Apennine, the trees growing less and thinner of leaves, till we came to Ingleton, 18 miles; it is a pretty village, situated very high and yet in a valley, at the foot of that huge monster of nature, Ingleborough: two torrents cross it, with great stones rolled along their beds instead of water; and over them are flung two handsome arches.

The nipping air, though the afternoon was growing very bright, now taught us we were in Craven;[140] and the road was all up and down, though nowhere very steep. To the left were mountain tops, to the right a wide valley, all inclosed ground, and beyond it high hills again. In approaching Settle, the crags on the left drew nearer to our way, till we descended Brunton Brow into a cheerful valley (through thin trees) to Giggleswick, a village with a small piece of water by its side, covered with cots—near it a church, which belongs also to Settle; and half a mile farther, having passed the Ribble over a bridge, I arrived there. It is a small market town, standing directly under a rocky fell. There are not in it above a dozen good-looking houses; the rest are old and low, with little wooden porticos in the front. My inn pleased me much (though small) for the neatness and civility of the good women that kept it: so I lay there two nights, and went

Oct. 13.   To visit the Gordale Scar, which lay 6 miles from Settle; but that way was directly over a fell, and as the weather was not to be depended on, I went round in a chaise the only way one could get near

¶ This scene opens just 3 miles from Lancaster on what is called the Queen's Road. To see the view in perfection, you must go into a field on the left. Here Ingleborough, behind a variety of lesser mountains, makes the background of the prospect; on each hand of the middle distance rise two sloping hills, the left clothed with thick woods, the right with variegated rock and herbage; between them, richest of valleys, the Lune serpentizes for many a mile and comes forth ample and clear through a well-wooded and richly pastured foreground. Every feature which constitutes a perfect landscape of the extensive sort is here not only boldly marked, but also in its best position.

it in a carriage, which made it a full 13 miles, half of it such a road! But I got safe over it, so there is an end—and to Malham (pronounced Maum), a village in the bosom of the mountains, seated in a wild and dreary valley. From thence I was to walk a mile over very rough ground, a torrent rattling along the left hand. On the cliffs above hung a few goats; one of them danced, and scratched an ear with its right foot, in a place where I would not have stood stock-still,

For all beneath the moon.[141]

As I advanced, the crags seemed to close in, but discovered a narrow entrance turning to the left between them. I followed my guide a few paces, and the hills opening again into no large space; and then all further way is barred by the stream that, at the height of about 50 ft, gushes from a hole in the rock, and spreading in large sheets over its broken front, dashes from steep to steep and then rattles away in a torrent down the valley. The rock on the left rises perpendicular, with stubbed yew-trees and shrubs starting from its sides, to the height of at least 300 ft.

But these are not the thing: it is the rock to the right, under which you stand to see the fall that forms the principal horror of the place. From its very base it begins to slope forward over you in one black or solid mass without any crevice in its surface, and overshadows half the area below its dreadful canopy. When I stood at (I believe) 4 yds distant from its foot, the drops which perpetually distil from its brow fell on my head; and, in one part of its top more exposed to the weather, there are loose stones that hang in the air and threaten visibly some idle spectator with instant destruction. It is safer to shelter yourself close to its bottom and trust to the mercy of that enormous mass, which nothing but an earthquake can stir.

The gloomy uncomfortable day well suited to the savage aspect of the place, and made it still more formidable; I stayed there, not without shuddering, a quarter of an hour, and thought my trouble richly paid; for the impression will last for life. At the alehouse where I dined in Malham, Vivares, the landscape painter, had lodged for a week or more; Smith and Bellers had also been there, and two prints of Gordale have been engraved by them.

Oct. 14. Leaving my comfortable inn, to which I had returned from Gordale, I set out for Skipton, 15 miles. From several parts of the road and in many places about Settle, I saw at once the three famous hills of this country—Ingleborough, Pennygant and Pendle—the first is esteemed the highest, and their features not to be described, but by the pencil.[142]

* * *

N.B: [Mr West adds] Without the pencil, nothing indeed is to be described with precision—and even then, the pencil ought to be in the very hand of the writer, ready to supply with outlines everything that his pen cannot express by words. As far as language can describe, Mr Gray has, I think, pushed its powers: for rejecting, as I have before hinted, every general unmeaning and hyperbolical phrase, he has selected (both in his journal and on other familiar occasions) the plainest, simplest and most direct terms; notwithstanding his judicious care in the use of these, I must own I feel them defective. They present me, it is true, with a picture of the same species, but not with the identical picture; my imagination receives clear and distinct, but not true and exact images.

It may be asked then, why am I entertained with well-written descriptions? I answer, because they amuse rather than entertain me; and because, after I have seen the places described, they serve to recall to my memory the original scene, almost as well as the rudest drawing or picture. In the meanwhile my mind is flattered by thinking it has acquired some conception of the place, and rests contented in an innocent error, which nothing but ocular proof can detect and which, when detected, does not diminish the pleasure I had received, but augments its, by supperadding the charms of comparison and verification; and herein I would place the real and only merit of verbal prose description.

To speak of poetical would lead me beyond the limits as well as the purpose of this note. I cannot, however, help adding that I have seen one piece of verbal description which completely satisfies me, because it is throughout assisted by masterly delineation. It is composed by Rev. Mr Gilpin, of Cheam in Surrey, and contains among other places an account of the very scenes which in this tour our author visited. This gentleman, possessing the conjoined talents of a writer and designer, has employed them in this manuscript to every purpose of picturesque beauty, in the description of which a correct eye, a practised pencil and an eloquent pen could assist him. He has, consequently, produced a work unique in its kind at once. But I have said it is in manuscript and, I am afraid, likely to continue so; for would his modesty permit him to print it, the great expense of plates would make its publication impracticable.*

* * *

Craven, after all, is an unpleasing country when seen from a height; its valleys are chiefly wide and either marshy or inclosed pasture, with few trees. Numbers of black cattle are fatted here, both of the Scotch breed and a larger sort of oxen with great horns. There is little cultivated ground, except a few oats.

Skipton, to which I went through Long Preston and Gargrave, is a pretty large market town in a valley, with one very broad street gently sloping downwards from the castle, which stands at the head of it.

* This excellent note [here taken into the text] seems to contain the justest criticism on the nature and powers of verbal description, as applied to landscapes and prospects. And now that the reader has gone through the author's specimens of it in the foregoing Guide, if it appear that he hath not availed himself of these precepts as much as he might have done, he may take a scrutiny into his errors, a critical lesson, in the next degree useful to instructions derived from such examples as Mr Gray's; and

thus reap improvements as well as amusement from the efforts of a hasty and redundant pen.

Mr Gilpin's tour has been since published. [Wm Cockin]

† Ann, Countess of Pembroke and Montgomery.

This is one of the good Countess's buildings,† but on old foundations; it is not very large, but of a handsome antique appearance, with round towers. A grand gateway, bridge and moat, surrounded by many old trees. It is in good repair, and kept up as the habitation of the Earl of Thanet, though he rarely comes thither.

What with sleet and a foolish dispute about chaises that delayed me, I did not see the inside of it, but went on 15 miles to Otley—first up Shode Bank, the steepest hill I ever saw a road carried over in England, for it mounts in a straight line (without any other repose for the horses than by placing stones every now and then behind the wheels) for a full mile; then the road goes on a level along the brow of this high hill over Rumbald Moor, till it gently descends into Wharfdale—so they call the vale of the Wharf—and a beautiful vale it is, well wooded, well cultivated, well inhabited, but with high crags at a distance, that border the green country on each hand. Through the midst of it, deep, clear and full to the brink, and of no inconsiderable breadth, runs in long windings the river. How it comes to the pass that it should be so fine and copious a stream here, and at Tadcaster (so much lower) should have nothing but a wide stony channel without water, I cannot tell you.

I passed through Long Addingham, Ilkely (pronounced Eecly) distinguished by a lofty brow of loose rocks to the right, and Burkley, a neat and pretty village among trees. On the opposite side of the river lay Middleton Lodge, belonging to a Catholic gentleman of that name; Welston, a venerable stone fabric with large offices, of Mr Vavasour, the meadows in front gently descending to the water, and behind a great and shady wood; Farnley (Mr Fowke's), a place like the last, but larger and rising higher on the side of the hill.

Otley is a large airy town, with clean but low rustic buildings and a bridge over the Wharf. I went into its spacious Gothic church, which has been new-roofed, with a flat stucco ceiling; in a corner of it is the monument of Thomas, Lord Fairfax, and Helen Aske, his lady, descended from the Cliffords and Latimers, as her epitaph says. The figures (which are not ill cut, particularly his in armour, but bare headed) lie on the tomb. I take them to be the parents of the famous Sir Thomas Fairfax.

Article IV

Ode to the Sun

By Mr Cumberland,[143] *Published 1776*

> Soul of the world, refulgent sun!
> Oh, take not from my ravished sight
> Those golden beams of living light,
> Nor, ere thy daily course be run,
> Precipitate the night.
> Lo! Where the ruffian clouds arise,
> Usurp the abdicated skies,
> And seize the ætherial throne:
> Sullen sad the scene appears,
> Huge Helvellyn streams with tears!
> Hark! 'tis giant Skiddaw's groan,
> I hear terrific Lowdore roar;
> The sabbath of thy reign is o'er,
> The anarchy's begun;
> Father of light! Return, break forth, refulgent sun.
>
> What if the rebel blast shall rend
> These nodding horrors from the mountain's brow—
> Hither glad deliverance send,
> Ah, save the votarist, and accept the vow!
> And say, through thy diurnal round,
> Where, great spectator, hast thou found
> Such solemn soul-inviting shades,
> Ghostly dells, religious glades?
> Where Penitence may plant its meek abode,
> And hermit Meditation meet its God!
>
> Now by the margin of the glassy deep
> My pensive vigils let me keep;
> There, by force of Runic spells,
> Shake the grot where nature dwells
> And in the witching hour of the night,
> Whilst thy pale sister lends her shadowy light,
> Summon the naked wood-nymphs to my sight.
>
> Trembling now with giddy tread,
> Press the moss on Gowdar's head.

But lo! Where sits the bird of Jove,
Couch'd in his eyrie far above;
Oh! lend thine eye, thy pinion lend
Higher, yet higher let me still ascend.
'Tis done—my forehead smites the skies,
To the last summit of the cliff I rise:
I touch the sacred ground,
Where step of man was never found;
I see all nature's rude domain around.

Peace to thy empire, queen of calm desires,
Health crown thy hills, and plenty robe thy vales;
May thy groves wave untouch'd by wasteful fires,
Nor commerce crowd thy lakes with sordid sails!

Press not so fast upon my aching sight,
Gigantic shapes; nor rear your heads so high,
As if meant to war against the sky,
Sons of chaos and primæval night.
Such were the heights enshrined Bruno trod
When on the cliffs he hung his tow'ring cell,
Amongst the clouds aspir'd to dwell
And half-ascended to his God.
The prim canal, the level green,
The close-clipped hedge that bounds the flourished scene,
What rapture can such forms impart,
With all the spruce impertinence of art!

Ye pageant streams, that roll in state
By vain windows of the great,
Rest on your muddy ooze, and see
Old majestic Derwent force
His independent course,
And learn of him and nature to be free;
And you, triumphal arches, shrink;
Ye temples, tremble; and ye columns, sink,
One nod from Wallow's craggy brow
Shall crush the dome
Of sacerdotal Rome,
And lay her glittering gilded trophies low.

Now, downward as I bend my eye,
What is that atom I espy?
That speck in nature's plan,
Great heaven! is that a man?
And hath that little wretch its cares,

Its freaks, its follies and its airs?
And do I hear the insect say,
"My lakes, my mountains, my domain?"
O weak, contemptible, and vain!
The tenant of a day.—
Say to old Skiddaw, "change thy place,"
Heave Helvellyn from his base,
Or bid impetuous Derwent stand,
At the proud waving of a master's hand.

Now with silent step, and slow,
Descend; but first forbear to blow,
Ye felon winds; let discord cease,
And Nature seal an elemental peace:—
Hush! not a whisper here,
Beware! for Echo, on the watch,
Sits with erect and list'ning ear,
The secrets of the scene to catch,
Then swelling, as she rolls around,
The hoarse reverberated sound,
With loud repeated shocks,
She beats the loose impending rocks,
Tears down the fragment big with death,
And hurls them thund'ring on the wretch beneath.

Not so the Naiad;‡ she defies
The faithless Echo and her yelling cries,
Howls on the summit of rude Lowdore's brow;
Then with a desperate leap,
Springs from the rocky steep,
And runs enamour'd to the lake below.
So the Cambrian minstrel stood,
Bending o'er old Conway's flood,
White as foam his silver beard,
And loud and shrill his voice was heard,
And all the while down Snowden's side,
Winding slow in dread array,
He saw the victor king pursue his way;
Then fearless rush'd into the foaming tide,
Curs'd him by all his idol Gods, and died.

Ah! Where is he that swept the sounding lyre,
And while he touch'd the master string,
Bade ruin seize the ruthless king,
With all a prophet's fire?—
Mourn him, ye naiads, and ye wood-nymphs mourn;

‡ This alludes to the great waterfall at Lowdore.

But chiefly ye, who rule o'er Keswick's vale,
Your visitor bewail,
And pluck fresh laurels for his hallow'd urn.
He saw your scenes in harmony divine,
On him indulgent suns could shine;
Me turbid skies and threat'ning clouds await,
Emblems, alas! of my ignoble fate.

But see! The embattled vapours break,
Disperse and fly,
Posting like couriers down the sky;
The grey rock glitters in the glassy lake:—
And now the mountain tops are seen
Frowning amidst the blue serene;
The variegated groves appear,
Deck'd in the colours of the waning year;
And as new beauties they unfold,
Dip their skirts in beaming gold.
Thee, savage Wyburn, now I hail,
Delicious Grasmere's calm retreat,
And stately Windermere I greet,
And Keswick's sweet fantastic vale:—
But let her naiads yield to thee,
And lowly bend the subject knee,
Imperial lake of Patrick's dale!¶
For neither Scottish Lomond's pride,
Nor smooth Killarney's silver tide,
Nor aught that learned Poussin drew,
Or dancing Rosa flung upon my view,
Shall shake they sovereign undisturbed right,
Great scene of wonder and sublime delight!

Hail to they beams, O Sun! — for this display,
What, glorious orb, can I repay?
Nor Memnon's costly shrine,
Not the white coursers of imperial Rome,
Nor the rich smoke of Persia's hecatomb;
Such proud oblations are not mine;
Nor thou my simple tribute shall refuse,
The thanks of an unprostituted muse;
And may no length of still returning day,
Strike from my forehead one refulgent ray,
But each tuneful, each attendant sphere,
To latest time thy stated labours cheer,
And with new Pœans crown the finish'd year.

¶ This alludes to the great lake of Ullswater, situated in Patterdale— viz Patrick's dale—a scene of grandeur and sublimity far superior, in my opinion, to the lake of Keswick.

Article V

A Night-piece on
the Banks of Winderemere

Written at Ambleside, Westmorland,
in the summer of 1797
By the Rev. James Plumptre[144]

PALE goddess of the serious night,
Arise, and cheer my anxious sight;
O'er dun twilight's gloom prevail,
Invigorate the drooping vale,
Shedding o'er mountains, woods and streams
Thy quiver full of silver beams,
Whilst amber, light and darkest shade
Alternate all the scene pervade.
In full-orb'd majesty arise,
Illume the azure vaulted skies.

Lo! From behind yon mountain's height
She comes—the chaste-eyed Queen of Night,
Thro' heaven's high cope, her course to run,
Till frightened by the garish sun.

Hark! Along the rocky shore,
I hear impetuous Brathay roar;
In sullen majesty he leads
Among the narrow winding meads
His tributary tides.
Thee, Rothay, in thy course he meets
Descending from thy flow'ry bed;
Swift to thee he fondly glides,
With strong embrace thy beauties greets:

Then, with all your glittering train
Together your proud course maintain
And with imperial Windermere
All your boastful honours share;
With load acclaim, exulting, hail!
The monarch of the stately vale.

* The Langdale Pikes.

† Wrynose.

‡ Colwith Force is a very fine, though a small cascade in Little or Higher Langdale. The features of it are very wild; and the ruins of a mill, on one side of the rock, have a very good effect.

¶ The River Brathay is formed chiefly from two streams —the one rising in Little Langdale, the other in Great Langdale, where it passes the Pikes and the slate quarry: these join in the small lake of Elterwater. Another of its feeders is the stream from Loughrig Tarn, a very small, but beautiful lake in the bottom of the mountains, a little to the right of the road as you cross over Elterwater, or Skelwith Bridge, to Grasmere.

Say, Brathay, as I walk your side,
List'ning to your murmuring tide,
What sights, what wonders have you seen
Passing your barrier hills between?
View'd you old Langdale's solid towers*
And Elterwater's peaceful bowers,
Where the quarry's yawning scar
Hangs hideous in the midnight air!
Or, rather higher Langdale's rocks,
Hardknot and his mountain twin†
At whose rude base your streams begin,
Where the widely-straying flocks
And the fragrant-smelling kine
Their ample wealth combine,
And to their happy peasant's board
A frugal, friendly meal afford,
Bestowing health and calm content,
The greatest blessings heaven has lent.
I heard you rattling through the wood
And pass by Colwith's‡ foaming flood,
His loose, dishevel'd hoary head
Affrighted, seeks a calmer bed,
Tumbling, from rock to rock, his course
With wild majestic, sullen force;
Still to his sister's¶ arms he flies
And, wide expanded to the skies,
On oosy bed supinely lies—
Again behold him raise his head
As if awaken'd from the dead,
Plumb down the rock of Skelwith dash
With hoarse reverberated crash,
And boist'rous boiling from below
Again across the peaceful meadow flow.

So the lorn maniac, in his moods,
Sullen o'er his sorrows broods;
With unaverted eye, he strays
Along the lonely desert ways
With solemn, measur'd, thoughtful pace,
Despair depicted in his face:
Then starts, and with a stedfast gaze
Replete with horror and amaze,
From rock to rock, from steep to steep,
Reckless he takes the dang'rous leap;
Then scours along the level plain
Till, all his strength exhaust again,

He sinks upon the earth's cold breast,
Toil-worn, to take his broken rest.

But, Rothay, you a gentler tide,
Serenely through the vallies glide;
Peaceful Grasmere's woody hills
Pour forth for you their tinkling rills.
Through Rydal's lake, with placid stream,
You, murmuring, in the valley gleam
And, at the neighbouring water's fall,
Pass your Fleming's stately hall;
For, O 'tis your delight to boast
The falls down Rydal's mountains tossed;
The high cascade,* with dashing spray,
O'er rugged rocks maintains its way
With stubbed trees, by storms despoil'd—
A scene most picturesquely wild.
Sublime the next cascade appears;
The lower, softer features wears.

Such scenes nor Poussin could, nor Claude,
In living canvas e'er afford;
For Nature ev'ry effort tried
To form your Fleming's wat'ry pride.
Nor be forgot thy force, Stock Gill,
Rushing from the shatter'd hill,
Down in frothy torrents tossed
Till in the dark abysm lost,
And foaming through the woody glen
Thund'ring from rock to rock amain
You seek a refuge in the plain.

O Rothay! Yours and Brathay's stream
Enfold (well worth the Muses' theme)
A spot where Art with Nature vies
To catch the enraptur'd poet's eyes.
But be it most his pride to tell:
There Elegance and Virtue dwell,
There Hospitality is found
Dealing delight to all around,
With innocence the hours beguiles
And joys to see another's smiles.

Oh! 'twere endless to declare
Thy charms, imperial Windermere:
Thy prospects, op'ning to the view,

* Besides the two cascades in the grounds of Sir Michael le Fleming, there is another higher up, which, when there is plenty of water, is well worth the notice of the picturesque traveller.

At ev'ry turn delight renew:
The skimming bark, with feath'ry sail,
Flying before the fresh'ning gale,
While Music's voice in æther floats,
And Echo still prolongs the notes—
What villas on thy banks arise,
T' arrest the far-exploring eyes;
Their vary'd beauties to rehearse,
Might claim for each a Muse's verse,
—Yet let not praise quite keep aloof
From Rayrig's hospitable roof;
And ever be the spot admir'd
Where learned Watson lives retir'd
Like Cincinnatus, tir'd of state
And factions of th'aspiring great;
Withdrawn from party's fierce alarm,
He daily tends his little farm.
And, oh! Had I my utmost will,
I'd dwell on yonder woody hill:
That humble mansion pleases best
Nam'd from the turtle's peaceful nest.

But, soft——the rustling leaflets sigh,
Responsive, as the breeze moves by,
In solemn accents, trembling, say
That Storm and Tempest move this way
From yonder murky, lab'ring cloud.
Hark! Thunder's voice rebellows loud,
Heav'n's crystal portals open fly
And light'ning blazes through the sky;
Wind sweeps along the' affrighted vale
And pattering rain, with pelting hale,
Commission'd by great Nature's Lord,
Come to fulfil his mighty word,
In many a mingling torrent fall,
While deep to deep, loud answering call.

† See *King Lear*, Act 3, Scene 2.

Now tremble, wretch,† whose guilty breast
Labours with crimes yet unconfess'd;
Hide thee, appal'd, thou bloody hand;
Thy crime, thou perjur'd, understand;
Thou simular of virtue's life,
Adulterer with thy neighbour's wife,
These high-engender'd warnings hear,
These dreadful summoners revere;
To all creation they proclaim

The Great JEHOVAH's hallow'd name:
Him, and Him only must we fear—
Mighty to judge, and merciful to spare.
Let me, O Lord, thy favour win—
I am both sinn'd against, and sin;
But as against my foes I deal,
So let me, God, thy mercy feel;
And, through the merits of thy Son,
Let me, my earthly race when run,
Thy everlasting kingdom share
With all I've ever held most dear,
From this world's storms and tempests free
To dwell with Happiness and Thee,
To hail the Dayspring from on high,
My Saviour's name to magnify.

And now the elemental war
Onward drives his clattering car,
Resounding fainter from afar.—
By slow degrees it dies away,
Whilst jocund comes returning Day
From out his chamber in the east,
Fresh as the bridegroom newly dress'd,
Chasing Midnight, thick and dark,
Usher'd by his herald lark.
Nature wears again her smile,
And labour stalks forth to his toil;
Fragrance breathes, and perfumes sweet
Th' exhilarated senses meet:
All, all is joy and gay delight
When day succeeds to fearful night.

'Tis thus in all his dealings still
The God of Nature speaks his will,
And never threatens but to save
And awe that wretch who dares to brave
That power, which only with a thought
Could make him vanish into naught;
And having chastened, will forgive
If he return, and bid him live
To fairer joys and brighter skies,
Where neither storms nor tempests rise—
The everlasting, bright abode
Of an all-righteous, bounteous God.

Article VI

A Description of Dunald Mill Hole[145]
by Mr A. Walker[146]

Taken from the *Annual Register* for 1760

Lancaster, August 26th, 1760

Last Sunday I visited a cavern about 5 miles from hence, near the road to
Kirkby Lonsdale, called Dunald Mill Hole—a curiosity, I think, inferior
to none of the kind in Derbyshire, which I have also seen. It is on the
middle of a large common, and we are led to it by a brook, nearly as big
as the New River,[147] which, after turning a corn-mill just at the entrance
of the cave, runs in at its mouth by several beautiful cascades, continuing
its course two miles under a large mountain and at last making its
appearance again near Carnforth, a village on the road to Kendal.

The entrance of this subterraneous channel has something most
pleasingly horrible in it. From the mill at the top, you descend for about
10 yds perpendicularly, by means of chinks in the rocks and shrubs of
trees; the road is almost then parallel to the horizon, leading to the
right a little winding, till you have some hundreds of yards thick of
rocks and minerals above you. In this manner we proceed—sometimes
through vaults so capacious we could not see either roof or sides, and
sometimes on all four, from its narrowness—still following the brook,
which entertained us with a sort of harmony well suiting the place, for
the different heights of its falls were as to many keys of music, which,
all being conveyed to us by the amazing echo, greatly added to the
majestic horror which surrounded us.

In our return we were more particular in our observations.
The beautiful lakes (formed by the brook in the hollow part of the
cavern) realize the fabulous Styx; and murmuring falls, from one rock
to another, broke the rays of our candles, so as to form the most
romantic vibrations and appearances upon the variegated roof. The sides
too are not less remarkable for fine colouring: the damp, the creeping
vegetables and the seams in the marble and limestone parts of the rock
make as many tints as are seen in the rainbow, and are covered with a
perpetual varnish from the just weeping springs that trickle from the
roof. The curious in grottos, cascades &c. might here obtain a just taste
of nature.

When we arrived at the mouth and once more hailed all-cheering
daylight, I could not but admire the uncouth manner in which nature
has thrown together those huge rocks which compose the arch over the

entrance; but, as if conscious of its rudeness, she has clothed it with trees and shrubs of the most various and beautiful verdure, which bend downwards and with their leaves cover all the rugged parts of the rock. As I have never met with an account of this place in any other author, I therefore think it the greater curiosity; but its obscure situation I take to be the reason.

Parties returning from the tour of the lakes to Lancaster, who choose to see the above natural curiosity, must leave the Lancaster road to the left at the guide post for Kellet, about 4 miles from Burton. When in the village, a mile farther on, enquire for the road to the mill, which is then near 2 miles distant.

Perhaps, when arrived at the cavern, if the traveller should not think it equal to his expectation and troubles, it may yield some compensation to enjoy one of the best prospects in the country, which is about a mile off. Though hitherto unnoticed, a good deal I think might be justly said in its praise; but previous description is generally more tiresome then welcome. To find this view, proceed eastward in the direction of the last lane leading to the mill, to the top of the highest rise that you will see on the common before you, and you will be at the station. A very little to the east, you will see a good road on the moor leading to Lancaster, distant about 4 miles, and the ride will soon entertain with several agreeable objects on the bank of the Lune.

Article VII

A Tour to the Caves in the West Riding if Yorkshire

in a letter[148] to a friend‡

‡ This work, written by the late Rev. John Hutton, BD, Vicar of Burton—with the addition of some philosophical conjectures on the deluge, remarks on the origin of fountains and observations on the ascent and descent of vapours, occasioned by facts peculiar to the places visited; also a glossary of old words used in the North of England—may be had of the publishers, price 1s. 6d.

> Of antres vast, and deserts idle,
> Rough quarries, rocks and hills whose heads touch heav'n,
> It was my hint to speak.
> (Shakespeare's *Othello*, Act I)

Sir,

According to promise, I sit down to give you an account of our summer excursion. After having made the tour of the lakes, we were induced to proceed from Kendal, by Kirkby Lonsdale, Ingleton, Chapel in the Dale, Horton and Settle, in order to see the caves and other natural curiosities in Craven, in the West-Riding of Yorkshire.

This second part was more entertaining to most of the party than the first, being peculiarly adapted to our taste for natural history, for the great and sublime. While some are pleased with the gay and beautiful, others are only to be roused and affected by the grand and terrible. The strong and nervous sensations require objects proper for their gratification, no less than most nice and delicate tastes. If elegant prospects and refinements of art are suited to *these*, the rough, irregular and stupendous works of nature are no less adapted to the enjoyments of the former. Objects accommodated to the genius of a hardihood truly sublime are only to be met with, in this island, among the wild and irregular mountains of the north, among the roaring cataracts that roll foaming down precipitate from their lofty summits, and huge and dreary caverns or profound and yawning chasms they contain within their sides. It is here that Nature delights, as it were, to perform her magnificent works in secret, silently satisfied with self-approbation.

As the most amusing part of our tour was in a country not much frequented by the curious and speculative traveller, and never yet described to the public, an account of the objects we met with may perhaps not be unentertaining; it may also tend to excite the curiosity of visiting those unfrequented parts of our own native country, and try to communicate that rational pleasure which a benevolent mind wishes every one of the same sentiments to partake of.

About 6 o'clock one morning in June, we set off from Kendal and, after travelling about a dozen miles along a good turnpike road over

Endmoor and Cowbrow, we arrived at Kirkby Lonsdale soon after 8. About the midway we left the little steep white mountain, Farlton Knot, on the right about a mile. It is all composed of solid limestone and is 200 or 300 yds in height. Those who have seen both say, on the west side, it is like the rock of Gibraltar. There were several good mansion houses by the roadside, which at the beginning of last century were inhabited by a substantial set of yeomanry and country gentlemen, the most useful members of the community. They are now however mostly let out to farmers, the desire of improving their fortune in trade, or the pleasure of living in towns, have induced the owners to leave them—reverses of fortune, or new attachments, have caused many to sell them, after they had been continued many centuries in their families.

Kirkby Lonsdale, is a neat, well-paved, clean town, ornamented with several genteel houses, adjoining to some of which are elegant gardens. The houses are covered with blue slate, which has an agreeable effect on the eye of a stranger. A small brook runs through the market street, which is useful and commodious to the inhabitants; afterwards it turns several miles, in its deep descent to the River Lune. The church is a large and decent structure; the roof is covered in lead, and supported by three rows of pillars. The steeple is a square tower containing six bells, the music of which we were entertained with at 9 o'clock, they being played on by the chimes every three hours.

Opposite to the church gates is the old hall, taken notice of 150 years ago by drunken Barnaby in his *Itinerary*.[149] It is still an inn, and no doubt keeps up its ancient character.

> *Veni Lonsdale, ubi cernam,*
> *Aulam factam in tabernam;*
> *Nitidæ portæ, nivei muri,*
> *Cyathi pleni, paucæ curæ;*
> *Edunt, bibunt, ludunt, rident,*
> *Cura dignum, nihil vident.*

> I came to Lonsdale, where I stayed
> At hall, into a tavern made:
> Neat gates, white walls—naught was sparing,
> Pots brim-full—no thought of caring;
> They eat, drink, laugh, are still mirth making—
> Naught they see that's worth care taking.

On our entrance into the churchyard we were struck with the neatness and elegant simplicity of the vicarage house, which faced us. The pleasant garden adjoining, ornamented with a neat octagonal summer-house, commanding one of the most delightful prospects of nature, must render this sweet retreat a happy abode to the worthy vicar.

We walked through the churchyard, which is large and spacious, along the margin of a high and steep bank, to a neat white mansion house full in view, somewhat above half a mile distant, called Underlay. The prospect was of the most amusing kind. At the foot of the steep bank on which we walked, being about 40 or 50 yds perpendicular, glided the large pellucid River Lune amongst the rocks and pebbles which amused the ear, whilst the eye was entertaining itself with a vast variety of agreeable objects. A transparent sheet of still water, about half a mile in length, lay stretched out before us: at the high end of it was a grotesque range of impending rocks of red stone, about 30 yds in perpendicular height, which had an excellent effect in the scene, both by their colour and situation. We were told that in the winter this precipice was in some parts so glazed over with ice, from the water trickling down the surface, as to make it appear like a sheet of alabaster. From other parts of the impending rocks hung great and enormous icicles, which made it appear like a huge organ.

After the eye had travelled over a rich and fertile vale, variegated with woods and country houses, the prospect was terminated with a chain of lofty mountains, which runs in a direction south to north parallel to the course of the river. The nearest were not above 2 or 3 miles off and looked like the bold and surly sentries of a legion, that seemed stationed behind them. On our return we were amused with prospects of a different nature. The church and town before us enlivened the scene: some mill wheels, between them and the river, added to an agreeable variety with their motion. The vale beneath seemed to dilate and expand itself: the few parts of it that were visible afforded sufficient ground to the imagination to conceive an assemblage of the most entertaining objects. Ingleborough, whose head was wrapped in a cloud, stood the farthest to the south in the rank of the mountains which faced us.

After breakfast, we walked by the side of the river to the bridge. The channel is deep, the stream rapid among rocks, the banks on each side covered with trees of various foliage, which serve both as a defence and ornament. The bridge is the most lofty, strong, ancient and striking to the eye of a stranger, of any I have seen. It is built of freestone, has three arches (two large and one smaller); the height from the surface of the water to the top of the centre arch, except in flood, is about 12 yds. The arches are of the ribbed sort, which makes the appearance the more grotesque. There is no memorial of its foundation—a negative argument of its vast antiquity. We were indeed amused by one anecdote of its founder, which seemed to be a remnant of the ancient mythology of the north and one instance among many of easily accounting for anything that is marvellous. The country people have a tradition that it was built by the Devil one night in windy weather; he had but one apron full of stones for the purpose and unfortunately, his apron-string breaking as he flew with them over Casterton Fell, he lost many of them out, or the bridge would have been much higher.

From the top of the bridge the prospect down the river is delightful: the sides of the deep channel covered with trees, and nearly parallel for half a mile, and the water one continued surface, save here and there where a pointed rock lifts up its head above the stream. We walked down by the side of the river about a mile, and as we continued were continually presented with new prospects, while the soft murmurs of the river afforded a variety of different notes. The vale of Lonsdale dilating by degrees, presented to us in succession with the different seats and villages adorn it: Whittington and Arkholme to the west, Tunstal, Melling and Hornby, and its castle to the south, and Leek to the east. The brown and blue mountains of Burnmore and Lyth Fell terminated the view, which we could have wished had extended still further to the south.

While we were selecting various objects for our amusement, we suddenly and insensibly arrived at Overborough, the seat of Thomas Fenwick esquire, a modern house and one of the largest and most elegant in the county of Lancaster, being situated on a rising ground, though near the River Lune, its different fronts command all the delightful prospects which the vale affords.

During our excursion through the gardens and pleasure grounds adjoining, we were presented with views of a different sort to any we had hitherto enjoyed: sometimes were embowered with woods and lofty trees—nothing of the adjacent country to be seen, save here and there the blue peak of Ingleborough or some neighbouring mountain, till we crossed a broad vista, which suddenly exhibited a new and unexpected scene of the widening vale beneath. A stranger, in going from the hall to the gardens, must be struck with a surprise bordering on terror, on viewing the profound and gloomy glen by the side of his way. The trees which guard this steep bank prevent the eye from seeing the River Leck, which flows through a chasm amongst rocks at the bottom: imagination is left to conceive the cause of the deep and solemn murmurs beneath.

Our idea of the beauties of art and nature were mellowed and refined by those of venerable antiquity. We were now on classic ground, Overborough being undoubtedly a Roman station and garrison—the *Bremetonacæ* of the emperor Antoninus, as may be collected from Tacitus and other ancient writers.

Bremetonacæ is placed 20 Roman (or 18 English) miles north of Coccium or Ribchester, and 27 Roman (or 24 English) miles south of Galacum, which some antiquaries conceive to be Apulby, though others with more probability think it was Brough; the distances correspond, beside the additional argument of their being nearly in the same direction whether we conceive Galicum to be Apulby or Brough. The Roman road is easily traced from Ribchester into Yorkshire, running on the north side of Slaidburn, through Crossa-Greta, then on the north side of Tatham Chapel, through Bentham to Overborough;¶ afterwards the Roman road goes through Casterton and Middleton; and, as some think, by Borrowbridge and Orton, to Apulby. Others, and perhaps from better

¶ A full account of the antiquities of *Bremetonacæ*, or Overborough, may be seen in a quarto volume, published by Richard Rauthmell.

* Chester or Caster is derived from the Latin word *castrum*, 'camp'. Street is derived from the Latin word *stratum*, 'military road, causeway'. Brough, or Burgh, from the Greek word *purgos*, 'watch tower'.

† If the traveller is distressed for time, and has no inclination to take a second view of the River Lune and its environs, he may order his horse to be sent to Cowan Bridge, and walk through the park of Brough Hall, where he may be entertained with a variety of other prospects.

reasons, are of opinion, the road went to Sedbergh, or Sedburgh,* over Blewcaster, along Ravenstondale Street and through Kirkby Stephen to Brough, or Burgh.

For Antoninus's tenth Itinerary[150] runs from Glanoventa (Lanchester, in the county of Durham) by Galacum, Bremetonacæ, Coccium and Mancunium (or Manchester) to Glenovento (or Drayton in the county of Salop). In various places by the side of this road are high artificial mounts of earth, which were without doubt the stations of sentinels, to prevent any insurrections or being surprised by an enemy: these may be now seen entire at Burton in Lonsdale, Overborough, Kirkby Lonsdale and Sedbergh. There are several lateral ones, as at Lune Bridge near Hornby, at Melling and Wellington.

On our return we had the bridge full in view most of the way: its antiquity and greatness made its presence venerable and respected. About a furlong before we arrived at the bridge, the town of Kirkby Lonsdale appeared in a point of view peculiarly pleasing: the high walls of a gentleman's garden, which were between us and the town, made it like a fenced city in miniature; the tower steeple of the church rising proudly eminent above the blue slated houses, with which it was on every side surrounded.

We mounted our horses at the bridge about 11 o'clock, having them down thither in order to save half an hour going up the town for them.†
We travelled near the bottoms of the mountains on the side of Lonsdale, along the turnpike road, about an hour, being in three counties in that short interval—Westmorland, Lancashire and Yorkshire—and amidst a variety of entertaining prospects. The number of small carts laden with coals, and each dragged by one sorry horse, that we met, was surprising to a stranger. Many of the smaller farmers betwixt Kirkby Lonsdale and Kendal earn bread with carrying coals, during most part of the year, from the pits at Ingleton, Black Burton, or properly Burton in Lonsdale, to Kendal and the neighbouring places, for fuel and burning lime in order to manure the land. These beds of coal, we were informed, are 6 or 7 ft in thickness. A steam-engine was erected at Black Burton, more commodiously to work their best collieries. A survey was lately subscribed to be made, in order to have a canal from these pits to Lancaster, where coals might be exported, as also to Kendal and Settle, which are towns much in want of fuel.

After we had got about 6 miles from Kirkby Lonsdale, to a public house called Thornton Church-Stile, we stopped to procure a guide, candles, lanthorn, tinder-box, &c. for the purpose of seeing Yordas Cave in the vale of Kingsdale, about 4 miles off. By the advice of a friend, we took also with us a basket of provisions, which we found afterwards were of real service.

When we had gone about a mile, we were entertained by a fine cascade called Thornton Force, near some slate quarries, made by the river issuing out of Kingsdale. This cataract had some features different to any we had yet seen among the Lakes, but which greatly conducted it to render it peculiarly engaging. Part of the river tumbled with impetuosity from the top of the stratum of huge rocks, perpendicularly about 20 yds; another part of it, in search of a nearer and less violent course, had discovered a subterranean passage and gushed out of the side of the precipice, when they immediately again united their streams in a large, round, deep and black basin at the bottom.

From the margin of this pool the view may be taken to the greatest advantage: the high rock on the south and opposite side about half a dozen yards higher than the cascade, and mantled with shrubs and ivy, leaves nothing on that hand for the imagination to supply. If the archetype was not in being, it might be thought the subterranean stream was added to the picture by ingenuity of the artist, in order to give a finishing stroke to the beauty of the scene. This little river is worthy the company of the curious tourist for about a mile along its course through a deep grotesque glen, fortified on each side by steep and impending rocks.

About a mile higher we came to the head of the river, which issues from one fountain called Keld's Head,‡ to all appearance more copious than St Winifred's Well in Flintshire, though there is a broken, serpentine, irregular channel extending to the top of the vale, down which a large stream is poured from the mountains in rainy weather.

‡ *Keld* seems the ancient Saxon or British word for 'spring' or 'fountain', and is often made use of it in that sense in these parts of Yorkshire.

We now found ourselves in the midst of a small valley about 3 miles long and somewhat more than half a mile broad, the most extraordinary of any we had yet seen. It was surrounded on all sides by high mountains, some of them the loftiest of any in England—Whernside to the south-east and Gragareth to the north. There was no descent from this vale, except the deep chasm where we saw the cascade. It seemed opened in some distant age, either by the gradual effect of the washing of the river, or some violent and extraordinary flood bursting open the rugged barrier that pent it up. The vale above has all the appearance of having been once a lake, from the flatness of its surface and its rich soil, like a sediment subsided on the bottom of a stagnant water. We were informed that the subterranean cascade beneath, just now mentioned, has but lately made its appearance and is every day more and more enlarging.

We were quite secluded from the world, not an habitation for a man in view but a lonely shepherd's house, with a little wood and a few inclosures near it, called Breada Garth: it is on the north side of a high mountain, seldom visited by man and never by the sun for near half a year. The shepherd, its solitary inhabitant, with longing eyes looks for returning verdure, when the sun begins to throw his benign rays on the solitary abode. No monk or anchoret could desire a more retired situation for his cell to moralize on the vanity of the world, or disappointed lover to bewail the inconstancy of his nymph. The soil seemed the deepest and richest, in some parts of the vale, of any we had ever observed and no doubt is capable of great improvement. We could not but lament that, instead of peopling the wilds and deserts of North

America, our fellow subjects had not peopled the fertile wastes of the north of England. We have since indeed been informed, that a plan is in agitation for having them inclosed, when no doubt but it will support some scores of additional families.

While we were musing on the many bad effects of peopling distant countries and neglecting our own, we arrived at the object of this excursion, Yordas Cave: it is almost at the top of the vale, on the north-west side of it under the high mountain Gragareth. We discovered it by some sheep-folds, at the mouth of a rugged gill or glen in which we safely pent up our horses. In rainy seasons, we were told, a copious stream is poured down this gill and a cascade falls over the very entrance into the cave, so as to prevent any further approach. We were, however, favoured by the weather, and met with no obstacle of that nature to stop our ingress, but boldly entered a large aperture to the left into the side of the mountain, like the great door of some cathedral.

Having never been in a cave before, a thousand ideas, which had been for many years dormant, were excited in my imagination on my entrance into this gloomy cavern. Several passages out of Ovid's *Metamorphoses*, Virgil and other classics crowded into my mind together. At one time I thought it like the den where Cadmus met the huge serpent—

> *Silva vetus stabat, nulla violata securi;*
> *Est specus in medio virgis ac vimene densus,*
> *Efficiens humilem lapidum compagibus arcum;*
> *Uberibus fæcundus aquis. Hoc conditus antro*
> *Martius anguis erat.*

> Within this vale there rose a shady wood
> Of aged trees: in its dark bosom stood
> A bushy thicket, pathless and unworn,
> O'errun with brambles and perplex'd with thorn,
> Amidst the brake a hollow den was found
> With rocks and shelving arches vaulted round;
> Deep in the dreary den, conceale'd from day,
> Sacred to Mars, a mighty dragon lay.¶

Indeed there wanted nothing but an ancient wood to make one believe that Ovid had taken from hence its lively description.

As we advanced within this *antre* vast, and the gloom and horror increased, the den of Cacus and the cave of Poliphemus came into my mind. I wanted nothing but a Sybil conductress with a golden rod to imagine myself, like Æneas, going into the infernal regions.* The roof was so high and the bottom and sides so dark that, with all the light we could procure from our candles and torches, we were not able to see the

¶ Ovid, *Metamorphoses*, Bk 3, fab. 1; translated by Addison.

* See Virgil, *Æneid*, L.3, l. 616 and L.6, l. 205 and L.6, l. 234.

dimensions of this cavern. The light we had seemed only darkness visible, and would serve a timid stranger, alone and ignorant of his situation,

> To conceive things monstrous, and worse
> Than fables yet have feign'd, or fear conceiv'd –
> Gorgons, and hydras, and chimeras dire.†

† Milton.

‡ Virgil, *Æneid*, Bk 6, l. 542, translated by Addison.

The height of this cave was somewhat between a dozen and twenty yards; the breadth about the same dimension with the height; and the length at least 50 or 60 yds. Some of the party, who had seen both, thought it much more stupendous and magnificent than the famous Peak's Hole in Derbyshire.

Having passed a small brook, which one of the party called the Stygian Lake, we came to the western side of the cave. It is a solid perpendicular rock of black marble, embellished with many rude sketches and names of persons now long forgotten, the dates of some being above two hundred years old. After we had proceeded 30 or 40 yds northward, past some huge rocks that had at some time fallen from the roof or side, and arrived at the colonnade of rude massy pillars standing obliquely on their bases, the road divided itself into two parts, but not like that Æneas, when descending in the realms of Pluto—

> *Hoc inter Elysium nobis; at læva malorum*
> *Exercet pænas, & ad impia Tartarus mittit.*

> 'Tis here in different paths the way divides:
> The right to Pluto's golden palace guides,
> The left to that unhappy region tends,
> Which to the depth of Tartarus descends,
> The seat of night profound and punish'd fiends.‡

—No, they both had a divine tendency: on the right was the bishop's throne, and on the left the chapter house—so called from their resemblance to these appendages of a cathedral. Here we could not but lament the devastation made in the ornaments of these sacred places: some Goths, not long since, having defaced both throne and chapter house of their pendant petrified works, which had been some ages in forming.

The little cascades, which fell in various places from the roof and sides with different trilling notes, serving to entertain the ear with their watery music; while the eye was busy in amusing itself with the curious reflections which were made by our lights from the streams and petrifactions which appeared all around us. We were told by our guide, what a great effect the discharge of a gun or pistol would have upon our ears; but, not being desirous to carry our experimental philosophy so far as to endanger or give pain to the organs of hearing, we were not disappointed in having no apparatus for that purpose.

We followed a winding passage amongst high and grotesque pillars, being led by the noise of a falling stream, till we arrived at the chapter house. From the dome of this natural edifice fell a fine and clear cascade into a basin of transparent water, which served in peculiar manner to embellish the works of nature in a style superior to anything we can have in those of art. We were shown a low and narrow passage on one of the shelves of the rock near the chapter house, which, we were informed, led to a wider path extending itself into the heart of the mountain; but our curiosity was satisfied without crawling among the rocks besmeared with slime and mud.

If we had not been cautioned to beware of coming out too suddenly lest the quick transition from the dreary gloom of the cavern into the glare of sunshine should injure the sense of seeing, the curiosity for exploring every part in our return, now when our eyes were more opened, was sufficient to retard our steps and prevent a too hasty egress. While we were regaling ourselves with the provisions we had brought, we enquired of our guide if he could furnish us with any curious anecdotes relative to this cave. After informing us that it had been alternately the habitation of giants and fairies, as the different mythology prevailed in the country, he mentioned two circumstances we paid some attention to.

About fifty or sixty years ago, a madman escaped from his friends at or near Ingleton and lived here a week in the winter season, having had the precaution to take off a cheese and some other provisions to his subterranean hermitage. As there was snow on the ground, he had the cunning of Cacus (see Virgil's *Æneid*, Bk 8, l. 209) to pull the heels off his shoes and set them on inverted at the toes, to prevent being traced—an instance, among many others, of a madman's reasoning justly on some detached part of an absurd plan or hypothesis. Since that time, he told us, a poor woman, big with child, travelling alone up this inhospitable vale to that of Dent, was taken in labour and found dead in this cave.

We now proceeded to examine the pits and chasms apparently caused by the water after it has run through the cave. We ascended the hill a little higher, to view the gill above the cave. A stream of water flowed down it, which entering an aperture in the rock, we could see descend from steep to steep a considerable way. We made no doubt but it was the same stream which afterwards falls down through the roof of the chapter-house. Here was also a quarry of black marble, of which elegant monuments, chimney-pieces, slabs and other pieces of furniture are made by Mr Tomlinson at Burton in Lonsdale. When polished, this marble appears to be made up of entrochi, and various parts of testaceous and piscosous relics.

We were persuaded to climb up to the top of the base of Gragareth, the mountain in whose side Yordas is situated, in order to see Jingling Cave. It is on the edge of the flat base of the mountain, on a green plain by the side of a brook, looking down into the vale—Ingleborough appearing a little to the left, or north-east of Breada Garth, which was almost opposite.

This natural curiosity is a round aperture, narrow at the top, but most probably dilating in its dimensions to a profound extent. The stones we threw in made a hollow jingling noise for a considerable time. At intervals we could hear nothing of their descent; then again we heard them resound in deeper keys, till they were either immersed in some deep pool or were arrived at too great a distance to be heard; for there seemed a variety of different passages for their descent, some being much sooner intercepted in their career than others. Two dogs that were with us, and a small horse brought up by one of the party, seemed violently agitated, and under fearful trepidations, under horrors resembling those we are told the animal creation are seized with preceding or during an earthquake.

Though our reason convinced us of the impossibility of the ground falling in beneath us, we could not but feel many apprehensions, accompanied with sensations hitherto unknown. We could not learn that any swain had ever been adventurous enough to be let down by ropes into this vast hiatus, to explore those unseen regions, either from a principle of curiosity or to search for hidden mines. We were informed of some other openings into this mountain, of a like kind with Jingling Cave, but being at a distance and of an inferior nature, we returned to Yordas for our horses, which we had pent up in the sheep-folds, and proceeding down the vale, we crossed over it at the bottom to Twistleton, and soon arrived at Ingleton.¶

After we had regaled and rested ourselves comfortably at the Bay Horse, we took an evening walk about a mile above the town, to the slate quarries by the side of the River Wease, or Greta, which comes down out of Chapel-in-the-Dale and joins the Kingsdale river at Ingleton. Here we had objects both of nature and art to amuse ourselves with. On one hand was a precipice 10 or 12 yds perpendicular, made by the labour of man, being a quarry of fine large blue slate affording a useful and ornamental cover for the houses in the adjoining parts of Yorkshire, Lancashire and Westmorland; on the other hand was the river, rolling down from rock to rock in a narrow, deep chasm, where there was no room for human foot to tread between the stream and the rugged, high, steep rocks on each side.

Several pieces of the slate were bespangled with yellow marcasites, of a cubic form and different sizes; others were gilded over with the various foliages of ferns, pines, oaks and other vegetables. This bed of slate runs nearly from south to north by this place and the quarry near Thornton Force. Its length may be traced 2 or 3 miles, though about 200 or 300 yds in breadth—and indeed of good slate, but a few yards broad. The plane of the stratum is nearly perpendicular to the horizon, and may afford matter of speculation to the natural philosopher as to its cause, whether from some melted and liquid matter being forced up there at the

¶ If the tourist would proceed immediately to Chapel-in-the-Dale, he may go either below Breada Garth to Twistleton, and then turn up the vale to Chapel-in-the-Dale; or, which is a nearer road, he may cross Kingsdale above Breada Garth and ascend the mountain, pursing a rough and not well-defined road, taking care to keep on the south-west side of a swamp, near a hill or heap of stones called a hurder, on the base of Whernside, and then to turn round the west corner of the mountain; afterwards he must turn his course easterly, along the base of the mountain, till he come to some lanes, any of which will lead him by some houses down to the chapel in the middle of the vale between Whernside and Ingleborough.

deluge, or some subsequent volcano, as it is limestone rock on both the east and west side of it, and apparently severed asunder by the weight of the western stratum separating from the above by its inclination to the vale beneath.

We crossed the river by means of the broken fragments of rocks, which afforded us their rugged backs above the surface of the water to tread on. Here we met with a fine field for our entertainment as botanists. There was the lady's slipper, the fly-orchis (rarely to be met with elsewhere), and many other scarce and curious plants. We crossed over to take a second view of Thornton Force, on the south side of the Kingsdale river, and followed its murmuring stream down a deep glen, fortified with high precipices on each side, to Ingleton; nor did we think ourselves ill repaid for all the difficulties we had to encounter in our road amongst rocks and streams, as something new and amusing presented itself almost every step we took.

Ingleton is a pretty village pleasantly situated on a natural mount, yet at the bottom of a vale near the conflux of two rivers, over which are thrown two handsome arches. If the streams are sometimes small, the huge stones and fragments of rocks which are rolled down the beds of these rivers will serve to show that at other times they are remarkably full and impetuous. The churchyard, in the middle of which stands a neat sacred edifice,* commands a fine view of the vale of Lonsdale, almost as far as Lancaster. The murmurs of the streams below soothe the ear, while the eye is selecting a variety of objects for its entertainment.

On the background are the lofty mountains of Gragareth, Whernside and Ingleborough, the summits of which, when they are not enveloped in the clouds, can scarcely be seen for their high intervening bases. When the top of Ingleborough is covered with a thick white mist (or, as the country people say, when he puts on his night-cap), there are often strong gusts, called helm winds, blowing from thence to that part of the country which adjoins to its base. The like observation is made by mariners of the table-land of the Cape of Good Hope, on the coast of Africa. They are called helm winds from their blowing from the cloud or helmet that covers the head of the mountains. Amongst other entertainments, the civil usage and good accommodation we met with at our inn contributed not a little to heighten the amusements and pleasures of the day.†

Early next morning we set off for Ingleton Fells, or Chapel-in-the-Dale, along the turnpike road leading to Askrigg and Richmond. We had not travelled much above a mile before we came into the dale, which is about three quarters of a mile broad. For near 3 miles it had something in its appearance very striking to the naturalist: there were high precipices of limestone rock on each side; and the intermediate vale, to a lively imagination, would seem once to have been of the same height, but sunk down by the breaking of pillars which had supported the roof of an enormous vault.

* The editor of *Barnaby's Journal* has this distich on Ingleton:

Purgus inest sano, sanum sub acumine collis;
Collis ab elatis actus & auctus aquis.
The poor man's box is in the temple set:
Church under hill, and hill by waters beat.

† The writer of this Tour to the Caves was informed of a deep and curious chasm on the western extremity of the base of Ingleborough, above the village of Caldecoates, about a mile or two from Ingleton; but, as did not see it himself, he has not attempted a description of it from tradition.

About 3 miles from Ingleton is the head of the River Wease or Greta, on the left-hand side of the road, only a few yards distant from it. It gushes out of several fountains at once, all within 20 or 30 yds of each other, having run about 2 miles underground, though making its appearance in two or three places within that distance. When there are floods, it runs also above ground, though not in all places except the rains are extraordinary great. This is the subterranean river mentioned by Dr Goldsmith in his entertaining *Natural History* (Volume I) by the name of 'Greatah'.

When we had gone about a mile farther, being 4 miles from Ingleton, we turned off the turnpike road to some houses near the chapel, where we left our horses. At first we imagined we had here met with an exception to the maxim of poet Butler,[151] the author of *Hudibras*, viz—

> A Jesuit never took in hand
> To plant a church in barren land.

For the chapelry produceth neither wheat, oats, barley, pease, nor any other sort of grain; nor apples, pears, plus, cherries, nor any kind of fruit—a ripe gooseberry was a natural curiosity in the summer season in most parts of the district; even their potatoes they have from other places. Yet though they were destitute of these productions, they were blessed with others as valuable by way of compensation. They abound with excellent hay ground and pastures, and were rich in large flocks, and herds of cattle, which enabled them to purchase every conveniency of life. Having little intercourse with the luxurious, vicious and designing part of mankind, they were temperate, substantial, sincere and hospitable. We found an intelligent, agreeable and entertaining companion and guide in the curate, who served them also as schoolmaster. As Dr Goldsmith observes on a like occasion:[152]

> A man he was to all the country dear,
> And passing rich with thirty pounds a year.

The first curiosity we were conducted to was Hurtlepot, about 80 yds above the chapel.‡ It is a round, deep hole between 30 and 40 yds diameter, surrounded with rocks almost on all sides, between 30 and 40 ft perpendicular above a deep black water in a subterranean cavity at its bottom. All round the top of this horrid place are trees, which grow secure from the axe: their branches almost meet in the centre and spread a gloom over a chasm dreadful enough of itself without being heightened with any additional appendages.

It was indeed one of the most dismal prospects we had yet been presented with: almost every sense was affected in such an uncommon manner as to excite ideas of a nature truly horribly sublime. Whenever we threw in a pebble or spoke a word, our ears were assailed with a dismal hollow sound, our nostrils were affected with an uncommon complication

‡ About 100 yds below the chapel there are the ruins of an old cave called Sandpot; the top has apparently sometime fallen in and has covered the bottom with its ruins. A large cascade is distinctly heard through this rubbish. If a descent were opened, no doubt but a subterranean passage would be discovered leading either to the caves above the chapel or, more probably, to Douk Cave on the base of Ingleborough, if not to both.

of strong smells, from the ramps and other weeds that grew plentifully about its sides and the rank vapours that exhaled from the black abyss beneath. The descent of Æneas into the infernal regions came again fresh into my imagination, and the following passage out of Virgil obstruded itself on my memory:

> Spelunca alta fuit, vastoque immanis hiatu
> Scrupea, tuta lacu nigro nemorumque tenebris;
> Quam super haud ullæ paterant impune volantes
> Tendere iter pennis: talis sese halitus atris
> Faucibus effundens supera ad convexa serebat;
> Unde locum Graii dixerunt nomine Avernum.

> Deep was the cave, and downwards as it went
> From the wide mouth, a rocky, rough descent:
> And here th' access a gloomy grove defends:
> And there th' unnavigable lake extends,
> O'er whose unhappy waters, void of light,
> No bird presumes to steer his airy flight:
> From hence the Grecian bards their legends make,
> And give the name Avernus to the lake.¶

¶ Virgil, *Æneid*, Bk 6, l. 237, translated by Dryden.

After viewing for some time, with horror and astonishment, its dreadful aspect from the top, we were emboldened to descend by a steep and slippery passage to the margin of this Avernian lake. What its depth is, we could not learn; but, from the length of time the sinking stones we threw in continued to send up bubbles from the black abyss, we concluded it to be very profound. How far it extended under the huge pendant rocks, we could get no information of, a subterranean embarkation having never yet been fitted out for discoveries. In great floods, we were told, this pots runs over: some traces of it then remained on the grass.

While we stood at the bottom, the awful silence was broken every three or four seconds by drops of water falling into the lake from the rocks above in different solemn keys. The sun shining on the surface of the water illuminated the bottom of the superincumbent rocks only a few feet above; which, being viewed by reflection in the lake, caused a curious deception, scarcely anywhere to be met with—they appeared at the like distance below its surface, in form of a rugged bottom. But, alas! How fatal would be the consequence, if any adventurer should attempt to wade across the abyss on this shadow of a foundation!

While we were standing on the margin of this subterranean lake, we were suddenly astonished with a most uncommon noise on the surface of the water, under the pendant rocks. It is called by the country people Hurtlepot boggard and sometimes the fairy churn, as a churn it resembles. It is no doubt frightful to them and would have been so to us, if we had not been apprised of the cause: we found it was effected by the glutting of the surface of the water against the bottom of some rocks, or passages worn into them to a considerable distance, when it was descending after rain as then happened to be the case. This deep is not without its inhabitants: large black trouts are frequently caught in it by the neighbouring people. Botanists find here some rare and curious plants.

On our return from the margin of this Avernian lake, we found the observation of the poet Virgil very applicable:

Facilis descensus Averni:
Nocles atque dies patet atri janua Ditis;
Sed revocare gradum, superasque evadere ad auras
Hoc opus, hic labor est.

The gates of hell are open night and day;
Smooth the descent, and easy is the way.
But to return, and view the cheerful skies,
In this the task and mighty labour lies.*

When we arrived in the superior region, we pursued our journey about 150 yds farther up a very narrow grotesque glen, over a natural bridge of limestone above 10 yds thick, having the subterranean River Wease, or Greta, underneath. When we got to the head of this gill, we were stopped by a deep chasm called Jinglepot, at the bottom of the precipice. It is of an oblong and narrow form. An enterprising person, with a steady head and active heels, regardless of the fatal consequences from a false step, might leap over it. It is filled with smooth pebbles at the bottom except the south corner, where there is a deep water which, in floods, swells up to the top and issues out in vast torrent. The length of this chasm is about 10 yds and the perpendicular depth at the north corner about 20 yds.

In our way from Hurtlepot, we could not help remarking the ruins of two small artificial mounts of earth which, we were told, formerly served as butts, when the inhabitants exercised themselves in the ancient military accomplishment of archery. The naturalist must also be entertained with the successful efforts that had been made by the roots of some old ashes to get across the dry and broad bed of rocks to a rich bed of sandy soil, in order to support their aged parents, forever doomed to dwell on the steep side of a barren and rugged cliff.

Returning back a little way from Jinglepot in order to find a passage out of this dreary glen, we proceeded about 120 yds higher, when we came to Weathercoat Cave or cove,† the most surprising natural curiosity of the kind in the island of Great Britain. It is stupendous subterranean cataract, in a huge cave, the top of which is on the same level with the adjoining lands.

On our approach to its brink, our ears and eyes were equally astonished with the sublime and terrible. The margin was surrounded

* Virgil, *Æneid*, translated by Dryden.

† The word cave is pronounced by the country people cove or coave. This hint may be of service to a stranger in his enquiries. This cave is not above 100 yds from the turnpike road from Lancaster to Richmond: it is on the left-hand side of the 22nd milestone from Lancaster, from whence the cascade may be distinctly heard. The delicate and timid may neither be afraid of their persons or clothes, if they have no mind to descend: they may stand safe on the margin of either Hurtlepot, Ginglepot or Weathercoat Cave. They will there see enough to astonish them, and imagination will supply the rest.

with trees and shrubs, the foliage of which was of various shapes and colours, which had an excellent effect both in guarding and ornamenting the steep and rugged precipices on every side. Where the eye could penetrate through the leaves and branches, there was room for the imagination to conceive this cavern more dreadful and horrible, if possible, than it was in reality.

This cave is of a lozenge form, and divided into two by a rugged and grotesque arch of limestone rock; the whole length, from north to south, is about 60 yds and the breadth about half the length. At the south end is the entrance down into the little cave, on the right of which is a subterranean passage under the rocks, and a petrifying well. A stranger cannot but take notice of a natural seat and table in a corner of this grotesque room, well suited for a poet or philosopher. Here he may be secluded from the bustle of the world, though not from noise; the uniform roaring, however, of the cascade will exclude from the ear every other sound and his retirement will conceal him from every object that might divert the eye.

Having descended with caution from rock to rock, we passed under the arch and came into the great cave, where we stood some time in silent astonishment to view the amazing cascade. The perpendicular height of the north corner of this cave was found by an exact admeasurement to be 36 yds. Near 11 yds from the top issues a torrent out of a hole in the rock, about the dimensions of a large door in a church, conveying usually as much water as the New River at London. It rushes forwards with a curvature, which shows that it has had a steep descent before it appears in open day, and tumbles precipitately 25 yds perpendicular down on the rocks at the bottom, with a noise that amazes the most intrepid ear. The water sinks as it falls amongst the rocks and pebbles, running by a subterranean passage about a mile, when it appears again by the side of the turnpike road, visiting in its way the other caverns of the Jinglepot and Hurtlepot.

The cave is filled with the spray that arises from the water dashing against the bottom; and the sun happening to shine very bright, we had a small vivid rainbow within a few yards of us, for colour, size and situation perhaps nowhere else to be equalled. A huge rock, that had sometime been rolled down by the impetuosity of the stream, and was suspended between us and the top of the cascade, like the coffin of Mahomet at Medina, had an excellent effect in the scene. Though the stream had polished the surfaces of the pebbles on which it fell at the bottom, by rolling them against each other, yet its whole force was not able to drive from its native place the long black moss that firmly adhered to the large immovable rocks.

We were tempted to descend into a dark chamber at the very bottom of the cave, covered over with a ceiling of rock above 30 yds thick, and from thence behind the cascade, at the expense of having our clothes a little wet and dirtied; when the noise became tremendous and the idea for personal safety awful and alarming, as the rocks on which we stood, and every one about us, seemed to shake with the vast concussion. We were informed that in a great drought the divergency of the stream is so small that we might with safety go quite round the cascade.

At the bottom we were shown a crevice, where we might descend to the subterranean channel which would lead us to Jinglepot and perhaps much farther. We were also shown, above, a shallow passage between the strata of rocks, along which we might crawl to the orifice out of which the cascade issued, where it was high enough to walk erect and where we might have the honour of making the first expedition for discoveries, no creature having yet proceeded in that passage out of sight of daylight; but, as we were apprehensive the dangers and difficulties to be encountered in our progress would not be compensated by the pleasure, we did not attempt to explore these new regions.‡

After a little rain another cascade, similar to the former, falls nearly from the same height on the west side of the cave, appearing and disappearing with great variety amongst the rocks, as if it fell down the chimney of a ruinous building, where several holes were made into it in the gable end. If the rains still increase, a large stream sets in out of the room by the side of the little cave; and, in great floods, a vast river falls into the great cave, down the precipice on the eastern side.

Nothing can be more grotesque and terrible than to view this cave when about half full of water: a variety of cascades issue from crannies in every quarter—some as small as a tap in a hogshead, and others as copious as rivers—all pouring with impetuosity into this deep and rugged basin. With their united streams they are sometimes able to fill the whole capacity of the cavern and make it overflow, the subterranean crannies and passages of this leaky vessel not being able, with the increased pressure from above, to carry off the water as fast as it is poured in: but this happens only about six or seven times in 20 years.¶

Having satisfied our curiosity in viewing this wonder of nature and moralised on the insignificancy of all human attempts in producing anything like it, we ascended into our native regions and proceeded to another, called Douk Cove, about a mile south on the other side of the turnpike road, towards the foot of Ingleborough, whose height now appeared to great advantage from the nature of our own elevated situation. Douk Cove is something similar to that of Weathercoat, but not heightened so much with the vast and terrible: the cavity indeed is longer and wider, but not deeper; the rocks not so high and steep, except on the east side, where the hawks and other birds build their nests, not dreading the approach of human foot.

They both seem once to have been covered over, like Yordas, but the roofs have fallen in, by some inundation or other accident. The stream of this cascade does not fall above 5 or 6 yds and is not so large as the former; though, like it, is immediately absorbed among the rocks beneath. The subterranean passage out of which it issues is very curious.

‡ The writer of this Tour, in company with the owner of the cave and some others, has since been in the passage out of which the cascade issues, but is not able to tell how far it extends, as it was high and wide enough to admit passengers much farther than they were. The owner of the cave and others have been in the passage beneath, halfway to Jinglepot. They have no doubt but it leads thither; they did not get so far, owing to the water deepening more than the height lessening. Another subterranean river, that from Gatekirk above, meets this cascade directly underneath it, along which there is a passage and which the above party (in some measure through mistake) explored, having missed their way in their return and gone far beyond the cascade, before they were convinced of their error by the noise of the cascade gradually decreasing.

¶ The owner of the cave says that it ran over in the back end of the year 1757 (before Christmas), in 1759, in 1771 two or three times (all in the back end of the year), in February 1782 and November 1783. But during this interval, the water has been several times near the top of the cave. Before it runs over, a large stream issues out of the well before Weathercoat House.

By the help of a ladder we ascended, and went along it to some distance, by means of candles. When we had gone about 40 or 50 yds, we came to a chasm 12 or 15 yds in depth from the surface, through which we could see broad day. How far we could have proceeded, we know not: we returned after we had been about 100 yds. This would be looked on as a great curiosity in many countries; but, after those we had seen, our wonder was not easily excited. No doubt but another subterranean passage might be discovered by removing the rubbish at the bottom of the cave, where the water sinks.

We were now on the base on which Ingleborough stands* and greatly elevated above all the western country. Our distance from the bottom, where the steep ascent of this high mountain begins, was about a mile in a direct horizontal line over rocks and pits. The fineness and clearness of the day, however, induced us to ascend its side and gain its summit. Though we had many a weary and slippery step, we thought ourselves amply repaid when we got to the top with the amusement we received in viewing the several extensive and diversified prospects and in making our observations, as botanists and natural historians, on its productions and contents.

All the country betwixt us and the sea, to the extent of 40, 50 and 60 miles from the north-west by the west to the south-west, lay stretched out beneath us like a large map, with the roads, rivers, villages, towns, seats, hills and vales, capes and bays in succession. Elevation is a great leveller: all the hills and little mountains in the country before us appeared sunk in our eyes and in the same plane with the adjacent meadows. To the north-west, the prospect was terminated at the distance of 40 or 50 miles by a chain of rugged mountains in Westmorland, Lancashire and Cumberland, which appeared as barriers against the fury of the ocean. To the west, the Irish Sea extends as far as the eye can penetrate, except where the uniformity of the watery prospect is interrupted by the isles of Man and Anglesey. The blue mountains in Wales terminated our further progress, after we had traced out the winding of the coast all the way from Lancaster, by Preston and Liverpool.

A curious *deceptio visus* presented itself: all the vales between us and the sea appeared lower than its surface, owing to the sky and earth both apparently tending to a line drawn from the eye parallel to the horizon, where they at last appeared to meet. To the east and north, the prospect was soon terminated by a number of black, irregular, chaotic mountains which, by their indentations and winding summits, gave us reason to believe they contained habitable vales between them. Their sides afford a hardy and wholesome pasture for sheep, and their bowels contain rich mines of lead, some of which are wrought with great advantage to the proprietors.

The immense base on which Ingleborough stands is between 20 and 30 miles in circumference. The rise is in some places even and gradual;

* The word *Ingleborough* seemed to be derived from the Saxon word *ingle*, which signifies a lighted fire, and *borough* or *burgh*, which comes originally from the Greek word *purgos* and signifies a watch tower (the labials *p* and *b* being often changed into each other), for here a beacon is erected on which a fire used to be made for a signal of alarm in times of rebellion or invasion.

in others, as to the north and west, it is rugged and almost perpendicular. The top is plain and horizontal, being almost a mile round, having the ruins of an old wall about it, from which some ingenious antiquaries endeavour to prove that it has once been a Roman station and a place of great defence.

Of late years it has never been frequented by any except the shepherds and the curious in prospects, and the neighbouring country people who resorted to the horse races, which were formerly annually held on its top. On the western edge there are the remains of what the country people call the beacon, some three or four yards high, ascended by a flight of steps. The ruin of a little watch-house is also adjoining. No doubt, in time of wars, insurrections and tumults, and particularly during the incursions of the Scots, a fire was made on this beacon to give the alarm to the country round about

The soil on the top is so dry and barren that it affords little grass, the rock being barely covered with earth; a spongy moss is all the vegetable that thrives in this lofty region. The stones on the summit and for a great way down are of the sandy gritty sort, with freestone slate amongst them; upon the base the rocks are all limestone, to an enormous depth. Near the top indeed on the east side is a stratum of limestone like the Derbyshire marble, full of entrochi. Several springs have their origin near the summit, particularly one on the north side of pure and well-tasted water, called Fair-Weather Syke, which runs down by the side of a steep fence wall into a chasm called Meir Gill. All the other springs, as well as this, when they come to the limestone base, are swallowed up and after running perhaps a mile underground make their appearance once again in the surrounding vales and then wind in various courses to the Lune or the Ribble, which empty themselves into the Irish Sea.

A naturalist cannot but observe a number of conical holes with the vertexes downwards, not only all over the base of Ingleborough, but particularly a row near the summit. They are from 2 to 4 or 5 yds in diameter and from 2 to 3 or 4 yds deep, except Barefoot Wives Hole (hereafter mentioned) which is much larger. They resemble those pits about Mount Etna, Vesuvius and the various parts of Sicily and Calabria, as described by Hamilton and other writers. What may have been the cause of them, is left for the determination of the ingenious naturalist.

The other stones and fossils on and about Ingleborough are black and brown marbles, abounding with white sea-shells, sparks of spar and flakes of entrochi; spars of various sorts, the stalactical and icicle in the caves; slates, pale and brown, and near Ingleton blue; black shiver, Tripoli or rotten stone, blood stone and lead ore.

The soil on the base and sides of Ingleborough (where there is any) is chiefly peat moss, which the country people get up and burn for fuel. The cover is in general ling or heath; other vegetables are ferns of various kinds, reindeer moss and various other mosses, heleborines, white and red, the different sorts of sedums, crane's bills, scurvy grass, bird's eyes, various liverworts, orchises, rosewort, lily of the valley, mountain columbines, the hurtle-berry or bilberry, knoutberry, cranberry, cloudberry and cowberry. The shrubs are mountain vine, bird cherry, mountain ash, gelder rose, burnet rose, stone bramble, red and black currants. In the Foalfoot, which is the north-west corner of this mountain, are found the vivaperous grass and the rose-of-the-root, which has a yellow flower and is like house-leek. Near Ingleton, as was before observed, are the lady's slipper and fly orchis. The chief animals found on and about Ingleborough are grouse, the ring ousel and wheatear, the fox, mountain cat, wild cat, polecat, weasel, stoat, badger and pine marten.

The perpendicular height of this mountain above the level of the sea is 3,987 ft, as taken by a neighbouring country gentleman.[153] The country people are all persuaded that Whernside, on the north side of the vale of Chapel-in-the-Dale, is higher than Ingleborough, from snow continuing linger on its top and other circumstances. The elevation appears so nearly the same to the eye, that nothing but an exact admeasurement can determine this honour for these rival, soaring candidates. The top of Ingleborough is the first land, however, that sailors descry in their voyage from Dublin to Lancaster, though above 30 miles from the sea, which shows the great height of this mountain, though not an argument for its being higher than Whernside, which is not so well situated to be seen from the Irish Sea.

In our return we visited the long, deep and dreadful chasm of Meir Gill, on the west side of the sheep-fence wall running north and south over the base of Ingleborough. It is about 80 yds long, but in most places so narrow that a person may stride over it and is nowhere above 2 or 3 yds wide: in one place there is a curious natural bridge over it. The depth is very different in different places: at one place we found it 100 ft, 48 of which were in the water. One part will admit a bold and active adventurer down almost to the water, by a gradual but slippery descent. Here the shadow of the superincumbent rocks, like that in Hurtlepot, forms a deceitful appearance in the water: the bottom seems not above two feet below the surface, but how fatal would be the attempt to wade this abyss in quest of further discoveries, from this shadow of encouragement!

The narrowest of this crevice at the top has something dreadful and alarming in it: how fatal would one false step prove to the unwary shepherd amongst the snow when the mouth is drifted up, or to a stranger bewildered in a fog and looking forward with eager eyes for some habitation or frequented path! Harmless and heedless sheep have often been suddenly swallowed up by this gaping wonder of nature. To say that no living creature ever came out of its mouth would be a proposition too general; trouts of a protuberant size have been drawn out of it, where they had been long nourished in safety, their habitation being seldom disturbed by the insidious fisherman.

A little further to the east, we came to another curiosity of nature, called Barefoot Wives Hole: we had noticed it in our ascent up the side of Ingleborough. It is a large round pit in form of a funnel, the diameter at top being about 50 or 60 yds and its depth 26. It is easily descended in most places, though on the south side there is a high rocky precipice, but is dry—the waters that are emptied into it being swallowed up among the rocks and loose stones at the bottom. In our way back we also saw Hardrawkin and some other subterranean passages of less note, which had been formed by the waters in their descent from the mountain adjoining to Ingleborough to the vale beneath. Indeed the whole limestone base of this monster is perforated and excavated in all directions like a honeycomb.†

From the Chapel-in-the-Dale we shaped our course towards the south-east corner of Whernside, along the road leading to the village of Dent. As we proceeded, the curate entertained us with an account of some singular properties observable in the black earth, which composes the soil in the higher parts of the vale in various morassy places. It is a kind of *igneum lutum*, or rather a sort of putrified earth, which in the night resembles fire when it is agitated by being trod upon. The effects it produces in a dark evening are truly curious and amazing. Strangers are always surprised and often frightened to see their own and horses' legs besprinkled to all appearance with fire, and sparks of it flying in every direction, as if struck out of the ground from under their feet. They are as much alarmed with it as the country people are with the *will-with-a-wisp* or mariners with the luminous vapour of the delapsed Castor and Pollux. Though the dark and dreary moor is broken into thousands of luminous particles, like so many glow-worms, when troubled by the benighted traveller, yet if any of this natural phosphorus is brought before a lighted candle, its splendour immediately vanishes and shrinks back into its original dull and dark state of sordid dirt.

While we were endeavouring to account for this curious phenomenon on the principles of putrefaction and electricity, we arrived at the first object of this lateral excursion from the turnpike road, Gatekirk Cave.‡ The brook which runs through it forms a fine natural basin of transparent water at its egress, where we entered the cave, gradually increasing in depth till about 5 or 6 ft at the most. I believe every one present thought it resembled the cave described by Ovid in the second of his *Metamorphoses*, where Actaeon unfortunately met with Diana and her nymphs amusing themselves with bathing, when separated from his companions during the chase—

> *Vallis erat piceis & acuta densa cupressu,*
> *Nomine Gargaphie; succinctæ cura Dianæ;*
> *Cujus in extremo est antrum nemorale recessu,*
> *Arte laboratum nulla; simulaverat artem*
> *Ingenio natura suo: nan pumice vivo,*
> *Et levibus tophis nativum duxerat arcum.*
> *Fons sonat a dextra, tenui pellucidus unda,*

† Limestone has all the appearance of having been once in a soft state and easily soluble in water. This principle will account for the scallops on the surface of limestone rocks, being made perhaps by the water draining off while the stone was soft; also for the chinks and crevices amongst them, made by their shrinking together when dried by the sun. The caves themselves proceed, most probably, from a great part of the rock being dissolved and washed down by the stream pervading the different strata.

‡ A furlong or two before we arrived at Gatekirk, we passed a little cascade, amongst some hollow limestone rocks, which would be a fine embellishment to a gentleman's garden or park. All the ground about seemed hollow, and we saw various chasms and empty spaces between the strata of rocks, though none worth a particular description in a country abounding with such a variety of a superior nature.

Margine gramineo patulos succintus hiatus.
Hic Dea silvarum venatu fessa solebat
Virgeneos artus liquido perfundere rore.

Down in a vale, with pine and cypress clad,
Refreshed with gentle winds, and brown with shade,
The chaste Diana's private haunt there stood,
Full in the centre of a darksome wood,
A spacious grotto, all around o'ergrown
With hoary moss, and arch'd with pumice-stone:
From out its rocky clefts the waters flow,
And trickling swell into a lake below.
Nature had everywhere so play'd her part
That every where she seemed to vie with art.
Here the bright goddess, toil'd and chaf'd with heat,
Was wont to bathe her in the cool retreat.¶

¶ Ovid, *Metamorphoses*, Bk 3, *fab.* 2,
translated by Addison.

Over the cave where the water flows is another subterranean passage,
of about 24 ft in length and from 3 to 10 in height. It enters the other
obliquely and looks like a natural orchestra, and where indeed a band of
music would exhibit to great advantage to an audience below. The roof
of the cave at the entrance by the stream is about 2 yds high, but soon
increases to 6. When we had proceeded out of sight of day, a new train
of ideas were excited in our imaginations. We could not but fancy that it
was like the caves of Polyphemus or of some giant in modern romance,
who hung up the mangled limbs of the unhappy victims that fell into his
hands, to the dome of his murky den. From the roof were pendant large
pertrifactions in every grotesque shape: some like hams, other like neats'
tongues, many like the heads and various parts of different animals.
Some parts of this cave appeared like dreary vaults or catacombs, where
we deposited the relics of ancient heroes or martyrs; some rocks at the
bottom appeared like huge stone coffins, and some large petrifactions on
the shelves like virgins or children represented in alabaster.

As we proceeded along, we met with several bye-streets or lanes,
down some of which came tinkling little currents; but they seemed not to
admit a passenger with ease to any great distance. As we went along, we
observed that the way divided for a considerable part of the whole length
into two main streets, which united again, made by the current dividing
above into two streams. After we had gone near a hundred yards, we
met with an orifice which easily admitted us above ground. We had no
curiosity to explore any farther, as the roof was now become only some
4 ft high and not admitting us with ease beyond this aperture. The brook
which runs through this cave is the main stream of the River Greta, which
runs underground for at least 2 miles, making its appearance here, at
Weathercoat and a few other places in its way down to its open channel.

The pools that are formed by the brook after its exit out of the cave exhibit a pleasing and rural scene, being shaded with rocks, weeping willows and mountain ash.

Having travelled a mile or two further and passed through the little remote village of Winterscales, we came to the natural curiosity we were in quest of, Greenside Cave: it is under the south-east corner of the lofty mountain Whernside. The mouth was wide and high, and the road rugged, but the roof gradually sank, or the bottom arose, till it was troublesome getting along soon after we were out of sight of day. A small brook ran along the bottom, as in the other caves; but there were none of the curious petrifactions we saw in most of them, to delight the eye. Churchill's description of the Caledonian cave of Famine,[154] with a few alterations, will convey a just idea of Greenside Cave:

This lonely cave (hard tax on Scottish pride!)
Shelter at once for man and beast supply'd.
Their snares without, entangling briers spread,
And thistles arm'd against th' invader's head.
Here webs were spread of more than common size,
And half-starv'd spiders prey'd on half-starv'd flies.
In quest of food, efts strove in vain to crawl:
Slugs, pinch'd with hunger, smear'd the slimy wall.
The cave around with falling riv'lets rung,
And on the roof unhealthy vapours hung.

Near the mouth of this cave is a thin stratum of coal not many inches thick. Some attempts have been made to work it, but affording so small gains and the inhabitants being so well supplied with this article from Ingleton, it was soon deserted. Being so near the top of Whernside, we ventured to ascend to the summit. The prospects were not diversified with many pleasing objects, being surrounded almost on all sides with brown and blue chaotic mountains. We had a peep into the pleasant vale of Dent beneath us, which made us wish to see it all. Pendle Hill appeared over the top of Ingleborough, which gave us a high idea of our own elevation, this latter mountain being much higher than the former.

We were surprised to see four or five tarns, or pools of water, on a plain very near the summit of Whernside. Two of them were large, being 200 or 300 yds in length and nearly of the same breadth (for one was almost circular, but the other oblong). There was a very thin bed of coal almost on the top of this mountain, and we were told another corresponded with it on the top of the great Colm, a lofty mountain on the other side of that branch of the vale of Dent called Dibdale. We were told some curious anecdotes of the vast cunning and sagacity of the sheepdogs in this country in discovering the sheep that had been buried under large drifts of snow for some days, and that must inevitably have perished with hunger or been drowned with the melting of that vapour, if not discovered by these useful animals.

We now shaped our course back to Winterscales and from thence to a public house called Gearstones, by the side of the turnpike road at the bottom of the mountain Cam. Here we refreshed ourselves and left our horses, while we went about half a mile to the south to explore another subterranean wonder of nature, called Catknot Hole. The entrance into it is at first not above 3 or 4 ft high, but almost immediately increases to as many yards. We had not gone out of sight of day before we were obliged to wade up to the mid-leg a few yards, through a little pool made by the rill that comes out of this cave. The passage grew narrower, but wide enough to walk along with ease, except in one or two places, where we were in danger of daubing our clothes with a red slime. We proceeded above a quarter of a mile, when the road grew wider, but the roof was so low that we could not go on with ease and pleasure. Perhaps if we had mustered humility and fortitude enough to have crouched and crawled a little, we might have come to where the roof again would have been as high as we should have desired.

In some places there were alleys out of the main street, but not extending to any great distance so as to admit of passengers. The rocks jutted out and were pendant in every grotesque and fantastic shape; most of them were covered over with a fine coating of spar, that looked like alabaster, while icicles of various shapes and colours were pendant from the roof all generated by the fine particles of stone that exist in the water, which transudes through the roof and sides, and leaves them adhering to the rock in their descent to the bottom. The various-coloured reflections made by the spars and pertrifactions that abounded in every part entertained the eye with the greatest novelty and variety; while, at the same time, the different notes made by the rill in its little cascades, and reverberated from the hollow rocks, amused the ear with a new sort of rude and subterranean music, but well enough suited to our slow and gloomy march.

This was the longest subterranean excursion we had yet made and, if we might have formed our own computation of its extent from the time we were in going and coming, and not from the real admeasurement of our guide, we should have thought it two or three times as long as it was—so much were we deceived in our estimate of a road unlike any we had ever before travelled. The romantic cascades, pools and precipices in the channel of the River Ribble that runs by the mouth of this cave, are not unworthy the notice of a stranger.

We were in some suspense whether we should pursue the turnpike road over Cam, to see the natural curiosities in Wensleydale; but, as we learnt there was only one remarkable object of the genus of those were now in quest of, Hardraw Scar, we desisted as we should have lost others more valuable, which lay in a different route. The description, however, which was given of it by our own reverend guide, was so lively and picturesque, that its own merit will be a sufficient apology for its insertion.

Hardraw Scar is near the town of Hawes, in Wensleydale, and bears some distant affinity to the tremendous Gordale *[hereafter taken notice of]*. The chasm is pervious at the bottom and extends above 300 yds in length, fortified with huge scattered rocks on each side, which are in some places 33 yds perpendicular, and the intervallum above 80. At the far end is an amazing cataract, which pours forth a vast quantity of water, that falls into a deep basin. Behind the waterfall is a deep recess excavated out of the solid rock. Here the spectator may stand behind the stream, secure from its madifying effects, and may go quite round it upon one of the numerous *saxa sedilia*, at the distance of ten yards from the water. In the years 1740, when fairs were held on the Thames, this cascade was frozen and constituted a prodigious icicle of a conic form, 32¾ yds in circumference, which was also its height.

After having determined to go to Settle, we had our doubt whether we should proceed by Ling Gill—which is a curious and romantic channel of a small river, having high and grotesque rocks on each side—or take a more western direction on the other side of the River Ribble, in order to see some other caves and chasms. Our taste for curiosities of this sort induced us to adopt the latter plan. We returned about a mile before we left the turnpike road, and then turning off to the left, proceeding almost to the same distance, we came to Alan or Alumn Pot, two or three furlongs above the little village of Selside.

It is a round steep hole in the limestone rock, about 8 or 10 yds in diameter and of a tremendous depth, somewhat resembling Elden Hole in Derbyshire. We stood for some time on its margin, which is fringed round with shrubs, in silent astonishment, not thinking it safe to venture near enough to its brim to try if we could see to its bottom. The profundity seemed vast and terrible, from the continued hollow jingling noise excited by the stones we tumbled into it. We plumbed it to the depth of 165 ft, 43 of which were in water, and this is a extraordinary dry season. As the direction of this hole was not exactly perpendicular, but somewhat sloping, it is very probable we were not quite at the bottom. A subterranean rivulet descends into this terrible hiatus, which caused such a dreadful gloom, from the spray it raised up, as to make us shrink back with horror when we could get a peep into the vast abyss.

We were informed that not long since some animals—an ox and a calf, at different times—had the misfortune to tumble into this dreary pit, being tempted by the untested herbage to venture too far on its slippery margin. Only a low mound of earth surrounds its brim, for a stone wall would answer no other purpose than to afford the curious traveller materials to throw in for his amusement. Any advantage arising from the skins and carcases of these animals was not a sufficient inducement to tempt a neighbouring adventurous youth to be let down by ropes to the bottom of this frightful chasm. The waters ran from its bottom above a mile underground, and then appear again in the open air below the little village of Selside.

After having excited the several passions of curiosity, dread and horror, from the negative knowledge we got of the capacity and depth of this huge pot, we went a little higher up the mountain and came to another hiatus, called Long Churn. We descended down till we came to a subterranean brook. We first ascended the cavern down which the stream ran, proceeding in a western direction for (at least as we imagined) a quarter of a mile till we came to a crevice which admitted us into our native region. We measured the distance between the two extremities above ground, and found it 241 yds; but it must be nearly double that distance along the passage below, on account of all the turnings and windings. The petrifactions here were the most numerous of any we had yet seen, few people coming either to break them off or deface them.

When we were almost arrived at the western extremity, we came to a fine round basin of pellucid water from 3 to 12 ft deep, known by the name of Dr Bannister's Hand Basin. A lofty, spacious and elegant dome is placed immediately over it, which nicely corresponds to the hollow receptacle at the bottom. Into this basin a rivulet falls down a steep rock above 6 ft high, which is very dangerous to get up and must be done at the expense of a wet skin, except a ladder is taken along with the party or the waters are less copious than when we were there: there is also some danger lest the adventurer should fall back, and have his bones broken by circumjacent rocks or be drowned in the doctor's basin. After having surmounted this obstacle and proceeded some yards farther, we were favoured with an egress into our own element, as was before observed; no unwelcome change after having been so long excluded from it.

After having rested ourselves a little, we returned to the chasm where we first entered Long Churn and, descending again, pursued the rivulet eastward along another extensive subterranean passage called Dicken Pot, which slopes and winds by degrees till it enters the ghastly and tremendous Alan Pot. We went 157 yds along this "antre vast" till we came to a steep rock full 12 ft perpendicular. Here we stopped—a wise consideration! We might have descended perhaps without danger, but the question was how were we to get up again; which, without ropes or a ladder, would be totally impracticable. At the far end was an elegant lofty dome, called by the country people St Paul's. There is no doubt but if we had ventured further we night have come to Alan Pot, at least so near as either to have seen the water that stagnates at its bottom or the light that is admitted into this gaping monster of nature.

There are several other caves, all along from hence, on the south side of Ingleborough, above the village of Clapham, to Ingleton; but we postponed the pleasure of exploring these hidden recesses of nature till another summer. We descended from hence along the banks of the River Ribble 4 or 5 miles farther, to the village of Horton, situated at the bottom of the lofty and elegant mountain Pennegant.

As we went along we passed a large heap of small round stones called a *hurder*. We were told there were two others by the side of the turnpike road, in a field called the Slights: one about a mile, and the other a mile and a half east of the Chapel-in-the-Dale. They seem evidently placed there by human hands; and what was most extraordinary, they were all small, round, sandy and gritty stones, and all the stones on the surface of the ground near them are limestone. No doubt they were *tumuli* of some deceased chieftains in the neighbourhood, or who died on their travels.

Before we left Horton we visited some natural curiosities of the cavern kind on the base of Pennegant.* Dowgill Scar, a little above Horton, is a grotesque amphitheatre of limestone rocks, composing a high precipice, which must appear awful and grand in a flood, when a large torrent of water falls from the top full in view; a small subterranean passage was able to take all the water when we were there. A romantic gallery, on the north side of the rocks, had a good effect in the scene.

About a mile or two above Horton, upon the base of Pennegant, we visited Hulpit and Huntpit Holes. The one, if we could have descended into it, would have appeared like the inside of an enormous old Gothic castle, the high ruinous walls of which were left standing after the roof was fallen in; the other was like a deep funnel, and it was dangerous to come near its edges. Horton Beck, or brook, runs through the one, and Bransil Beck through the other of these pits, but through which I cannot remember. They each run underground near a mile: Horton Beck appearing again at Howgill Scar, and Bransil Beck at a place called Bransil Head. But what is most extraordinary, these subterranean brooks cross each other underground without mixing waters, the bed of one being on a stratum above the other: this was discovered by the muddy water, after a sheep-washing, going down the one passage, and the seeds or husks of oats that were sent down the other. About a couple of miles from Horton, on the right-hand side of the road to Settle, is a curious stone quarry at a place called Culms, or Coums. The stones are of a blue kind, like slate, from one to three inches thick: some are 2 or 3 yds broad and 5 or 6 yds long. They are made use of for floors in houses, being sometimes laid over cellars, on joists: they are also used for gate-posts, footbridges and partitions between the stalls in stables and cow-houses.

At Stainforth, which is about 3 miles from Horton and 2 from Settle, we were entertained with two cascades, one in the Ribble, near the road, about 6 or 8 yds high; and another a little above the village, perhaps 20 or 30 yds perpendicular.

* The word *Pen* is of Phoenician extraction, and signified head or eminence. It was first introduced into Cornwall, where the Phoenicians had a colony who wrought the tin mines. Hence we have many names in Cornwall which begin with *Pen*. Most mountains in Wales begin with *Pen*. In Scotland, the labial letter *P* is changed into *B* and *Pen* into *Ben*; as Benlomond, Benevish, &c.

About a quarter of a mile before we arrived at Settle, we turned to the right along the road towards Kirkby Lonsdale, about a mile, under the high and romantic rocks called Giggleswick Scar, in order to see the well by the wayside that ebbs and flows. We were in luck, seeing it reciprocate several times while we were there, and not staying above an hour. We could not however learn with any degree or certainty by what intervals of time, and to what heights and depths, the reciprocation is carried on. We were informed that, if the weather was either very droughty or very wet, the phenomenon ceased. I have seen some philosophical attempts to solve this extraordinary curiosity on the principle of the siphon, but in vain; as, on that hypothesis, if the siphon is filled by the spring, it will flow on uniformly for ever. We were told by drunken Barnaby, 150 years ago, that it puzzled the wits of his age:[155]

> *Veni Giggleswick, parum frugis*
> *Profert tellus, clausa jugis:*
> *Ibi vena prope viæ*
> *Fluit, refluit, nocte, die;*
> *Neque norunt unde vena,*
> *An a sale vel arena.*

> Thence to Giggleswick, most steril,
> Hemm'd with shelves and rocks of peril.
> Near to the way, as a traveller goes,
> A fine fresh spring both ebbs and flows,
> What procures it, salt or gravel.

As we approached towards Settle in our return, a white rock, like a tower, called Castlebar, immediately above the town and about 20 or 30 yds in perpendicular height, engaged our attention. This precipice is partly natural and partly a work of art. It is made deeper and more dangerous every day, in consequence of stones being got from its bottom and sides, to supply an adjoining lime-kiln.

Settle is irregularly built, has a large and spacious marketplace and some good houses in it. Though by no means an inconsiderable town, either for trade, riches or number of inhabitants, it has no church or chapel: the church is at Giggleswick, about a mile off, which appeared to be the court end of the parish, consisting chiefly of gentlemen's houses.

From Settle we proceeded eastwards, over the moors and mountains, about half a dozen miles, to Malham, or Maum, in order to see some other natural curiosities of the precipice and cataract kind. We had already indeed seen so many, that our wonder could not easily be excited, except there were more great and terrible. As such we had them represented at Settle, or else we should scarce have left the turnpike road; and when we saw them we were not disappointed, for great and terrible they are.

The first was Malham Cave (or vulgarly Maum Cove), though it has properly nothing of the cave about it. It is a fine amphitheatre of perpendicular limestone rock, on the side of the moor, at least 100 yds high in the middle. The rocks lie stratum upon stratum, and on some there are *saxa sedilia* or shelves, so that a person of great spirit and agility, but of small and slender body might almost walk round. A small brook springs out at the bottom of the rocks, but in floods the narrow subterranean passage is not able to give vent to all the water, when there pours down a stupendous cataract, in height almost double that of Niagara. This is the highest perpendicular precipice I have ever seen, and I think not enough known and admired by travellers for its greatness and regularity.

After pursuing our journey near a mile, by the side of the deep and romantic channel of the River Air, which washes the base of many a rugged and high precipice in its impetuous course to the vale beneath, we came to Gordale, the highest and most stupendous of them all. The prospect of it, from the side of the opposite western bank, is awful, great and grand. After viewing for some time its horrid front with wonder and astonishment, we were tempted to descend, with care and circumspection, down the steep bank on the west side, to this river, which being interspersed with trees and shrubs, enabled us to rely on our hands, where we could find no more sure foothold. The water being low, we met with no difficulty in stepping from one broken fragment of the rocks to another, till we got on the other side, when we found ourselves underneath this huge impending block of solid limestone, near 100 yds high. The idea for personal safety excited some awful sensations, accompanied with a tremor.

The mind is not always able to divest itself of prejudices and unpleasing associations of ideas: reason told us that this rock could not be moved out of its place by human force, blind chance or the established laws of nature: we stood too far under its margin to be affected by any crumbling descending fragment (and a very small one would have crushed us to atoms, if it had fallen upon us) yet, in spite of reason and judgement, the same unpleasing sensations of terror ran coldly through our veins, which we should have felt if we had looked down, though secure, from its lofty top. Nothing, however, fell upon us, but a few large drops, which sweat from out its horrid prominent front. Some goats frisked about, with seemingly a wanton carelessness, on the brink of this dreadful precipice, where none of use would have stood for all the pleasant vales washed by the River Air. Some lines in Virgil's *Eclogues* seemed to receive additional beauties when repeated in this grotesque scene:

> *Non ego vos posthac, viridi projectus in antro*
> *Dumosa pendere procul de rupe videbo.*

No more extended in the grot below,
Shall I e'er see my goats high up the brow,
Eating the prickly shrubs, or void of care,
Lean down the precipice, and hang in air.†

† Virgil, *Eclogues*, 1, l. 76.

‡ If Kilsey-Crag should not be thought
an object worth going 6 or 7 miles
to see, the best way from Gordale to
Skipton will be Kirkby, Malhamdale
and Gargrave.

A little higher up is a fine cascade, where the river, striving for an easier and gentler descent, has forced a way through the rocks, leaving a rude natural arch remaining above. If a painter wanted to embellish his drawing of this romantic scene with some grotesque object, he could add nothing which would suit his purpose better, if nature had not done the work for him.

From Gordale, we proceeded to a curious lake called Maum or Malham Tarn, abounding with fine trout, upon the top of the moor; and from thence by Kilscy Crag to Grassington on the banks of the River Wharf.‡ Coming unexpectedly to the crags of Kilsey, I was a good deal amazed at the prospect. They are by the side of the vale along which descends the River Wharf. Like those at Giggleswick, they extend in a line to some distance, but are higher and more prominent. The road we came along wound down amongst these crags so that we were presented with a full view of them on a sudden, which caused the greater surprise. After having refreshed ourselves at Grassington, we travelled about 9 miles farther and came to Skipton.

The country all around is uneven and rugged; the vales are fertile on the surface, and the mountains beneath it abound with rich mines of lead. After we had visited the castle (which belongs to the Earl of Thanet) and the curious canal behind it, above the mills, which leads to the limestone quarry by the side of a romantic deep glen, we left Skipton. Before our departure, we were for some time in doubt whether we should ascend the steep and black hill of Rombaldsmoor, and so proceed down the vale of Wharfdale, one of the pleasantest in England, to Otley and so to Leeds; or go by Keighley, Bingly and Bradford along the side of the new canal, and view the locks and other contrivances on this new and useful work of art. Most of us having been the former road, and this with its objects being quite new, we were induced to proceed along it.

At Kildwick, about 4 miles from Skipton, we passed under this aqueduct, where it was banked up a great height above the adjoining lands, at a vast labour and expense. There have been some violent struggles between the elements of earth and water—the mounds have not always been able to keep the water within its proper limits, they oftener than once been broken through by the pressure on their sides.

About a mile further, at Steeton, we could not but observe the steep ascent and descent of the road over a hill, when a level path might have been made almost equally near along the side of the river. The inconveniences that must attend carriage in carts and waggons from such ill-concerted roads perhaps might suggest the expediency of a canal. The use and practicability of such an undertaking in a mountainous country, one would imagine, might give the inhabitants a hint to make their roads wind with easy ascents and descents along the sides of the vale. From Skipton to Otley the road is carried up and down the corner of the steep mountain Rombaldsmoor, when as near a one might have been conducted along the vale beneath. The inhabitants might have carried to the market the produce of their lands and brought coals and manure at a little expense if this plan had been adopted: but the prejudices against improvements and innovations are not easily removed.

At Bingly we were entertained with the locks: there are five or six of them together, where the barges ascend or descend 80 or 90 ft perpendicular, in the distance of about 100 yds. They are elegant and well finished, but seem too deep not to leak and be frequently out of repair.

About 4 miles before we arrived at Leeds, in our way from Bradford, we were suddenly presented with the grand and venerable ruins of Kirkstal Abbey, full in view from the road. We stood some minutes looking with silent respect and reverence on the havoc which had been made by time on this sacred edifice. How much soever we might condemn the mistaken notions of monkish piety that induced the devotees to lethargic supineness, and to forsake all the social duties of life in order to be good men, yet we secretly revered that holy zeal which inspired them to exert every power in erecting structures the magnitude and beauty of which might excite ideas worthy of the Deity to whom they were dedicated, and also reprobated that fanatic bigotry which suffered them to decay and go to ruin because they were once inhabited by a set of christians whose manner of worship was not orthodox. While we were moralizing thus on religious prejudices, the instability of the work of men's hands and the fading glories of this world, we came to Leeds.

As the largeness and extent of this thriving manufacturing town, with all the elegant buildings in and about it, are well known to you, and as you have seen everything worth notice in and near the road from thence, I shall here take my leave of you, and no longer tire you with a relation of the adventures and curiosities I met with in my summer's journey.

Address

To the Genius of the Caves[156]

—————Hail, kindred glooms!
Congenial horrors, hail!
(Thomson)[157]

————————Thou Spirit dread,
That hover'dst o'er this rocky region erst,
With burning sulphur and volcanic stream
Of fire extinct, all hail! ——thou, whose loud shriek,
Midst scowling tempests, oft the list'ning swain
Hast heard aghast; oft in slow-pacing clouds,
That drag their sweeping trains o'er Gragareth's steep,
Has trac'd thy wild fantastic form. Thy steps,
Through many a rugged, uncouth path, well pleas'd
I follow. Whether, from the dread abyss
Of some unfathom'd cavern,¶ Echo's groans
With many a dreary pause between, from rock
To rock rebound, and break upon my ear
Like distant thunder;— or my raptur'd gaze,
E'en from the yew-fring'd margin, down the steep
Pursues the foaming cataract's* headlong course,
Till, spent and dazzled on those wat'ry hues,
Midway it rests, where light refracted paints
Each clustering dew-drop's glassy orb, and vies
With melting Iris' vernal tinctur'd bow;—
Or whether, by the taper's glimm'ring ray
Led on, my steps pervade thy secret shrine,
Yordas, where, hid from Phoebus' garish eye,
With Contemplation, thy compeer, thou sit'st,
And, like a curtain, spread'st thy cloud of night
Around thy throne;— I feel, I feel thee near.
Full many a young idea, that ere this
Hath slept in silence, at thy thrilling call
Starts from its trance and, kindling into life,
With joy and mingled awe attemper'd swells
My crowded soul; and ever and anon,
As at the wizard's call, my straining eye,
Quick glancing, sees a thousand fleeting shapes,
Scatter'd from bright-ey'd Fancy's dewy plume.

¶ Jingling Cave, on Gragareth.

* Weathercoat Cave, in Chapel-in-the-Dale.

Parent of Horrors, hail! To my fix'd eye
Thy sacred form in these, these solemn scenes
Reveal'd descends; and O! more awful far
This great design, grav'd by fair Nature's hand,
These frowning rocks and mineral roofs, reflect
Thy semblance, than could Raphael's warmth devise,
Than Phidias' featur'd marble: and thy voice,
Borne on the panting wing of each low blast
That sighs along the vault, awakes the soul
To feelings more ennobled than the lyre
Of Orpheus, or the rapture-breathing strains
Of Handel, e'er inspir'd. O, may I oft,
In this Egerian cave, Great Power, attend
Thy sacred presence, here with nature's self
Hold converse till, by just degrees, my mind
Through Science's footsteps pierce the harmonious maze
Of sacred order, and to brighter views
From day to day aspiring, trace at length,
Through all the wonders of this nether world,
Th' Eternal Cause; to him on rapture's wing
Dart her swift flight, and scale the walls of heaven.

Article VIII

Further account[158] of Furness Fells

or Observations on placing objects on the eminences and planting trees in the valleys seen on this tour (being the note intended for page 43)

Furness Fells, and the adjacent parts here alluded to, are so peculiarly distinguished with *picturesque* beauty that they deserve a more minute description. This country consists of a succession of mountains and valleys, formed and intermixed in all the possible variety of rural nature. Much of the valleys and the bases of most of the hills are covered with young wood, which at certain periods is cut down and charred for the use of the neighbouring furnaces.

On this account the copses, which consist of various kinds of trees, constantly in the summer exhibited every pleasing colour of youthful vegetation. The main shoots also spring up so straight, and the collateral ones at such small angles with them, that they give an uncommon idea of vegetating vigour; and when they are seen rooted in the clefts of rocks, fancy will conceive them not unlike the streams of some fluid bursting forcibly from its prison. Among these copses are found several neat villages, houses and spaces of cultivated land, which, with a number of brooks and rivers tumbling and tinkling among them, constitute a scene of sylvan beauty exceedingly lovely and singular.

But what still enhances the whole is the goodness of the highways, of which, in fine weather, it is not extravagant to say in general that they are more like the walks of a gentleman's pleasure ground than roads for ordinary occupation. This circumstance, though in part owing to the peculiar goodness of the materials, is nevertheless much indebted to the neatness and public spirit of the inhabitants.

A laudable taste for adorning nature has led us from ornamented gardens to ornamented farms, and being in the possession of good roads (an essential article for the display of rural beauty) there seems to be but one thing wanting to make this a truly ornamental country. What I mean here is artificial objects raised on proper parts of the mountains and eminences, which at every turn are presented to us through some agreeable opening or other.

Eminences are as naturally fit places for objects intended to attract the distant eye as they are for enabling the eye to survey distant objects. Hence to decorate them with columns, obelisks, temples, &c. has the sanction of natural fitness. And if to this consideration we add that of the inherent beauty of the objects themselves and remember that there is nothing sets off the beauties of nature so much as elegant works of art; justifying motives for these erections can never be wanting to any one who has a taste for rural beauty, and is willing to accomplish as much of it as is in his power.

But this is not all: the practice is certainly patriotic; for such elegant ornaments will at least naturally contribute to diffuse a serenity and cheerfulness of mind in every beholder; and thence (if we may be pardoned the figure) like electrical conductors, they may be supposed to bring down a little of the happy placidity of better regions, to add to the natural quantity shooting about on the earth. As another motive, it may be observed that it is pleasing in any country to see the inhabitants so much at ease in mind and circumstances as to pay attention to these fanciful undertakings; and moreover, that as a man of sense appears the more so for seeming conscious of the importance of what he says, so every traveller will conceive the better of a people who, sensible of the natural advantages of their country, are found disposed to make the best of them.

How these objects should be formed, or situated, must for the most part be determined by circumstances under the eye of taste. One thing, however, seems worthy of particular notice in this place, which is that erections of this sort would have the most grand and characteristic effect placed on eminences, so as to have the sky for a background. When this is the case, the hills they are raised upon should be bounded by agreeable lines, seen at a great distance, and much in sight of the principal roads.†

The most simple of these erections are obelisks and properly formed summer-houses.‡ But a series of columns constituting a temple, or supporting arches, pediments &c. would have by much the best effect, provided they were properly large for the ordinary points of view. Through the openings of these columns, the sky would always give them a striking appearance; but in the evening, if the sun set behind them, no spectacle of the kind could be imagined more grand and attractive or more accordant with the sublimity of the surrounding mountains. Perforated doors and windows, in the imitation of old Gothic ruins, it is true, would yield part of this effect; but their gloomy and irregular appearance renders them, in the case before us, generally improper.

Something of this kind (on the bolder eminences particularly) seems to be all the essential article that is wanting to perfect the rural beauties of this country; except, indeed, it may be thought that a little more attention paid to the removal and planting of trees would be of use for that end; and concerning which I beg leave to lengthen this article with a few observations.

Trees are certainly the ornament and pride of vegetable nature. A bird despoiled of its plumage scarcely seems more mutilated and ungainly than countries and inclosures destitute of trees. They have a good effect planted even (in their worst situation) anyhow in hedgerows; but, if they be lightly scattered with taste, in proper parts of the

† If they be not intended also for a near inspection, they need not be of any expensive materials. Provided they be well formed in outline (and for the design of which, artists of taste should always be applied to) common stone and mortar will do very well.

‡ This kind of summer-house should either be octagonal or at least have more than four sides. And if either of these sorts of erections be not placed on very pointed hills, care should be taken to raise them (either by raising the earth on which they stand, or by giving them a high rustic base &c.) so that the sides of the hills will not prevent a complete sight of their elevation from the principal points of view. Nothing can be worse managed than to see these objects as if rising beyond the top of a hill, or from the bottom of a fish-pond. Perhaps a summer-house standing on proper rustic arches (through which the

sky might be seen) would, for the following reason, in some cases have a good effect.

inclosure itself, they become infinitely more pleasing. Hence, though Nature has done wonders in the disposition of trees in some of her favourite haunts, yet still (if not in them) she may be improved upon in others by the assistance of Art.

And let not the lips of Sordidness object to the purport of this hint, that if put into practice, it would ask some care and expense, and probably prevent the growth of what is more profitable to the owner and serviceable to man; for the God of Nature has far from having fully proportioned the animals of the earth to its produce: and as he renders fruitless innumerable seeds of almost every vegetable and animal creatures, so the application of a part of our care and a portion of the earth to its own ornament is, I am persuaded, so far from being culpable or improper that (in humble imitation of the divine love of beauty and liberality) it seems to be as much required from the pious votary of nature as his admiration of what comes immediately from its own efforts. In both cases God is alike honoured; and honour to God is certainly too nearly connected with religion to make it in any case an act of indifference.

Do then, ye affluent and prosperous landholders pay some attention to this particular. Study the subject through the medium of books and pictures; and sometimes spare, and sometimes plant a tree for ornament's sake. And (if you think them unreasonable ones) observe all the few following remarks, humbly offered to your consideration. They shall be made as brief as possible.

The greatest nicety and perfection in the arts of planting trees lies in the use of exotics and in ingenious mixture of foliage, in order to decorate for near inspection the marginal view of a lawn, walk &c. But if ever a fondness for agriculture, built upon a love of simple nature and sober piety (of which there are too, *too* few indications in our present manners) shall turn the general taste of the kingdom towards ornamented farms, such an event cannot be supposed to be suddenly brought about: hence the precepts that relate to this elegant part of gardening, will in this place be wholly unnecessary, and our attention must be confined to the management of the larger trees, which are already found in these regions.

Scotch firs, though a favourite tree with many people, seem to require a good deal of judgement in their use for they may be so planted as to injure a landscape more perhaps than they are generally seen to adorn it. In hanging woods (with which this country abounds) they frequently appear to disadvantage, however disposed. A single tree in this case often looks like a blot, and a plantation like a daub—especially in winter, when the most is expected from their verdure. The reason for this seems to be the darkness of their colour, and the obviousness of their whole form and outline: from the first particular they always attract the eye more than anything else; and only from the second hurt the imagination with presenting to it only a parcel of small limited streaks or patches, awkwardly inclined to the horizon. When slightly and irregularly interspersed in woods of this kind, they may now and then please from variety; but in general they come so forward to the eye, and at a good distance in winter to resemble yew, holly and the like gloomy and barren-looking trees, that they do a real injury to the soft and pleasing tints which result from the native items and which, from use, best accord with the idea of thriving woodlands.

For these reasons, Scotch firs look best when they are seen in large horizontal plantations, on low (or at least not high) ground, when the front only is exposed to sight (hence their depth backwards imagined very great) and when the blue vapours of an extended horizon are seen over their tops: in this case they have a very grand effect, and form a fine dark contrast to the pale and distinct features of the overlooking hills.

Those circular groups of trees called clumps are oftener seen than worthy of praise. They appear to have the best effect (if they must be used) for near views, or when they are found in the middle of a level open vale of fine lawn or meadow; but on the sides of distant hills or mountains (where they are seen all around) their appearance is truly paltry. The more smooth and large these eminences are, the more improper this species of ornament becomes; and, in short, I apprehend the features of a lady's face would scarce be more injured by the mark of her thimble than the features of several hills would be by these unnatural circles. At the same time, however, that we censure this mode of decorating mountains, it may be proper to observe, that if they be wholly covered with wood, or lightly interspersed with single trees, the effect will be natural and pleasing.

But the most absurd decoration of these eminences in vogue is a few trees placed on their top, so that the whole boles of the foremost ranks may be seen, down to their very roots. Trees, we know, are chiefly the produce of the lower parts of the earth's surface; and to see the roots of some above the heads of others as it were, tier above tier, is not natural and therefore not beautiful. Houses, which are the work of art, seldom look well in this form. In short, whatever be the circumstances of the base of a fine mountain as to wood, its top should either be wholly naked or ornamented with one of those artificial erections spoken of before.

These observations will also hold good with respect to little abrupt prominences, or swells, in ornamented grounds; which (if they must be tampered with) would receive more improvement from being encircled with an assortment of shrubs, over whose tops the crown of the hills (either plain or terminated with some agreeable erection of stone) might be fairly seen, than from a few large trees planted, as we often find, on their summits: for where these swells are pretty frequent (as they mostly are in uneven countries) art is better applied in lowering them, as it were, to the eye, than in giving them real additional height.

As to avenues of tall trees, they have certainly a noble effect for a private walk, or the first part of an approach to a gentleman's seat; but, seen from distant eminences, they often betray a good deal of the formality of a common fence.

¶ Respecting houses, I would just observe by the bye that to any person, save a naïve inured to them, buildings of blue rag without mortar have a very mean and depressing look; and that, if it fall conveniently within reach, the common rough-cast of limestone countries has the most neat and cheerful appearance of any outside finish of an easy expense, and of easy management.

* The great advantage that any town receives in appearance merely from the letters on the various signs &c. being elegantly done is very evident. And were the finger posts on the roads executed with proper taste, they might be made as ornamental as they are useful and hence yield due credit to the public spirit of the townships to which they belong, instead of being thought (as they often are at present) lamentable indications of their ignorance and poverty.

† It may also be here proper to remind the husbandmen and farmers of another slovenly practice they are frequently guilty of in most countries: I mean the custom of throwing stones, weeds and other kinds of rubbish from their fields upon the face of the roads, with no more regard to the seemliness of its appearance than to the moral honesty of the deed. If they cannot comprehend that they have no more right to make use of the roads for this purpose than of a neighbour's field and that, though generally connived at, the practice is wrong, the surveyors would do very well to teach them this decent piece of knowledge by the proper severities of the law.

To close the subject with a maxim or two more. Keep all large trees at a good distance from every neat-looking house.¶ Always consider extensive, unevenly-bounded forests to have an infinitely better effect in a landscape than an equal quantity of trees dispersed over it in crowded, formally enclosed patches. And, above all things, never forget the superlative beauty which (for a new view) may be given to a park, farm or cultivated country by single trees lightly and irregularly placed out of the hedgerows.

The bounds of this article will not admit of more than a few leading remarks on this subject; but, I fancy, if the above hints were observed, they would be sufficient, under the influence of taste, for the intended purpose. And though they are thrown out more particularly with a view to one part of the country included in this tour, yet it is all so much alike, in several respects, that they might be attended to with the same advantage in every other. And were these ideas verified, I flatter myself this northern district would be worthy of being termed the British Arcadia and exhibit, nearly to the utmost pitch of the poet's fancy,

An ample theatre of silvan grace.
(Mason's *English Garden*)[159]

This to the more wealthy of its inhabitants. To the more humble I will just subjoin a finishing word. That you are placed in one of the most beautiful districts in the kingdom, the number of its visitors of all ranks constantly testify; and you will see it is one purpose of this book to make it still more known. And if you be not the happiest people, the fault must be in yourselves; since nature has bountifully bestowed upon you every essential requisite of enjoyment.

Be therefore content to pursue your innocent though humble vocations, without letting a wish wander beyond your peaceful vales; and now and then turn your thoughts towards those particulars which annually bring among you so many wealthy and respectable visitors. Keep your highways in good order (for, as observed before, their beauty is essential to rural beauty).* Preserve your native modesty, and never let envy mar your civility. When you prune a fence joining to a public road, put the branches where they can be no annoyance;† and then, as you are already exemplary in many moral virtues, you will set a pattern of rural decency worthy of the imitation of several politer parts of the kingdom.

Article IX

Account of Ennerdale[160]

In a ride from Keswick to Ennerdale, the mountains, between whose bases an irregular avenue opens for the curious tourist, are more variegated than those in other regions of this little world of wonders. In the course of ten minutes' travelling he will behold the most beautiful verdure climbing to the summit of one, a bushy wood creeping to the top of another and the most tremendous fragments of rock scowling from the front of a third. The Pillar challenges particular notice.

If a transient storm disturb or intercept the view, which frequently happens in the serenest days of summer, the appearance is not only awful, but pleasing; and the traveller will frequently behold a tempest without feeling it. The commotion is far above him and where he treads all is calm, solemn and silent. As he approaches the vale of Ennerdale, in whose bosom one of the most enchanting of the lakes is seated, he will find the rugged scenery of the country gradually refining; and as he winds round the foot of the Pillar, he will discover a vista which cannot fail to strike the most indifferent observer with astonishment and pleasure.

The mountains which serve to heighten this scene and enhance its surprise are Sty Head, Honister Crag, Wastdale, the Pillar and Red Pike. The Liza waters the base of the latter and on its margin lies an even, level road not formed by the hand of man, but presenting to the eye the appearance of a pavement. The delighted tourist will insensibly confine his view (though it is not in reality bounded by any of the lofty objects already mentioned) to the verdant island of Gillerthwaite, whose romantic situation must be *seen* – description cannot furnish an idea of its beauty.

An essayist in the provincial paper of this country, speaking of the place, says:

> It forms a picture such as the canvas never presented; it embraces a variety so distributed as no pencil can ever imitate. No designer in romance ever allotted such a residence to his fairy inhabitants— I had almost said no recluse ever wooed religion in such a blessed retirement. … The genius of Ovid would have transformed the most favoured of his heroes into a river and poured his waters into the channel of the Liza, there to wander by the verdant bounds of Gillerthwaite—the sweet reward of patriotism and virtue.

Gillerthwaite is not, however, an island, though almost as much contrasted in the landscape as land with water. It is a patch of enclosed and apparently highly-cultivated ground on a stony desert of immeasurable extent—for the mountains on each side of it are the most barren in their aspect and continue that appearance till their heads mix with horizon. There are two decent farmhouses on the inclosure, and from the serpentine tract of the valley no other habitation of man is visible.

From Gillerthwaite, the road already briefly described (and which a very little industry might make convenient for most occasions) leads towards the pride of the valley, once the seat of power and splendour, of which some faint remains are yet to be traced. The place here alluded to is How Hall, a mansion formerly of some note. The estate, by purchase, came into possession of the Senhouses and is now the property of Joseph Tiffin Senhouse esquire of Calder Abbey. The following inscription, in Saxon characters, is yet visible over the principal door of How Hall:

> This house was built, A.D. 1566, by William Patrickson, and Frances his wife, daughter of Sir Thomas Swynburn, one of the privy counsellors to King Henry VIII.

Within these few years, several visitors of the lakes extend their tour by taking in Whitehaven, and proceeding from thence by Cleator and Kinnyside to Ennerdale Bridge; at which place guides can be procured to conduct them by the best route to Ennerdale Broad Water—and, if they choose, from thence to Loweswater, Buttermere &c. This part of the journey (without which the tour is incomplete) cannot, however, be performed in a carriage, but a ride on horseback will amply recompense the trouble, for the scenery is delightful and the objects have been pronounced (as well by many gentlemen of taste as by artists of much celebrity) highly interesting. Many such have ventured to prefer these views even to some of those which have attracted so much attention from the patrons of the fine arts.

Certain it is, the approach to the lake of Ennerdale, to Loweswater and to Buttermere is from no other quarter so magnificent and captivating. The lake of Ennerdale appears in view. To the left a majestic wood, rising gradually up the side of Cold Fell from the opposite shore of the water, imparts the most graceful ornament to the entrance into a region perfectly different from the last. A short turn to the right lays the whole lake and valley open to the view, and Herd House presents his tawny front, as regent of the scene. The furniture of the lake (if the expression may be allowed) is totally changed: on the traveller's side (the east) the farms are stretched out and exhibit a verdure seldom exceeded in the most fertile parts of this kingdom, and in a compass of a few miles the number of small tenements seem to say, with Goldsmith,

Here every rood maintains its man.

On the opposite shore of this little ocean (which is frequently seen vexed with little storms of short duration), the mountain towers with great dignity, neither terrible nor inviting in its aspect, but suited to the serenity of the spot, which is calculated to inspire sentiments at once sublime and cheerful.

The language of poetry never applied "The clear mirror of the flood" with a propriety greater than that with which, on many accounts, a description of this lake might adopt it: the extent of the water is particularly calculated, with the height of the adjoining mountain, to produce the most astonishing reflection from its surface; and the situation of the neighbouring mountains occasions such frequent changes of the atmosphere in the course of the summer's day (and at no other season, it is presumed, are these parts visited by strangers) that the tourist will hardly be disappointed of viewing the picture in all its great variety of light and shade.

The following lines are an *impromptu* written by a gentleman in the year 1788 who has since distinguished himself by his ingenuity, and at present enjoys no inconsiderable rank as an artist; we might be justified in saying he now possesses a very honourable niche in the modern temple of pictorial fame in Somerset House.

HERE let the youth who pants for honest fame
By real genius led, whose classic taste
Delights to copy Nature, here employ
His pencil, and by boldest stretch of art,
Snatch all the transient colours of the lake,
That wildly on its surface mingling play.

And let the rapture that with speed pursues
The flying spectacle of light and shade
(And, instant, strikes the canvas with their tint)
Direct the eye, and guide the rapid hand,
Quick! As the chasing clouds and glancing light
Reflect their image on the glassy plain.

Now leave the varying beauties of the scene,
And dash the scowling mountain's brows sublime:
Sweep down their rugged sides, august and steep,
With many a furrow-mark'd, and shelving ridge,
And paint the pebbled margin of the flood.

But seize! ah, seize on Pillar's lofty top,
That passing mist which half obscures its peak.
Its evanescent form no art depicts!

No fancy wing'd so quick to give it shape!—
It flies, alas! and mix'd with common air,
Brightens and fades—insensibly—away!

Describe the dread serenity that dwells
In all this region of romantic view,
Of awful silence—silence undisturb'd
Save when, as gently mov'd by zephyrs bland,
The hedgerow mingles with its sweets a sigh,
Or the wing'd inmates of the wat'ry vale
Carol, responsive, to the general song
Of rising Nature. From her lap she throws
The richest offerings of the growing year;
And ev'ry tow'ring hill, and daisy'd bank,
Breathes choicest incense to th' Almighty Power,
Beneficent, whose works are only good.

(Pictor)

Article X

Specimens of the Cumberland Dialect[161]

These are taken from the poems of the ingenious and modest Relph—
an author of some estimation in those parts, and whose Pastorals
in particular are admired by all judges for their exact delineation
(after the best classic models) of the language and manners of his
rustic countrymen.

Harvest or *The Bashful Shepherd*
A Pastoral in the Cumberland Dialect

When welcome rain the weary reapers drove
Beneath the shelter of a neighbouring grove,
Robin, a love-sick swain, lagg'd far behind,
Nor seem'd the weight of falling showers to mind;
A distant, solitary shade he sought,
And thus disclos'd the troubles of his thought.—

Ay, ay, thur drops may cuil my outside heat,
Thur callar blasts may wear the boilen sweat;
But my het bluid, my heart aw' in a bruil.
Nor callar blasts can wear, nor drops can cuil.

Here, here it was (a wae light on the pleace!)
'At first I got a gliff o' Betty's feace:
Blyth on this trod the smurker tripp'd, and theer
At the deail-head unlickily we shear.
Heedless I glim'd, nor could my een command,
Till gash the sickle went into my hand:
Down hell'd the bluid; the shearers aw' brast out
In sweels of laughter; Betty luik'd about—
Reed grew my fingers, reeder far my feace—
What could I de in seck a dispert kease?
Away I sleeng'd, to grandy meade my mean:
My grandy (God be wud her now she's geane)
Skilfu' the gushen bluid wi' cockwebs staid,
Then on the fair a healen plaister laid.

Glossary
Thur, these. Cuil, cool. Callar, cold.
We'ar, cool or allay. Boilen, boiling.
Het, hot. Bluid, blood. Aw', all. Bruil,
broil. Wae, woe. Pleace, place. 'At, that.
Gliff, a transient view. Feace, face. Trod,
footpath. Smurker, smiler. Theer, there.
Deail-head, a narrow plat of ground
in a common field. Shear, reaped.
Glim'd, looked askance. Een, eyes. Gash,
to cut. Hell'd, poured. Aw', all. Brast,
burst. Sweels, swells or bursts. Luik'd,
looked. Reed, red. Reeder, redder. Feace,
face. De, do. Seck, such. Kease, case.
Sleeng'd, went creepingly away. Grandy,
grandmother. Meade, made. Mean,
moan. Wud, with. Geane, gone. Gushen,
Gushing. Bluid, blood. Cockwebs,
cobwebs. Sair, sore. Healen, healing.

Glossary
Arr, scar or mark. Neathing, nothing.
Mair, more..Sae, so. Bworn, born. Lang,
long. Mud, must. Fworc'd, forced. Pruive,
prove. Nin, none. Luive, love. Parfet,
perfect. Springin, springing. Owr, Over.
Aither, either. Luik'd, looked.

The healen plaister eas'd the painful fair—
The arr indeed remains, but neathing mair.

Not sae the other wound, that inward smart—
My granny could not cure a bleedin heart.
I've bworn the bitter torment three lang year,
And aw' my life-time mun be fworc'd to bear,
'Less Betty will a kind physician pruive,
For nin but she has skill to medcin luive.

But how should honest Betty give relief?
Betty's a parfet stranger to my grief.
Oft I've resolv'd my ailment to explain—
Oft I've resolv'd indeed—but all in vain:
A springing blush spread fast owr aither cheek;
Down Robin luik'd, and duice a word could speak.

Glossary
Neet, night. Spinnels, spindles. Wi',
with. Sae, so. Meade, made. Glop, stare.
De, do. Mud, must. Tak, take. Tuik, took.
Gangs, goes. Pleaugy, plaguy.

Can I forget that neet (I never can)
When on the clean-swept hearth the spinnels ran?
The lasses drew their line wi' busy speed;
The lads, as busy, minded ev'ry thread
When, sad! the line sae slender Betty drew,
Snap went the thread, and down the spinnel flew;
To me it meade; the lads began to glop.
What could I de? I mud, mud tak it up:
I tuik it up, and (what gangs pleaugy hard)
E'en reach'd it back without the sweet reward.

O lastin stain! E'en yet its eith to trace
A guilty conscience in my blushen feace.
I fain wad wesh it out, but never can;
Still fair it bides, like bluid of sackless man.

Glossary
Lastin, lasting. Eith, easy. Treace, trace.
Blushen, blushing. Feace, face. Wad,
would. Wesh, wash. Bides, abides.
Bluid, blood. Sackless, innocent. Wully,
Willy. Par, pair. Thar, them. Lows'd,
loosed. Sleely, slyly. Struive, strove.
Cowren, crouching. Mickle, much. Aw,
all. Watter'd, watered. Weel, well. 'At,
that. Bworn, born. Frae, from. Scworn,
scorn. Mun, must. Fash'd, troubled.
Stragglen, straggling.

Nought sae was Wully bashfu': Wully spy'd
A par of scissars by the lass's side;
Thar lows'd, he sleely drop'd the spinnel down.
And what said Betty? —Betty struive to frown;
Up flew her hand to souse the cowren lad—
But, ah! I thought it fell not down owr sad!
What follow'd, I think mickle to repeat:
My teeth aw' watter'd them, and watter yet.

E'en weel is he 'at ever he was bworn!
He's free frae aw' this bitterment and scworn.
What! mun I still be fash'd wi' stragglen sheep,
Wi' far-fetch'd sighs, and things I said asleep?

Still shamfully left snafflen by mysel
And still, still dogg'd wi' the damn'd neame o' mell?

Whare's now the pith (this luive! the Duice ga wi't)
The pith I show'd whene'er we struive to beat?
When a lang lwonin throught the cworn I meade;
And bustlin far behind the leave survey'd?

Dear heart! that pith is geane, and comes nae mair,
Till Betty's kindness shall the loss repair:
And she's net like (how sud she?) to be kind,
Till I have freely spoken out my mind,
Till I have learnt to feace the maiden clean,
Oil'd my slow tongue, and edg'd my sheepish een.

A buik theer is—a buik—the neame—sham faw't!
Something o' compliments, I think, they caw't—
'At meakes a clownish lad a clever spark.
O hed I this! this buik wad de my wark!
And I's resolv'd to hav't whatever't cost—
My flute; for what's my flute if Betty's lost?
But if sae bonny a lass but be my bride,
I need not any comfort lait beside.

Farewell, my flute, then, yet or Carlisle fair,
When to the stationer's I'll stright repair,
And bauldly for thur compliments enquear—
Care I a fardin?—let the 'prentice jeer.

That dune, a handsome letter I'll indite,
Handsome as ever country lad did write;
A letter 'at sall tell her aw' I feel,
And aw' my wants without a blush reveal.

But now the clouds brek off, and fineways run;
Out frae his shelter lively luiks the sun;
Brave hearty blasts the droopin barley dry:
The lads are gaen to shear, and sae mun I.

Glossary
Shamfully, shamefully. Snafflen, sauntering. Mysel, myself. Neame, name. O' mell, of the hindmost [mell, a beetle]. Whare's, where's. Luive, love. Ga' wi't, go with it. Lang, long. Lwonin, lane. Cworn, corn. Bustlin, bustling. Leave or lave, all the rest. Geane, gone. Nae mair, no more. Sall, shall. Sud, should. Feace, face. Een, eyes.

Glossary
Buik, book. Theer, there. Sham faw't, shame befall it. Caw't, call it. 'At meakes, that makes. Hed, had. Wark, work. I's, I am. Hav't, have it. Whatever't, whatever it. Lait, seek. Stright, straight. Bauldly, boldly. Thur, these. Enquear, enquire. Fardin, farthing. Dune, done. 'At sall, that shall. Aw, all. Brek, break. Sineways, sundry ways. Frae, from. Luiks, looks. Droopin, drooping. Gaen, gone. Shear, reap. Sae mun, so must.

Horace

Book II, Ode 7
Translated in the Cumberland dialect

The snaw has left the fells, and fled,
Their tops i' green the trees hev' cled;
The grund wi' sindry flowers is sawn,
And to their stint the becks are fawn:
Nor fear the nymphs and graces mair
To dance it in the meadows bare.
The year, 'at slips sae fast away,
Whispers we mun net thing to stay;
The spring suin thows the winter frost;
To meet the spring does simmer post;
Frea simmer, autumn clicks the hauld,
And back at yence is winter cauld.
Yit muins off-hand meake up the loss:
But soon as we the watter cross,
To Tullus great, Eneas guid,
We're dust and shadows without bluid.
And whae, Torquatus, can be sworn,
'At thame abuin 'ill grant to-mworn?
Leeve, than; what's war't I' murry cheer,
Frae thankless heirs is gitten clear.
When Death, my friend, yence ligs ye fast,
And Minus just your duim has past,
Your reace, and wit, and worth, 'ill mak
But a peer shift to bring you back.
Diana (she's a goddess, tee)
Gets not Hippolitus set free;
And, Theseus, aw' that strength o' thine,
Can never brek Pirithous' chyne.

Article XI

Mrs Radcliffe's
Description of the Scenery
in a ride over Skiddaw (1794)[162]

HAVING engaged a guide, and with horses accustomed to the labour, we began to ascend this tremendous mountain by a way which makes the summit 5 miles from Keswick. Passing through bowery lanes, luxuriant with mountain ash, holly and a variety of beautiful shrubs, to broad open common, a road led us to the foot of Latrig (or, as it is called by the country people, Skiddaw's Cub), a large round hill covered with heath, turf and browsing sheep.

A narrow path now wound along steep green precipices, the beauty of which prevented what danger there was from being perceived. Derwentwater was concealed by others that rose above them, but that part of the vale of Keswick which separates the two lakes and spreads a rich level of 3 miles was immediately below: Crosthwaite church in the centre, with the vicarage rising among trees. More under shelter of Skiddaw, where the vale spreads into a sweet retired nook, lay the house and grounds of Dr Brownrigg. Beyond the level opened a glimpse of Bassenthwaite Water—a lake which may be called elegant—bounded on one side by well-wooded rocks and on the other by Skiddaw.

Soon after, we rose above the steeps which had concealed Derwentwater and it appeared, with all its enamelled banks, sunk deep amidst a chaos of mountains and surrounded by ranges of fells not visible from below. On the other hand, the more cheerful lake of Bassenthwaite expanded at its entire length. Having gazed a while on this magnificent scene, we pursued the path and soon after reached the brink of a chasm, on the opposite side of which wound our future track; for the ascent is here in an acutely zig-zag direction. The horses carefully picked their steps along the narrow precipice, and turned the angle that led them to the opposite side.

At length, as we ascended, Derwentwater dwindled on the eye to the smallness of a pond, while the grandeur of its amphitheatre was increased by new ranges of dark mountains, no longer individually great, but so from accumulation—scenery to give ideas of the breaking up of a world. Other precipices soon hid it again, but Bassenthwaite continued to spread immediately below us, till we turned into the heart of Skiddaw and were inclosed by its steeps. We had now lost all track even of the flocks that were scattered over these tremendous wilds. The guide conducted us by many curvings among the heathy hills and hollows of the mountain; but the ascents were such that the horses panted in the slowest walk, and it was necessary to let them rest every six or seven minutes.

An opening to the south at length showed the whole plan of the narrow vales of St John and of Nadale, separated by a dark ridge of rocks called St John's Rigg, with each its small line of verdure at the bottom and bounded by enormous grey fells, which we were however now high enough to overlook. A white speck on the top of St John's Rigg was pointed out by the guide to be a chapel of ease to Keswick, which has no less than five such, scattered among the fells. From this chapel, dedicated to St John, the rock and vale have received their name; and our guide told us that Nadale is frequently known by the same title.

Leaving this view, the mountain soon again shut out all prospect but of its own valleys and precipices, covered with various shades of turf and moss, and with heath, of which a dull purple was the prevailing hue. Not a tree nor bush appeared on Skiddaw, nor even a stone wall anywhere broke the simple greatness of its lines. Sometimes we looked into the tremendous chasms, where the torrent, heard roaring long before it was seen, had worked itself a deep channel and fell from ledge to ledge, foaming and shining amidst the dark rock. These streams are sublime from the length and precipitancy of their course, which, hurrying the sight with them into the abyss, act as it were in sympathy upon the nerves and, to save ourselves from following, we recoil from the view with involuntary horror. Of such, however, we saw only two, and those by some departure from the usual course up the mountain; but everywhere met gushing springs, till we were within 2 miles of the summit, when our guide added to the rum in his bottle what he said was the last water we should find on our ascent.

The air now became very thin, and the steeps still more difficult of ascent; but it was often delightful to look down into the green hollows of the mountain, among pastoral scenes that wanted only some mixture of wood to render them enchanting. About a mile from the summit, the way was indeed dreadfully sublime, lying for nearly half a mile along the edge of a precipice that passed with a swift descent, for probably near a mile, into a glen within the heart of Skiddaw; and not a bush nor a hillock interrupted its vast length or, by offering a midway check in the descent, diminished the fear it inspired. The ridgy steeps of Saddleback formed the opposite boundary of the glen; and, though really at a considerable distance, had from the height of the two mountains such an appearance of nearness that it almost seemed as if we could spring to its side.

How much too did simplicity increase the sublimity of this scene, in which nothing but mountain, heath and sky appeared! But our situation was too critical, or too unusual, to permit the just impressions of such sublimity. The hill rose so closely above the precipice as scarcely to allow a ledge wide enough for a single horse. We followed the guide in silence and, till we regained the more open wild, had no leisure of exclamation. After this, the ascent appeared easy and secure, and we were bold enough to wonder that the steeps near the beginning of the mountain had excited any anxiety.

At length, passing the skirts of the two points of Skiddaw which are nearest to Derwentwater, we approached the third and loftiest, and then perceived that their steep sides, together with the ridges which connect them, were entirely covered near the summits with a whitish shivered slate, which threatens to slide down them with every gust of wind. The broken state of this slate makes the present summits seem like the ruins of others—a circumstance as extraordinary in appearance as difficult to be accounted for.

The ridge on which we passed from the neighbourhood of the second summit to the third was narrow, and the eye reached, on the side, down the whole extent of the mountain—following, on the left, the rocky precipices that impend over the lake of Bassenthwaite and looking, on the right, into the glens of Saddleback far, far below. But the prospects that burst upon us from every part of the vast horizon, when we had gained the summit, were such as we had scarcely dared to hope for and now rather venture to enumerate than to describe.

We stood on a pinnacle, commanding the whole dome of the sky. The prospects below, each of which had been before considered separately as a great scene, were now miniature parts of the immense landscape. To the north lay, like a map, the vast tract of low country which extends between Bassenthwaite and the Irish Channel, marked with the silver circles of the River Derwent in its progress from the lake. Whitehaven, and its white coast, were distinctly seen; and Cockermouth seemed almost under the eye. A long blackish line more to the west, resembling a faintly formed cloud, was said by the guide to be the Isle of Man—who, however, had the honesty to confess that the mountains of Down in Ireland, which have been sometimes thought visible, had never been seen by him in the clearest weather.

Bounding the low country to the north, the wide Solway Firth, with its indented shores, looked like a grey horizon; and the double range of Scottish mountains, seen dimly through the mist beyond, like lines of dark clouds above it. The Solway seemed surprisingly near us, though at 50 miles distance; and the guide said that on a bright day its shipping could plainly be discerned. Nearly in the north, the heights seemed to soften into plains, for no object was there visible through the obscurity that had begun to draw over the further distance; but towards the east they appeared to swell again, and what we were told were the Cheviot Hills dawned feebly beyond Northumberland.

We now spanned the narrowest part of England, looking from the Irish Channel on one side to the German Ocean on the other, which latter was, however, so far off as to be discernible only like a mist. Nearer than the county of Durham stretched the ridge of Cross Fell and an indistinct multitude of the Westmorland and Yorkshire highlands, whose lines disappeared behind Saddleback, now evidently pre-eminent over Skiddaw, so much so as to exclude many a height beyond it. Passing this mountain in our course to the south we saw, immediately below, the fells round Derwentwater, the lake itself remaining still concealed in their deep rocky bosom. Southward and westward, the whole prospect was "a turbulent chaos of dark mountains:" all individual dignity was now lost in the immensity of the whole, and every variety of character was overpowered by that of astonishing and gloomy grandeur.

Over the fells of Borrowdale and far to the south, the northern end of Windermere appeared, like a wreath of grey smoke that spreads along the mountain's side. More southward still and beyond all the fells of the lakes, Lancaster Sands extended to the faintly seen waters of the sea. Then, to the west, Duddon Sands gleamed in a long line among the fells of High Furness. Immediately under the eye lay Bassenthwaite, surrounded by many ranges of mountains, invisible from below. We overlooked all these dark mountains and saw green cultivated vales over the tops of lofty rocks, and other mountains over these vales, in many ridges, whilst innumerable narrow glens were traced in all their windings and seen uniting behind the hills with others that also sloped upwards from the lake.

The air on this summit was boisterous, intensely cold and difficult to be inspired, though below the day was warm and serene. It was dreadful to look down from nearly the brink of the point on which we stood upon the lake of Bassenthwaite, and over a sharp and separated ridge of rocks that from below appeared of tremendous height, but now seemed not to reach halfway up Skiddaw; it was almost as if

————the precipitation might down stretch
Below the beam of sight.————[163]

Under the lee of a heaped-up pile of slates, formed by the customary contribution of one from every visitor, we found an old man sheltered, whom we took to be a shepherd, but afterwards learned was a farmer and—as people in this neighbourhood say—a statesman, that is, had land of his own. He was a native and still an inhabitant of an adjoining vale; but, so laborious is the enterprise reckoned, that, though he had passed his life within view of the mountains, this was his first ascent. He descended with us for part of the way and then wound off towards his own valley, stalking amidst the wild scenery, his large figure wrapped in a dark cloak, and his steps occasionally assisted by a long iron-pronged pike, with which he had pointed out distant objects.

In the descent, it was interesting to observe each mountain below gradually reassuming its dignity, the two lakes expanding into spacious surfaces, the many little valleys that sloped upwards from their margins recovering their variegated tints of cultivation, the cattle again appearing in the meadows and the woody promontories changing from smooth patches of shade into richly tufted summits. At about a mile from the top, a great difference was perceptible in the climate, which became comparatively warm and the summer hum of bees was again heard among the purple heath.

We reached Keswick about four o'clock, after five hours passed in this excursion, in which the care of our guide greatly lessened the notion of danger.

Endnotes

[1] The connection between unspoilt Nature (specifically the Lake District) and the Garden of Eden is made explicit by West quoting John Milton's *Paradise Lost* at the start. Turner did just the same when exhibiting a painting of Coniston Fells.

[2] The *double entendre* in "with a curious, if not judicious and philosophic eye" is perhaps accidental. Does Cockin mean 'We may justifiably go so far as to call West judicious and philosophic'? Or does he mean 'West was inquisitive, certainly, but not (alas) judicious or philosophic'? It is hard to know: in person Cockin had the reputation of being diffident and upright, but in print he was capable of wit and mockery. For what we know of Thomas West himself, see p. xi.

[3] William Cockin (1736?–1801), born and was buried at Burton-in-Kendal. He was friend and assistant to George Romney, the painter, and a schoolteacher who wrote in a variety of genres, from short biographies of Lakeland worthies to an arithmetic textbook.

[4] See Addenda, Article III for Thomas Gray's journal.

[5] Thomas Pennant (1726–1798) came from a landed family in Shropshire, of Welsh origins. He wrote widely on natural history, most famously his *British Zoology* (1766), and corresponded with West. The 1772 visit to the Lakes must have been part of his second *Tour in Scotland* (1774–6), which was admired by Samuel Johnson.

[6] West had travelled on the Continent and seems to speak from personal experience of the Alps; he is less specific about the Apennines (which he generally spells 'Appenines'), but in view of his personal history he may well have been to Rome.

[7] See p. xv above.

[8] Burn's *Westmorland* is evidently his part in Joseph Nicolson and Richard Burn, *The History and Antiquities of the Counties of Westmorland and Cumberland* (1777). Richard Burn (1709–1785) was born at Winton, near Kirkby Stephen. The hermit was Hugh Garth, who later founded Cockersand Abbey.

[9] West is presumably quoting from 'Killarney' (1791) by Patrick O'Kelly, a very famous work in its day (the Prince Regent bought 50 copies), although the lines printed here do not seem to appear in later editions of Bard O'Kelly's epic poem.

[10] Arthur Young (1741–1820), best known as an agricultural improver, visited the Lakes in 1768 and wrote *A Six Months' Tour through the North of England* (1769), from which West quotes at length later in his guide.

[11] Claude, born Claude Gellée (1604/5–1682) in Lorraine, is often called Claude Lorrain. He spent most of his adult life in Rome and was regarded as the greatest master of ideal-landscape painting. His pictures often contain classical ruins or figures from classical mythology.

[12] Like Claude, Nicolas Poussin (1594–1665) spent most of his working life in Rome (from 1624). They sketched landscapes together in the 1630s around Rome and in the foothills of the Apennines. Poussin mainly painted classical, mythical and biblical subjects.

[13] Salvator Rosa (1615–1673), Neapolitan painter, etcher, satirical poet and actor, is several times cited by West, sometimes (like Claude) only by his first name. Rosa's pictures show a taste for the wild, the melodramatic and even the morbid. The grouping of these three painters from the previous century (see also p. 101) was not new. The poet James Thomson (1700–1748) wrote (*Castle of Indolence* I.xxxviii):

> What'er Lorrain light touched with softening hue
> Or savage Rosa dashed, or learned Poussin drew.

Thomson was still famous enough sixty years after his death for a monument to be erected to his memory.

[14] West refers here to the Claude mirror, often called a 'Claude glass'; see pp. xxv, 12. Elsewhere he calls it a 'perspective glass'.

[15] The *Notititia Dignitatum* is a list of office holders in the Roman Empire circa AD 400, which survives in several late mediaeval recensions.

[16] West naturally assumes that his readers will know the life of Gnaeus Julius Agricola (governor of Britannia, 78–84), written AD 98 by Tacitus, his son-in-law.

[17] Agricola campaigned against the Brigantes, a Celtic tribe whose territory covered almost the whole of northern England as well as south-east Ireland.

[18] West is an intelligent antiquarian, and not credulous. Here, as elsewhere, he looks for evidence and accepts hearsay only when it seems to come from a reliable source and to corroborate what he can see for himself.

[19] Pennant's 1772 visit has already been mentioned. William Camden (1551–1623), the antiquary, is most famous for his historical–topographical work *Britannia*. In 1600, with Robert Cotton, he visited the north, travelling as far as Carlisle, his last major journey. In the same year the 5th edition of the *Britannia* appeared. John Leland (1503–1552) was a diligent antiquary who travelled all over England in search of manuscripts and historic remains; he became insane about 1545 and his *Itinerary* was not published until 1710 onwards.

[20] Charles Leigh (1662–c.1705), physician, wrote *The Natural History of Lancashire, Cheshire and The Peak* (1700).

[21] The name is now spelt Quernmore.

[22] The Written Rock is in the gorge of the River Gelt, about two miles from Brampton. John Horsley (1685/6–1782), a Northumberland antiquary, travelled extensively in England studying Roman inscriptions. He published his well-documented research in *Britannia Romana* (1732), a work which was still highly regarded in the twentieth century.

[23] Cockin's footnote mentions the aqueduct of the Lancaster Canal; the map in West's guide shows the canal ending at Tewitfield, the site of

a flight of eight locks, the only locks on the whole of the Lancaster Canal. The Lancaster section opened in 1797, but work on the Tewitfield–Kendal section started only in late 1812. In 2008 work had started on reopening this section.

[24] The viewpoint is identified by the Norgates at grid reference SD4964. William Mason compiled an account of Gray's life and published it in *The Poems of Mr. Gray* (1775). He included verses that the poet had decided not to publish; he also burnt some of Gray's writings that he did not approve.

[25] The 'Ptol.' of the footnote is the *Geography* of Claudius Ptolemaeus, written *circa* AD 150. The next three paragraphs originally appeared as an extended footnote.

[26] The next seven paragraphs were added by William Cockin as an even more extended footnote.

[27] Peter's pence was a tax levied by the Vatican and used to help poorer parts of Christendom. It is now an annual, voluntary contribution by Catholics.

[28] West quotes Horace, *Epistles*, I.16: 'It flows with healing for headaches and sick stomachs'.

[29] Sir Daniel Fleming (1633–1701), antiquary, was born at Coniston Hall and died at Rydal Hall. He was noted for his use of original sources, particularly in compiling his family history. He wrote a history and topography of Cumbria (Cumberland, Westmorland and Furness), which however remained unpublished.

[30] Sir William Dugdale (1605–1686) published his great reference work, the *Baronage*, in 1676–7.

[31] The Claude landscape was one of the pictures destroyed in the 1870 fire.

[32] The opening lines of the *Epistle to Mr Addison* by Alexander Pope (1688–1744), written in 1715.

[33] Mount Edgcumbe in eastern Cornwall, built in the 1550s and much reconstructed since, was the first country house in England built deliberately to take advantage of the view. It overlooks a large park and the Tamar estuary.

[34] This viewpoint, somewhere between Broughton Beck and Lowick, may be near Wood Gate, grid reference SD283852.

[35] The Water Park viewpoint is identified by the Norgates at grid reference SD293902.

[36] The Peel Ness viewpoint is identified by the Norgates at grid reference SD29849187.

[37] The Beck Leven Foot viewpoint is identified by the Norgates at grid reference SD30959525.

[38] The viewpoint from a boat on Coniston Water is identified by the Norgates at grid reference SD30949620.

[39] The Hollin Bank North viewpoint is identified by the Norgates at grid reference SD32119845, and Hollin Bank South close by at SD32159830.

[40] Claife Station is identified by the Norgates at grid reference SD398954.

[41] Harrow Farm viewpoint is identified by the Norgates at grid ref SD3896.

[42] The Belle Isle South viewpoint was probably at grid reference SD393964.

[43] Belle Isle North was evidently at or close to the northern tip of Belle Isle, at grid reference SD395971.

[44] Cockin's account of Calgarth Park and its skulls originally appeared as a long footnote.

[45] The boating viewpoint is identified by the Norgates at grid reference SD3997.

[46] Rawlinson's Nab viewpoint, on the western shore, is identified by the Norgates at grid reference SD385931.

[47] Arthur Young's description of the view of Windermere from Bowness (he spells it 'Bonus', apologising that he did not discover how it was spelt) comes from *A Six Months' Tour through the North of England* (1771 edn), Letter xvii, in vol. iii, pp. 147–51.

[48] Brant Fell viewpoint is identified by the Norgates at grid reference SD40999613.

[49] The 'convex reflecting glass' is the Claude mirror. Youngs's comment, quoted by West, that a low viewpoint best suits the artist, may be compared with the multiple viewpoints that Smith and others used, as discussed in Mark Haywood's introduction.

[50] The Low Wood Inn (now Hotel) is at grid reference NY386021.

[51] Cockin cites 'Killarney' as the source, but again the lines quoted seem not to occur in later editions.

[52] The Rayrigg Hall viewpoint is identified by the Norgates at grid reference SD402981.

[53] This paragraph was added by William Cockin as a footnote.

[54] Again, this text and the excerpt from Patrick O'Kelly's poem 'Killarney' (1791) were added by Cockin.

[55] Taken from William Mason's life of Thomas Gray in *The Poems of Mr. Gray* (1775).

[56] Rydal Hall is at grid reference NY365064.

[57] Grasmere hill is Helm Crag. The viewpoint is identified by the Norgates at grid reference NY3209.

[58] Loughrigg Fell viewpoint is identified by the Norgates at grid reference NY3405.

[59] The battle and its results are accepted as history. The identity of King Dunmail remains unclear; see C. Phythian-Adams, *Land of the Cumbrians* (Scolar Press, 1996) for a discussion.

[60] The Dalehead Hall viewpoint is identified by the Norgates at grid reference NY314175.

[61] Cockshot Wood viewpoint is identified by the Norgates at grid reference NY2622.

[62] Crow Park viewpoint is identified by the Norgates at grid ref NY263230.

[63] The "bard of Loweswater" is presumably John Marshall (1762–1825), who was schoolmaster there from 1805. In 1810 his only published verse appeared under the title *The Village Pedagogue*.

[64] The tourist is told to follow the shore until they stand between Stable Hills and Walla Crag, but the viewpoint is evidently further south. It is identified by the Norgates at grid reference NY2720. The map (one of a series, 1783–94) by Peter Crosthwaite shows the viewpoint, where "Falcon Crag … hangs over your head", and it seems to be at NY271208.

[65] Niagara is about 170 ft high; Lodore no more than 100 ft, in several stages.

[66] From a long didactic poem by a Scottish physician, John Armstrong (1708/9–1779). The poem, called *The Art of Preserving Health* (1744), was often reprinted over the next hundred years.

[67] Castle Crag viewpoint is identified by the Norgates at grid reference NY249159.

[68] This aside and the lines from Patrick O'Kelly's 'Killarney' originally appeared in a footnote.

[69] Here and elsewhere the reference is to the Lake District as "This other Eden, demi-paradise", not to the Eden valley, some miles to the east.

[70] The next five paragraphs were originally set as a long footnote.

[71] Gray is quoting a line from John Milton's *Samson Agonistes*; here Samson speaks of his blindness.

[72] Swinside viewpoint is identified by the Norgates at grid reference NY24332245, altitude 801 ft.

[73] Foe Park or Fawe Park viewpoint is identified by the Norgates at grid reference NY25272271, altitude 407 ft.

[74] Latrigg viewpoint is identified by the Norgates at grid reference NY278246; its altitude is 1203 ft.

[75] The River Greta viewpoint is identified by the Norgates at grid reference NY2824.

[76] Mr Wren's house is identified by the Norgates as being in grid square NY22.

[77] Crosthwaite vicarage viewpoint is identified by the Norgates at grid reference NY261243.

[78] That is to say, Thomas Gray viewed the panorama in his Claude mirror, standing on a mounting block. See Addenda, Article III, 4 October.

[79] West made such a good guide partly because had done his research. Not only had he tried viewing the scenery from a boat, but he had looked up what five previous visitors had said and tested it for himself.

[80] The extended quotation is from Thomas Pennant, *A Tour in Scotland and Voyage to the Hebrides* (1774–6).

[81] John Brown (1715–1766), 'the Columbus of Keswick', was born in Rothbury, Northumberland, son of a Scottish clergyman. His father became vicar of Wigton, where Brown grew up. He too became a priest and tutored the boy William Gilpin, usually credited as the progenitor of the Picturesque. According to the *Cambridge History of English and American Literature* (1907–21), vol. X, "The credit of discovering the Lakes belongs really to neither of these [Gray and Wordsworth]. It belongs to poor crazy Brown, the author of *The Estimate*, who

187

wrote of a night scene near Keswick". His 'A description of the lake at Keswick and the adjacent country in Cumberland' was published anonymously in the *London Chronicle*, April 1766, and as a pamphlet in 1767 at Newcastle-upon-Tyne, where he was then vicar. Brown apparently also wrote a panegyric on the Jesuits, remarkably for an Anglican priest. West was a Jesuit. Did they perhaps know each other? Wordsworth reprinted Brown's Keswick poem beginning 'Now sunk the sun' in his *Guide to the Lakes*. Horace Walpole said "poor Dr. Brown was mad" and the *Oxford Dictionary of National Biography* says "On 23 September 1766, in his apartments in Pall Mall, Brown committed suicide by cutting his throat". He never married.

[82] The aside and verse extract appeared originally as a footnote. We are told that this fragment of Brown's poem beginning 'Now sunk the sun' (echoing a line from Homer's *Odyssey*) was preserved only because Richard Cumberland quoted it in the dedication of his *Odes* (1776). Wordsworth reprinted it in his *Guide to the Lakes*.

[83] This sentence and the following excerpt were originally set as a footnote.

[84] Thomas Pennant, *A Tour in Scotland and Voyage to the Hebrides* (1774–6). For Gray, see Addenda, Article III.

[85] Armathwaite Hall viewpoint is identified by the Norgates at grid reference NY207324.

[86] Scarness viewpoint is identified by the Norgates at grid reference NY213304.

[87] Broadness viewpoint is identified by the Norgates at grid reference NY22012969.

[88] The double foss was two parallel ditches; the agger is an earthwork forming a rampart or causeway.

[89] Beck Wythop viewpoint is identified by the Norgates at grid reference NY21542861.

[90] These two paragraphs were originally part of the extended footnote.

[91] This verse extract and the next come from *The Minstrel* by James Beattie (1735–1805), son of a Scottish tenant farmer. The poem, published in two volumes in the 1770s, made a big impression on Wordsworth among others. Both verse extracts, with their *chapeau* paragraphs, were originally footnotes.

[92] Pennant means 'cure' in the sense of a curacy, the care of souls.

[93] West seems to indicate that he has crossed both the Alps and the Apennines.

[94] Mont Maudit (14,648 ft) is part of the Mont Blanc massif.

[95] Highgap Yeat (Thrushbank) viewpoint is identified by the Norgates at grid reference NY13532126.

[96] Flass Wood viewpoint is identified by the Norgates at grid reference NY14352021.

[97] Dob Ley Head viewpoint is identified by the Norgates at grid reference NY15362135.

[98] Added by Cockin as a footnote, this account was originally in a letter

from a young clergyman to his friend, sent by John Locke to the Royal Society and published in their *Philosophical Transactions (1683-1775)*, Vol. 46 (1749–50), pp. 362–6.

[99] Here 'rood' evidently means a rod, pole or perch, a measure 5 ½ yds (16 ft 6 ins) long, and not a measure of area.

[100] The Chorographia is the document now known as the Ravenna Cosmology.

[101] A cultivated reader would be expected to recognise these two great reference works: John Horsley, *Britannia Romana* (1732) and William Camden, *Britannia* (1st edn, 1586; many subsequent editions).

[102] Dunmallet is identified by the Norgates at grid reference NY46792462.

[103] For the rest of Gray's journal, see Addenda, Article III.

[104] Stybarrow Crag is identified by the Norgates at grid reference NY38771785.

[105] Patterdale Hotel viewpoint is identified by the Norgates at grid reference NY39601585.

[106] William Hutchinson (1732–1814), *An Excursion to the Lakes in Westmorland and Cumberland, August 1773* (1774). This account was originally a footnote.

[107] The Watermillock station is identified by the Norgates at grid reference NY4422.

[108] A fathom is 6 ft, but the deepest point now is about 200 ft deep; the level was about 95 ft lower before the 1929 dam was built.

[109] Its etymology is now understood as Welsh *pen*, 'head, chief' and *rhyd*, 'ford' – 'the chief ford'.

[110] Henry Rowlands (1655–1723) wrote about Anglesey, his birthplace, in *Mona Antiqua Restaurata: An archaeological discourse* (1723). He believed bronze age sites were druidical.

[111] Penrith Beacon viewpoint is identified by the Norgates at grid reference NY5231, altitude 1020 ft.

[112] The bard is John Langhorne (1735–1779), born at Winton near Kirkby Stephen. In 1766 he published a 2nd edition of his *Letters to and from Select Friends* with the subtitle *Effusions of Friendship and Fancy*. The verse extract and its *chapeau* paragraph were inserted by Cockin as a footnote.

[113] Arthur Young, *A Six Months' Tour through the North of England* (1771).

[114] Stone Crag viewpoint is identified by the Norgates at grid reference NY530978.

[115] West explains 'Kendal cottons' but assumes his readers will know the other fabrics mentioned: linsey (a coarse linen first made at Lindsey, Suffolk), toilonet (a fine cloth made with a silk or cotton warp and woollen weft, used for fancy waistcoats and dresses), kerseymere (a medium-weight, twilled woollen cloth) and calico (a strong, unbleached cotton cloth, first imported from Calcutta).

[116] This paragraph was added by Cockin, in a footnote as was his habit.

[117] Thomas Gray's journal is printed in full in the Addenda, Article III.

[118] Abbot Hall was built in 1759 on the site of the abbot's residence; the church of Kendal was an outpost of St Mary's Abbey, York. Kendal Corporation bought the house in 1897, and the grounds became a public park. The house was opened as an art gallery in 1962.

[119] His daughter married Henry Howard, Earl of Suffolk, who gave it to his mother as her home. She left it to her grand-daughter, one of the Bagot family who still live at Levens.

[120] West often stayed at Sizergh and died there. The Strickland family were Catholics.

[121] 'End of the guide and the routes'. Lancaster was where West began.

[122] For comparison, the highest points of these mountains, taken from the 1966 edn of the OS one-inch map of the Lake District and other OS 7th series one-inch maps, were (in feet/yards):
Scafell Pikes 3206/1069
Helvellyn 3116/1039
Skiddaw 3054/1018
Bow Fell 2960/987
Rydal Head [Fairfield] 2863/954
Grasmoor 2791/930
Red Pike 2479/826
High Street 2719/906
Coniston Old Man 2631/877
Whernside 2419/806
Ill Bell 2476/825
Carrock 2174/725
Knoutberry Haw 2216/739
Gatescarth Pass (about) 1880/627
Pendle Hill 1831/610
Whinfell Beacon 1544/515
Rivington Pike 1498/499
Benson Knott 1040/347
Penrith Beacon 937/312
Kendal Fell 679/226
Kendal town (about) 150/50

[123] The letter was addressed to 'Lord Littleton' – George Lyttelton, 1st Baron Lyttelton (1709–1773) – and first published anonymously in the *London Chronicle*, April 1766. Dr John Brown (1715–1766), a Wigton man, also wrote essays, plays, poems, sermons and, most famously in his own day, *An Estimate of the Manners and Principles of the Times* (1757).

[124] This poem was printed in vol. 1 of George Pearch, *A Collection of Poems*, 4 vols (London, 1775), but it had been separately published much earlier. John Dalton (1709–1763) was son of the rector of Dean, in west Cumberland. He was a doctor of divinity and in 1748 became a canon of Worcester, where he was buried. The work from which this

extract comes was published as a *Descriptive poem, addressed to two ladies* [the two Misses Lowther] *at their return from viewing the mines near Whitehaven* (1755).

125 Thomas Gray (1716–1771) is famous for his *Elegy in a Country Churchyard*, begun in the 1740s and finished in 1750. He met his lifelong friend Thomas Wharton (1717–1794) when they were at Cambridge. Wharton became a physician in Yorkshire, where Mason also lived. On their 1769 tour, Wharton had to return home before they even reached the Lake District, having fallen ill at Brough. Gray wrote this long and detailed account in a series of letters to Wharton and he seems to have copied it more than once (he was proud of his calligraphy) for other friends. It was first published in 1775 after his death by William Mason (1724–1797), his biographer and literary executor. Christopher Alderson (1737–1814) was Mason's curate for many years.

126 Gray was evidently another user of the Claude mirror. The word 'usually' suggests that West knew or corresponded with Gray.

127 Gray had visited Wharton in 1767, and together they had travelled in the Peak District and the Lakes.

128 The classical version of paradise was just as evocative as the Garden of Eden for an eighteenth-century scholar, and had the advantage that Claude and Poussin had already pictured it in landscapes comparable to those of the Lake District.

129 The line is given to Virgil, dismissing the *ignavi*, the cowards too afraid to enter Hell in Dante's *Inferno*. It translates as 'Don't take any notice of them; just look and walk on'.

130 John Milton, *Paradise Lost*, Book 1, line 540.

131 The reference to Siserah and the butter comes from Judges 5:25.

132 'Erne' is an old name for the sea eagle, which became extinct in the British Isles about 1900 and was re-introduced to Scotland in the 1980s. The latest taxonomy for British birds at the time was that of Thomas Pennant, who also corresponded with West. Linnaeus had yet to prevail in Britain.

133 John Milton, *Samson Agonistes*.

134 The 'bard of Loweswater' also lamented the loss of the oak trees in Crow Park, in a poem quoted by West in the main text; see pp. 46–7.

135 West noted lower viewpoints for artists (see p. 38 and n.49), though perhaps he too took for granted that an artist would not choose the lowest viewpoint possible.

136 Either Cockin or the publisher, William Pennington, was cut to the quick by this slight on Kendal and rebutted it in a footnote.

137 It is noteworthy that Gray remarks that the Stricklands were an old Catholic family, whereas West – who knew them and had stayed there – does not. But West was a Catholic priest and evidently trying to keep a low profile.

138 It seems odd that Gray should use Bishop Auckland as his standard of

comparison for Lancaster's size; but perhaps this was the last town of any size that he and Wharton visited before the latter fell ill at Brough.

[139] In 2004, 23 cocklers drowned, working on these sands.

[140] Craven is the name for the limestone country of the West Riding of Yorkshire.

[141] Shakespeare, *King Lear*, Act IV, Scene vi, where Lear is on the edge of the cliff.

[142] The next three paragraphs, originally a footnote, are by West; the commentary in the remainder of the footnote is Cockin's. William Gilpin, a Cumberland man, was headmaster of a school in Cheam, Surrey, from 1753 to 1777. He published a series of illustrated *Observations … relative chiefly to picturesque beauty* from 1782 onwards.

[143] 'Mr Cumberland' is not a pseudonym, as might be thought, but Richard Cumberland (1732–1811), playwright (and sometimes plagiarist), also a novelist, essayist and writer upon Spanish art.

[144] The Revd James Plumptre (1770–1832) went on two or three walking tours in the Lake District in the late 1790s, taking with him Uvedale Price's *On the picturesque* as reading matter. One result of this was his best-known work, *The Lakers: a Comic Opera* (1798). It satirised the new craze and its devotees: the enthusiastic lady botanist, the tourists going native in carriages, and the hero (this would have pleased Alfred Wainwright), a solitary walker. In the north country, 'laiker' (or 'laker') means someone who plays about or plays truant.

[145] The cave is about a mile east of Nether Kellet, near Lancaster. It was visited by tourists, and eventually by coach parties, well into the twentieth century. It is now closed, having become unsafe as a result of large-scale quarrying nearby.

[146] Mr A. Walker may be the same as the writer about the caves on Ingleborough, who is mentioned by Haskett Smith: "an early description by Mr. Adam Walker in the Evening General Post for September 25, 1779, which is quoted by West" in W.P. Haskett Smith, *Climbing in the British Isles*, Pt 1: England (1894). A book appeared later: A. Walker, *Remarks made on a Tour from London to the Lakes of Westmorland and Cumberland in 1791*(1792). There is a painting of Dunald Mill Hole by James Campbell (1828–1893) in the Walker Art Gallery, Liverpool.

[147] The New River, 10 ft wide and 4 ft deep, was completed in 1613. It brought spring water from Ware in Hertfordshire to the centre of London – and still does, though the water is now treated on arrival.

[148] Revd John Hutton (1739–1806) was born in Westmorland and became vicar of Burton-in-Kendal in 1764. His book *A tour to the caves in the environs of Ingleborough and Settle* was published in 1781. It is possible that this account was written for publication; it was an eighteenth-century convention to expound a topic in letter form.

[149] Originally published in Latin as *Barnabae itinerarium, or, Barnabee's Journal*, by Corymbaeus (1638), Drunken Barnaby's riotous travels

between London and Kendal were later published in English as well, but still pseudonymously. A new edition appeared in 1817–18, edited by Joseph Haslewood, who established that the author was Richard Brathwaite (1587–1673), a Kendal man.

150 The *Itinerarium Antonini Augusti* was a 4th-century list in their correct order of the places to be found along each Roman road. West cites it several times.

151 The poet Samuel Butler (1613–1680) is remembered for *Hudibras* (1663–78), which has been regularly republished ever since.

152 Oliver Goldsmith, 'The deserted village'.

153 Its height, according to the OS 7th series one-inch map, was 2373 ft.

154 The reference is to Revd Charles Churchill (1732–1764) and his poem *The Prophecy of Famine: A Scots Pastoral*. It satirised the Bute administration of 1762.

155 Richard Brathwaite's *Barnabee's Journal* (see n.149).

156 The poem, of which this is only an excerpt, is presumably by John Hutton himself.

157 James Thomson (1700–1748), *The Seasons*, 'Winter', ll. 74–5.

158 Thomas West proposed this 2,500-word piece as a footnote (see p. 27). His idea of planting landmarks on prominent heights was sometimes carried into practice, especially in Scotland. The Forestry Commission began planting conifers in Lakeland valleys in the 1930s; the move to planting native, deciduous trees began in the 1980s.

159 William Mason (1725–1797) was a clergyman, but much more a poet, satirist, musician and gardener; he designed several unusual gardens. His poem *The English Garden* appeared in four volumes in 1772–81. He was the biographer and literary executor of Thomas Gray.

160 This anonymous account of Ennerdale by 'a friend of the publishers' lacks the signature 'X' that Cockin added to his contributions. It first appeared in the 4th edition of 1789. *Pictor*, who wrote the 1788 *impromptu* poem and became a noted exhibitor at Somerset House, may be Joseph Farington RA 1747–1821; he was painting his *Views of the Lakes* in 1788.

161 Revd Josiah Relph (1712–1743) was poet, curate and schoolmaster of Sebergham Grammar School. His poems were published in 1747, and again in a new edition in 1798 with woodcuts by Thomas Bewick. His father was priest at Sebergham before him.

162 Mrs Ann Radcliffe née Ward (1764–1823) was the first woman to ride to the top of Skiddaw. According to the *Oxford Dictionary of National Biography*, her travel book, *A Journey Made in the Summer of 1794*, appeared in 1795. However, she is much more famous for her romances, especially *The Mysteries of Udolpho* (1794). They featured picturesque landscape descriptions, but what made them hugely successful was their combination of innovation, clever plotting and high drama. At the height of her fame, she stopped writing; the reason is unclear.

163 Shakespeare, *Coriolanus*, Act III, Scene ii.

Plates

The Vale of Lonsdale

J. Emes delineavit
S. Alken fecit

Coniston Lake

J. Smith delineavit
S. Alken fecit

Windermere Lake

J. Smith delineavit
S. Alken fecit

Winandermere Lake from Calgarth

J. Smith delineavit
S. Alken fecit

Elter-water

J. Emes delineavit
C. Apostool fecit

Rydal Water

J. Smith delineavit
S. Alken fecit

Stock-gill Force near Ambleside

J. Emes delineavit
S. Alken fecit

Upper Cascade Rydal

J. Emes delineavit
S. Alken fecit

from a sketch by Laporte

Grasmere Lake

J. Smith delineavit
S. Alken fecit

Leathes Water

J. Smith delineavit
S. Alken fecit

Derwent-water from Castle-crag

J. Emes delineavit
S. Alken fecit

Derwent-water from Ormathwaite

J. Emes delineavit
S. Alken fecit

from a sketch by Laporte

Buttermere Water

J. Smith delineavit
S. Alken fecit

Lowes Water

J. Smith delineavit
S. Alken fecit

Ulleswater

J. Smith delineavit
S. Alken fecit

The upper end of Ulls-water

J. Emes delineavit
S. Alken fecit

Coniston Station 1   *Near Park Nab*

Coniston Station 2   *Near Peel Island*

Coniston Station 3   *Near Beck Leven*

Coniston Station 4   *Top of the Lake*

Windermere Station 1   *Claife Station*

Windermere Station 2   *South Side of Belle Isle*

Windermere Station 3   *North Side of Belle Isle*

Windermere Station 4   *Rawlinson Nab*

Windermere Station 5   *Brant Fell*

Derwent Water Station 1   *Cockshot Wood*

Derwent Water Station 2 *Crow Park*

Derwent Water Station 3   *Falcon Crag*

Derwent Water Station 4   *Castle Crag*

Derwent Water Station 5   *Swinside*

Derwent Water Station 6   *Fawe Park*

Derwent Water Station 7 *Latrigg*

Derwent Water Station 8   *Garden of The Old Vicarage, Great Crosthwaite*

Bassenthwaite Station 1   *Armathwaite Hall*

Bassenthwaite Station 2 *Scarness Headland*

Bassenthwaite Station 3   *Near Broadness Farm*

Bassenthwaite Station 4   *Near Beck Wythop*

John Darwell has worked as a photographer on environmental and post-industrial projects for over twenty years. He has had over 30 exhibitions around the world. His work has appeared in many magazines, including *Adbusters*, *Creative Camera*, *Portfolio*, *Photometro*, *Camera Austria*, *Fotographia*, *Zoo* and *Baby*, as well as in newspapers. He has published five books and his work is also featured in a number of major collections including The Victoria & Albert Museum, The National Museum of Photography, Film & Television/Sun Life Collection and The Metropolitan Museum of Art, New York.

Niki Thomas comes from a tradition of drawing and watercolours, but specialises in digital print. Inspired by this medium, in recent years she has worked largely with a digital camera and editing software, exhibiting widely and teaching in adult education. In 2005 Niki took a year to travel abroad and develop a body of work examining how people behave at, and interact with, tourist sites. In the Lake District, she has studied Thomas West, his ideas about viewpoints and how his 'viewing stations' are used today, leading to a solo exhibition in Keswick in 2008.

A modern edition of *A Guide to the Lakes* by Thomas West
Unspoilt. Unvisited. Until Thomas West wrote his guidebook, the Lake District
was unknown and unloved. No poets came, no tourists toured and the average
nymph or shepherd saw nothing worth a second look. Yet, before Wordsworth
was even born, one man was showing people the beauty of this wilderness
– through a *camera*, too.

Thomas West was a scholar who loved the Lakes and made the world
see what he saw. In this new edition of his guidebook, photographs match the
original views and the 'viewing stations'. West sketches the scene and highlights
the special features, 'verified by his own repeated observations' – a scholarly
introduction and notes fill in the background.

Why visit the Lakes? What will you see that the camera doesn't?
Suitable for 'the curious of all ranks', this is the guidebook that began it all.
Use it to look at the Lakes with fresh eyes.

ISBN 978-1-869979-25-6

9 781869 979256 >

looking at me

isabella rossellini looking at me

on pictures and photographers

SCHIRMER/MOSEL

The "Me Wall" — a prominent wall in my apartment covered with photos of me taken by different photographers — might have looked to guests like a display of narcissism in the entrance area of my apartment. So, fearing being labeled as such, I moved them to my private studio, away from all eyes, but it had taken me a while to realize how the "Me Wall" might look to others. For me as the viewer looking at the "Me Wall" did not make me wonder, like the bad Queen in Snow White, "'Mirror, mirror on the wall….who's the fairest of them all?" In fact, I didn't see myself at all for that matter but instead saw the photographers' work, their ideas, and our working collaboration in capturing fantasies.

I love photography. I can flip through any fashion magazine and tell who shot each layout without looking at the photo credits. Photography is just like handwriting — it is personal and unique to each photographer. I also love modeling. The more I worked, the more I realized that modeling was not as stupid as I had thought when I began my career. I grew to understand that my main responsibility was to listen and understand what the photographer wanted to express. I saw myself as an interpreter and a vehicle of their ideas. I did not only lend my nose, eyes and mouth to them, but also the expression of my emotions, though the emotions displayed were more theirs than mine. But I should say that the process of being an interpreter never made me feel like a *femme objet*. Instead, posing in front of a camera was like taking a trip in someone else's mind — the most interesting minds offered the most interesting trips.

The face and body in the "Me Wall" and in this book is always the same — mine. But what is interesting is how differently each photographer can portray the same person — proof that our five senses, or at least sight in this case, make each of us perceive reality differently, uniquely and relatively.

The "Me Wall" in my Manhattan apartment, photographed by Oberto Gili, 1996

Looking at Me may seem like a retrospective of my work. This idea makes me nervous — retrospectives imply an end, not a future, and that would not be such good news for me. I counterbalance this thought and possible bad omen by doing the "corna" horns like this…holding the little and index fingers out…a little Italian superstition that should bring me luck! Luck for me means to continue to be able to work because I love it. However, putting together this book offered me the opportunity to review what I have done up to this point. It has indeed made me proud of my work and thankful to the many photographers who used me as their model.

Strangely, it was working on this book that made me finally take down the "Me Wall" completely. Each photo is now wrapped up in plastic and stored in a corner in my studio. I got tired of looking my face and that big, nagging doubt kept coming back to my mind — is this book, like the "Me Wall," no matter what I want to believe, simply and unequivocally the ultimate display of my own narcissism? I hope you don't feel this way, but I must admit, it may just be that…DAMN IT!

★★★

Let's change subjects; this narcissism is such a bore. Let me tell you about something else. Let me tell you that I think that my love for modeling and photography might just be genetic. That's why this book opens with a photo of my maternal grandfather, Justus Bergman, who owned a portrait photography shop in Stockholm in the early 20th century.

Here he is with his immense camera in 1926. He liked experimenting with this new medium and used his family, especially my mother, as the subject of his experiments. A large number of his glass negatives are stored at the Ingrid Bergman Archives at Wesleyan University in the United States. (Ingrid Bergman was my mother.) These are the old-fashioned negatives created with pure silver dust on a flat surface known as the plate. By a chemical process that I still don't understand and that is pure magic to me, the plate, when exposed to light and shadow, reproduced, in black and white, the reality in front of the camera lens.

I never met my grandfather Justus or my grandmother Friedel. They both died when my mother was still a child. But my mother kept framed photos of her parents by her bedside table. These photos, taken by Justus, were covered with traces of my mother's lips. She must have kissed these images, and I suspect, asked her dead parents to be her guardian angels and to protect her.

Throughout my mother's nomadic life — from Sweden, where she was born, to Hollywood, where she established her legendary career as an actress, to Italy, where she fell in love with my dad, Roberto Rossellini, and had three kids, one of whom is me, and then to France and England — she carried a trunk containing her father's photos. For her, the emotions these photos elicited were the only tangible, true connection to her lost family.

I believe that is why mother took many photos of us, her children. It was one of the ways she parented us. She arranged the photos in elaborate and beautiful albums, which were presented as the diaries of our lives. I tried to do the same for my children, but failed. My photos are strewn about in total chaos in several boxes. Once, sitting on a plane next to an executive of Eastman-Kodak, I was told my organizational failure was not uncommon. "Technology has become so easy and accessible," he said, "that people take too many photos and then never organize the shots." I was also surprised to learn from him that already at the beginning of the last century, George Eastman was striving to develop a simpler camera technology to appeal to women because he alone in that business realized that it was women who were the traditional keepers of family records and memories. Isn't that what deserves to be called a stroke of genius?

But this book isn't about those kinds of photos. It is about "fictional" pictures — photos that either reconstruct realities or that represent realities that spring from the fantasy of the photographer. There are a few exceptions in this book, like the photos of Eve Arnold and Anton Corbijn. These photographers come from a photojournalism background and their assignment was to capture the real me, not one of my interpretations. There is also a photo captured by a paparazzo that is included because it apparently adorned Diana Vreeland's desk, the great dame of fashion. I took this as a compliment even thought I don't know why she kept it there.

Photos have always been important and powerful for me. A powerful photo is like an epitaph or a famous sentence — in one frame it can capture a complex reality. A good photo has the same power of a concise, profound sentence like "to be or not to be." BOOM! "To be or not to be"… immediately, your brain starts thinking, analyzing, and a cascade of emotions follow. The same is true for powerful images like Bob Capa's falling soldiers and D-Day photos, Henri Cartier-Bresson's portrait of Matisse with doves, Eve Arnold's photos of Marilyn Monroe or the gardening monk, Avedon's Dovima with elephants, and Penn's flowers. All these photos are seared in our brains and constitute a part of our collective visual culture.

Then there is the string of images, 24 frames per second, that make up film. My dad was a film director. His simple, stark, matter-of-fact images created a new film style called "neo-realism." This new style of film always reminded me of Robert Capa's photos. Both Capa and my father's images were so powerful, that in my mind and the minds of lots of other people, World War II is remembered in black and white. Isn't it? This is our collective visual culture.

My mom, you should know, was in love with Capa. As reported in her autobiography, he told her, "I cannot marry you. I cannot be tied down…If they say Korea tomorrow and we're married and we have a child I won't be able to go to Korea, and that's impossible… I am not the marrying kind." Mother wrote, "That part was not easy…not easy at all… I wanted so much to be with him."

Her biography begins with the story of her going to the movies to see *Open City*, a film my dad directed. When I asked her why she started the book with this, she replied, "Seeing *Open City* and the consequences of it was the most important event in my life." What she meant by consequences was that after writing a letter to Dad immediately after seeing the film to ask if she could work with him, they met, fell in love, and pregnancy followed before divorce from previous marriages could be arranged. Scandal! Big international scandal, followed by being chased out of Hollywood and being persecuted by the press…in other words hell. Into that chaos I was born.

Later on, as an adult I often wondered if my mother saw Capa's photos coming to life in dad's films. Working in dad's films was her opportunity to participate in something she deeply respected. If marriage to Capa was impossible, it was very possible with my father. Together Mom and Dad made 5 films and 3 kids.

So, how do you want me not to love photos or films? I am connected to them, derived from them, I came to life because of them and now I've lived by them. Oh, and by the way, I forgot to tell you that my grandfather, Angelo, built the first movie theater in Italy. Now, how could you possibly expect me not to love photography and films?

plates

MILES ALDRIDGE

SERGIO ALOCCI

EVE ARNOLD

KEVYN AUCOIN

RICHARD AVEDON

JAMES BALOG

ERIC BOMAN

JEFF BRIDGES

MICHEL COMTE

ANTON CORBIJN

PATRICK DEMARCHELIER

ARTHUR ELGORT

FABRIZIO FERRI

OBERTO GILI

MICHEL HADDI

MARY HILLIARD

HORST P. HORST

DOMINIQUE ISSERMANN

BILL KING

JOSEF KOUDELKA

BRIGITTE LACOMBE

ANNIE LEIBOVITZ

PETER LINDBERGH

DAVID LYNCH

ROBERT MAPPLETHORPE

ELLIOT MARKS

KURT MARKUS

STEVEN MEISEL

SHEILA METZNER

UMBERTO MONTIROLI

FRANÇOIS NARS

IRVING PENN

JIM RAKETE

ANDRÉ RAU

HERB RITTS

PAOLO ROVERSI

FRANCESCO SCAVULLO

IKÉ UDÉ

ELLEN VON UNWERTH

MAX VADUKUL

BRUCE WEBER

WIM WENDERS

1
PETER LINDBERGH
New York City, 1997

Amongst the strongest "signatures" in photography is the work of Peter Lindbergh. I can leaf through a magazine and recognize a Peter Lindbergh photograph instantly. Peter told me once that he doesn't think that fashion photography is art at all. To me, fashion and cosmetics photography can be art, because while its goal is commercial thereby restraining the photographer's artistic freedom, the photographer's "signature" is still allowed to come through. This is why I think of it as an art form. It is simply art in a straightjacket.

2

PETER LINDBERGH
New York City, 1997

Marcello Mastroianni's description of my loud laughter
captured by Peter Lindbergh's photo flattered me.

*Of all her faces the one I like best is the chubby-faced little girl
that I'm sure she once was, and still must be off-camera, letting
out one of those wonderfully fresh yet fierce bursts of laughter.*

P.S. Couldn't a photographer try to capture this laugh?
MARCELLO MASTROIANNI

3
PETER LINDBERGH
New York City, 1997

Walking in
Soho with my
dog Macaroni

4
FRANÇOIS NARS
New York, 1997

François Nars is an excellent make-up artist turned
photographer. For most of our lives, François and I have
made a living promoting make-up for different companies.
Now François has his own make-up line called *Nars*
and I have my own make-up line called *Manifesto*.
Yet, several years ago when we sat together in a studio,
François who was photographing me for a book on
make-up authored by him, decided to snap this unmade-up
version of me. It was as if, after all the different make-up
looks he had created on my face over the years, he
finally needed to see my face NAKED.

5
PATRICK DEMARCHELIER
New York, 1994

"Patrick," I said at the shoot, "the advantage of working with a good photographer like you is that it can all rest on your shoulders. I'll talk to Marina Schiano, the art director, while you snatch the photos." What I meant was that sometimes posing is not necessary. Relaxing in front of the camera and letting the photographer catch what he wants and what he likes sometimes works better. Donna Karan's art director had explained that she wanted a spontaneous expression from me for this shoot. What can be more spontaneous than just chatting with a friend?

Marina Schiano is my friend and was the stylist for this shoot. Marina, who went from modeling to being Yves St. Laurent's muse, then from *Vanity Fair* to jewelry designer, is a loud, eccentric Neapolitan consciously and unconsciously funny, meaning I laugh with her and at her too. She has a great sense of humor, talks with her hands, and is contagiously neurotic. Just seeing her makes my adrenalin rise and I find myself intoxicated with her exaggerated, theatrical emotions. In Marina's company, my gestures reverse to heavy Italian, my laugh grows deeper, my sense of humor grows broad and I lapse into obscene jokes, Marina's favorite. I knew talking to her would have this effect on me, and I believed I could use it for this shoot.

Reacting is part of acting. As an actress, I react to fellow actors. As a model, it's not so simple — I've got to hunt around the set for the best person to bounce off of to provoke emotions to use for the camera. Most of the time I use the photographers but I just couldn't use Patrick. My normal reaction to him is bewilderment and confusion. He makes me frown — an unacceptable expression in fashion and beauty shoots. The reason for this is that too much of an international lifestyle has reduced Patrick's communications skills to an incomprehensible mixture of languages. Aware of this, he adds a speech pattern which is the second fastest I've ever heard. (The first fastest speaker being my ex-husband Martin Scorsese.) Patrick's voice seems to be running away from him in a desperate attempt not to be caught at having forgotten one complete language.

This unfortunate habit is not uncommon among fashion people. Peter Lindbergh's language has suffered the same as Patrick's. Here is the note which Peter recently sent me concerning a TV commercial for my cosmetic line *Manifesto*. "Gran plan of Isabella augen. Cut to long shot of pelouse with ragazze bellisime laufen among the linge ou soleil. Il fodra dire Amour to remember de parlier ou sound man."

This translates as: "Close up of Isabella's face. Cut to a long shot of meadow with the beautiful girls laughing among the laundry hanging in the sun. I must tell Amour to remember to talk to the sound man"…evidence that we fashion people deal in images not speech!

6
RICHARD AVEDON
American Vogue*, November 1982*

On this shoot for American *Vogue* at Avedon's studio
in New York he instructed me, "Change your thoughts."
He seemed to be able to really see what I was thinking.
So, I tested him. I disobeyed and went back to my
original thought, the one he had asked me not to have.
He caught me immediately.

7
RICHARD AVEDON
American Vogue, *November 1982*

DOMINIQUE ISSERMANN
Venice, 1998

Dominique and I have worked together many times. One of our assignments was to create an advertising image for a jewelry company. During the shoot we decided to let a German TV crew film us working together for a behind-the-scenes look at modeling. We were shooting on the streets of Venice, and with so many cameras pointed at me — Dominique's, the TV crew's, and all the tourists fascinated with the photo shoot — it became IMPOSSIBLE to pose.

The atmosphere was so chaotic that Dominique and I could not create the intimacy that we were usually capable of. I could only maintain this dreamy, far away look on my face because that's where I wanted to be — far, far away.

9
MILES ALDRIDGE
New York City, 1996

look at me   I was trying to look like
James Dean, just as pho-
tographer Miles Aldridge
had instructed me to. But, it
turned out that I look like Gary Oldman.
It is said that in a long marriage couples start to look alike
over time. Yet I had only been going out with Gary Oldman
for several months when this photo was taken. Is it possible
that the camera, with its sharper eye, immediately registered
this symbiosis?

10 (overleaf)
MILES ALDRIDGE
Paris, 2000

I have worked with Miles on other projects, not only in
front of his camera, but behind it. In fact, I recently hired
him to shoot the advertising campaign to launch my
cosmetic line, *Manifesto*. Even more recently, Nicole
Wisniak, editor of the French avant-garde magazine *Egoïste*,
my dear friend Jean Paul Scarpitta (acting as art director)
and I staged a "manifestation" as a demonstration is called
in French. The resulting photo is bold and mirrors the
philosophy of my cosmetic line which promotes reexamin-
ing women's approaches to beauty.
  I loved doing this photo. We did not tell any of our
executives at *Manifesto* what we were doing for *Egoïste*
because often boldness and fun go out the window when
business is involved. I truly wish this image could be the
advertisement for my cosmetic line.

11

MILES ALDRIDGE
In a coffee shop, New York City, 1996

The first time that I worked with Isabella Rossellini
was for the "Sunday Times Magazine". For some
reason someone had decided that we do the pictures at
The Chelsea Hotel. I arrived late at the dark seedy
hotel room and she was already in make-up having her
signature red lipstick painted on. Her hair was being
coiffured in that glamourous "Blue Velvet" way and a
rack of sexy dresses, hung in a corner, were being
steamed. I introduced myself and she said how much
she liked my work. I took the compliment sure that
she had never seen any of my pictures, I had only been
working for a matter of months at this stage and was
certainly not well known. She asked how I liked the
hair style and the make-up and the dresses and weren't
they all wonderful... I replied that I thought it all
looked great but that I had this idea to make her into
a boy, James Dean in fact. "James Dean?" she said looking at her reflection, her red lips, her perfectly coiffured hair, her cleavage and those colourful dresses.

She thought about it for two seconds and then with
new enthusiasm for this idea wiped off the lipstick and
started to comb her hair into the familiar James Dean
pompadour quiff. The stylist meanwhile quickly
ordered some men's wear.

We took pictures in the hotel room, with one of the
bedside lights for illumination. At the first polaroid
she looked at herself and exclaimed "I look just like
Gary." We then carried on taking pictures outside on
West 23rd Street. We walked together, her sauntering
like James Dean, while I snapped away, arriving at
an old diner where she ordered a coffee. Seated beside
her was this wonderful, toothless old lady, one of the
many freaks of Chelsea, who was energetically trying
to eat a doughnut. I snuck out my camera and grabbed
the picture of the two of them together. They made
quite an interesting couple.

MILES ALDRIDGE

12
FABRIZIO FERRI
Advertisement for Bulgari, Rome, 1975

Fabrizio Ferri and I met on that night in 1975 when the Communist Party almost won the election in Italy. We were in our teens and a part of the huge crowd that had gathered in the little street near the Communist Party headquarters in Rome. (It was the same little street where years later, Aldo Moro, president of the Christian Democrats who had tried to create a coalition with the Communist Party, was found dead, shot by the terrorist group Red Brigade.)

I was standing in the crowd in that little street when I saw Fabrizio for the first time. He seemed a vision, taller than any other Italian, with big green eyes, all dressed in white, snapping photos of the crowd. He spotted me and took some photos of me while waiting for the final count of the election. A few days later, he called me at home. I don't know how he found my number…perhaps I gave it to him that night. He wanted to photograph me for an ad for the jewelry house Bulgari. I went and while he photographed me, I fell in love with him. But you have to know that everyone falls in love with Fabrizio.

In the brief year we were together, two tragedies struck. Fabrizio's mother died suddenly of a stroke and my Dad died unexpectedly of a heart attack. Since that time our lives have been bonded and connected forever and he has taken photos of me throughout my life. I feel an enormous closeness and tenderness toward Fabrizio Ferri, which I think you can see in my face in these pictures.

with my
son Roberto

13
FABRIZIO FERRI
Pantelleria, 1995

14
FABRIZIO FERRI
Long Island, 1993

with my dog
Macaroni

15
FABRIZIO FERRI
Pantelleria, 1995

16

SERGIO ALOCCI
Italian Vogue, *August, 1970*

I didn't really remember this particular photo of me until, strangely enough, I saw it included in a retrospective exhibit on fashion guru Diana Vreeland at New York's Metropolitan Museum. They had reconstructed Diana's office at *Vogue* magazine and it was there, this paparazzi photo of me at age 16, pasted up on an "inspiration board" filled with images torn from newspapers and magazines.

I grew up in Rome, paparazzi city par excellence. I couldn't stand them. During my childhood, my brother, sister and I always had paparazzi photographers following us and long lenses were always pointed at our home spying through our windows hoping to catch us off guard. We, the children, organized ourselves into a gang and declared war against the paparazzi. Armed with stones, bricks and slings, we regularly ambushed them to the dismay of my mother.

This paparazzo photo was taken of me at a party before I was a model and even before my parents allowed me to go out alone at night. This is how my father would sometimes catch me. A magazine or newspaper would publish a photograph of me at a party, with a boy, with a cigarette, with a drink or late at night, and the next day, my father would see it. That's the danger of having paparazzi around. What a nightmare!

The paparazzi were still there. Many years later, when I would travel to Italy with my young children, their constant following and photographing us became the reason why my children don't want to spend holidays in Italy. Once, one paparazzo asked me, while walking backwards as he was shooting photos, "But why do you dislike us so much? You should see us as your protectors…with all the kidnappings, terrorist attacks and even the simple *scippo* (the popular little crime of purse snatching) happening all the time, as long as we keep photographing you, no one will ever dare to come near you." You know, I had to admit that he might have a point.

17
EVE ARNOLD
During filming of White Nights*, Finland, 1985*

This photo was taken the day I did my first love scene in a film. I was offered a closed set which means anyone who doesn't need to be on the set when a difficult scene is being shot is asked to leave. For a situation like this, a crew of approximately 120 people can be shrunk to 5 people! Eve was on special assignment for Magnum photo agency to take on-set pictures and she wanted to be among these absolutely necessary people which included the director, the camera man, the sound man and my love scene partner, Gregory Hines. I was glad to have Eve around.

Eve took photographs barefoot to make sure that she was not noticed and that she did not intrude. As a photo reporter, she seizes images instead of arranging them and so, if she saw me even noticing the camera she stopped. I loved her presence around me. She had photographed Marilyn Monroe and Joan Crawford and she knew much more than I of the hardships of certain scenes. Her feminine presence and sensibility, both of which are apparent throughout her work, reassured me. On that day she felt like my guardian angel.

18
EVE ARNOLD
During filming of White Nights*, Finland, 1985*

I asked Eve what the driving force of her long, photographic career was which encompassed covering an extremely wide variety of subjects from Malcolm X to actresses, from childbirth to harems. She gave me this answer, "If I had to use a single word, it would be curiosity." Curiosity! That's my driving force too!

19

ANONYMOUS
With Muhammad Ali in the early 1970s, New York

Boxing is the maximum expression of masculinity and modeling is the maximum expression of femininity. Both professions involve primarily one's physique rather than one's mind and both fields share the unpleasant reputation of being filled with not so intelligent people.

I am, in fact, an expert on boxing (as well as in modeling), but I don't like it. I find it too brutal; it is the most recent evolution of the gladiator. When I first got involved in boxing, I couldn't believe real punches were legally allowed. Coming from films where everything is pretend, I assumed that the two men in the ring had choreographed their fights. In the early 1970s, I would often sit next to the boxing ring and every time a punch landed on a face I would say, "oops" as if it had been a mistake.

I was there because I had been hired by RAI Italian TV to assist the sports journalist Gianni Mina in America. I was 18 years old and it was my first job. I was immediately sent to stay at Muhammad Ali's training camp to follow his preparation for the Norton and Frazier fights. These matches were so popular that the worldwide TV audience demanded a daily update on the training of these heavyweights, especially focusing on Ali.

Ali was a godsend for journalists with his wonderful showmanship and constant clowning for the cameras. Most of all I think, Muhammad Ali elicited the interest of everybody, even people who did not care for the sport, like me. Although I often had to close my eyes during the fights, Ali was still immensely appealing because of his intelligence. I could stomach the fight only because Muhammad Ali's strategy in the ring was fascinating to watch.

I revere Muhammad Ali. When in his presence I sensed that he emanated the aura of a wise man, like the kind of man that is written about in old fairy tales.

20
DAVID LYNCH
Los Angeles, 1987

One day I went into a restaurant and I met three girls.
Two of them I knew. The other looked strangely familiar
and I said to her..."You know, you could be Ingrid
Bergman's daughter." The other girls laughed and said, "You
idiot...she is Ingrid Bergman's daughter." Later on I found
out she was a lot more than that.
DAVID LYNCH

This photo reminds me of a joke between David and
me. David has an unusually deep wrinkle in his forehead, just between his eyes. "It could be the sprouting
of your third eye," I used to tell him, "or the sprouting
of a second ass." Life signs are hard to interpret!

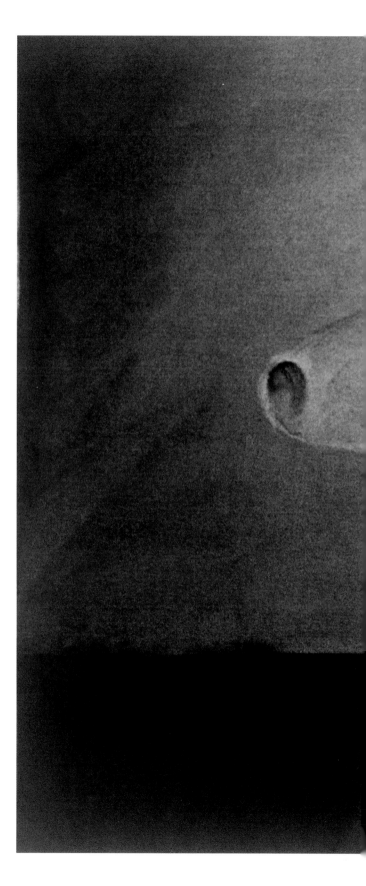

David's eyes and his
strange vertical
wrinkle.

21

KEVYN AUCOIN
The Diva, New York City, 1997

One of the world's leading make-up artists, Kevyn Aucoin, has turned photographer and for his photos, he loves to transform people. Here I am as Barbra Streisand. The metamorphosis took a surprisingly short time. Generally it takes two to three hours of make-up and hair to be ready for a photo shoot but for this shot, it only took half an hour to become Barbra.

The resemblance wasn't so striking when I looked at myself straight in the mirror but in profile I saw that Barbra and I were very similar. I asked Kevyn, "Did you always think I looked like Streisand?" He answered, "Of course — there is the nose. The NOSE is what makes Barbra and you."

22

MICHEL COMTE

For Dolce & Gabbana, "New Rock'n'Roll", Fall/Winter 1994/95
New York City, 1994

In this ad campaign for Dolce & Gabbana, Michel captures
me cloaked in an aura of sex, smoke and money. It is an
amusing image for me because I don't see myself as a sex
goddess and I don't smoke, but I do like money! My parents
didn't care about money and they didn't admire people
who had it. But I learned as an adult that my parents were
wrong: money is much more important than my parents
ever told me — it is the very basis of independence.
I wanted to work because I wanted to be on my own.

   When I started modeling, I couldn't get over those big
modeling fees. My agent would send me out on a day's
work — catalog shoot: $5000, runway: $15,000, day fitting:
$3500 — and would tell me to bring back a signed voucher
in order to be paid. As the day went by, I began to fear
that I had misunderstood the amount. The sums seemed
astronomical. By the end of the day, I would be sure that
I had misunderstood the amount. So, I inevitably pretended
that I had forgotten my voucher and I'd ask them to call
my agent to take care of it.

   At the end of each month, when I'd receive my check,
I'd always be shocked by how much I'd earned while left
feeling full of guilty pleasure.

My uniform: black pants white shirts

23–24
MICHEL COMTE
New York City, 1991

25
HORST P. HORST
Lancôme advertisement, New York City, 1984

"Horst?"…I kept asking myself as I was going to the set.
"The famous Horst, or a relative of Horst? Maybe a
grand-child or someone who took his name as an alias.
Could he be the Horst as in the mythical Horst?"

Well, he was the Horst as in Horst. Very old, very sweet,
very assisted by his collaborators who protected him so
much that I couldn't really talk with him. He was also almost
blind. Photographs are about light, shadows, expressions and
emotions. He managed to capture all of these qualities in
this shot probably with his sixth sense, which was the only
sense that had remained sharp in this old man.

26

ANDRÉ RAU
French Elle*, December 1993*

The first time André and I worked together he turned blue,
fainted behind the camera and was rushed to the hospital.
André is often red in the face, looks tired, and is stressed
by jet lag or whatever else, but he always keeps on working.
In spite of how bad he might feel or how difficult the
circumstances, he makes do.

   Make-do for me is an art. I appreciate people who get
creative and inventive with the little that they have or in
spite of what they have. A dish of pasta, a fresh hair cut,
or playing monster is enough to snatch a good picture.

27–30
ANDRÉ RAU
Spaghetti with Macaroni, French Elle, *December 1993*

31
FRANCESCO SCAVULLO
Harper's Bazaar, *New York City, 1986*

Do you think that when I see this photo I am not embarrassed? Of course I am, but my job as a model is to lend my
two eyes, one mouth, two hands, two feet and one body to
the photographer's lens to create his vision. The photo of me
in the hat is obviously not a portrait of *me*. It is Scavullo's
statement of womanhood within the context of the 1970s
"era of excess" when he was the photographer of the
moment. But I realize that the woman in the white shirt
could be interpreted as me. She is elegant and classy but
would not intrude or impose herself on anyone. And that,
my dear reader, certainly isn't me!

32
FRANCESCO SCAVULLO
L'Officiel, *New York City, 1994*

33
BILL KING
American Vogue, *March 1982*

In my speech at Bill King's funeral I said that most people say I owe my looks to my beautiful mother, Ingrid Bergman, but that I also owed my looks as well as my successful modeling career to Bill King. If Bruce Weber "discovered" me, and Avedon "crowned" me (9 covers for American *Vogue*, 4 of which were in one year, 1982, with 3 of them in a row — unprecedented), Bill King built my career. I went to his studio so often (almost daily) to be photographed for different assignments that I referred to it as "my office."

Bill was shy, mysterious, difficult and polite. He did not know how to direct me with words. Instead, I understood what to do by feeling his moods — bad when he wanted me to do something else, happy when I was doing what he wanted. He used big fans and often resorted to spraying cold water on models' faces. He liked us mad. He liked women with strong, angry emotions and hair flying all over like the Furies.

Once he got to know me well, he dared photograph me with soft, warm expressions. I think he could only photograph tenderness if he truly trusted the person in front of the lens. I always felt touched by his silence, his moods, his mysteriousness and his letting me look warmly into his camera. Bill died young and I miss him enormously.

34
JOSEF KOUDELKA
During shooting of White Nights
by Taylor Hackford, Finland, 1985
Isabella Rossellini and Gregory Hines

Misha Baryshnikov must have been the reason for war-
revolution–death–poverty–pain photographer Josef Koudelka
to come visit and photograph the set of *White Nights*.
Both were defectors — Misha from the Soviet Union, Josef
from Czechoslovakia. Josef did not come for me.

I know that I am not a subject he would volunteer to
photograph. At the time, I was the top model of the super
consumeristic world of fashion. I say that because I read
it in his eyes which were nearly always lowered and embarrassed in my presence. He was the photographer
of the 1969 Prague Spring Revolution, the person who
translated the famous 60s slogan that captured the mood
of the time, "make love, not war" into images.

The best shot of me is the one which came from Josef's
most comfortable point of view of me. With his eyes
lowered in my presence, he caught my legs flirtatiously
sticking out of Gregory Hines' big male body.

35 (overleaf)
JOSEF KOUDELKA
With Mikhail Baryshnikov, 1985

36
JEFF BRIDGES
During shooting of Fearless *by Peter Weir*
Los Angeles, 1991

Jeff Bridges played my husband in *Fearless,* by Australian director Peter Weir.
Jeff took lots of photos on the set. In this photo I am patiently trying on different
clothes for my character. To me, wardrobe is a major key to my character's
personality — who she is and how she wants to be perceived. It is probably my
modeling experience that makes all the details in a character's wardrobe so
important to my understanding of who she is.

OBERTO GILI
American Harper's Bazaar, *May 1997*

Oberto loves pets. All the photographs he takes of me
include my pets. Oberto photographed a birthday party for
my Jack Russell Macaroni that I organized to amuse my
children. He also photographed Spanky, my pig, who grew
up to be huge but never lost the habit of jumping on my
lap and sitting (affectionately) on me. Spanky almost killed
me several times and I had to run away from his displays of
love. When he died, I confess it was a relief, but since then
I have stopped eating pork.

OBERTO GILI
House & Garden, *June 1992*

39
MARY HILLIARD
With Madonna, American Vogue*, December 1997*

At the launch party for my first book, *Some of Me*,
Mary Hilliard caught me and Madonna chatting. We didn't
even notice that Mary was snatching moments of our
conversation.

   I had met Madonna with Steven Meisel. We all had
dinner together and I was asked to be in their book, *Sex*.
Sex is an interesting subject to me because it encompasses
the darkest aspects of life as well as the most luminous
and loving ones. Government, religion, societies, and families
legislate, command, and dictate how we should think about
sex and how we should do it. I loved what Madonna stated
in her book. She said, "My pussy has nine lives!"

40

IRVING PENN
American Vogue*, New York, 1997*

In the early years, I had gone several times to Penn's studio with my modeling portfolio to be hired but to my dismay, he never did. I told Anna Wintour, editor-in-chief of American *Vogue*, about my disappointment and years later, remembering my story, she sent me to his studio to be photographed for a story *Vogue* was doing on me as the author of *Some of Me*, my fictional memoirs.

Mr. Penn, as he likes to be called, said to me, "Don't do any modeling in front of my camera. I'm photographing you as a writer not as a model." I was a bit lost. What did he mean by wanting to photograph me 'as a writer'? What do writers do, anyway? These sorts of questions thrashed around in my brain but I was too embarrassed to ask Mr. Penn for a clarification of his directions. I tried my best to appear "writerly." Here is the result:

41–42
SHEILA METZNER
German Vogue*, February 1995*

Sheila photographed me spoofing my mother, Ingrid
Bergman, in *Casablanca* for a short comic film directed by
Robert Zemeckis (*Who Framed Roger Rabbit* and *Forrest
Gump*). People ask me all the time what it is like to be the
daughter of Ingrid Bergman. I tell them that since I haven't
been the daughter of anyone else, I really wouldn't know.

43 (overleaf)
MAX VADUKUL
Town & Country, *May 1995*

Max Vadukul's homage to Jacques-Henri Lartigue

What inspires the new generation of photographers like
Max Vadukul is not only the fantasy or reality in front
of them but also the collective memories – the visual
culture established by other photographers before them
like Henri Lartigue.

44
ELLEN VON UNWERTH
New York City, 1992

I think people assume that female photographers will photograph femininity differently from male photographers. With Ellen, I find this not to be true. She seems to capture in her photos the forbidden fantasies of men or rather what we women think is the ultimate male dream of what we should be. Whorish, provocative and with a dirty sex appeal. Maybe Ellen, because she is a woman, free of this embarrassing male fantasy, is able to capture a point of view on femininity that is more male than male.

45
ELLEN VON UNWERTH
American Vogue, *January 1993*

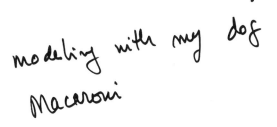

modeling with my dog
Macaroni

46

JIM RAKETE
Berlin, 1993

This photo was taken in Germany while I was shooting
The Innocent directed by John Schlesinger, the man I credit
with making me feel comfortable and legitimate as an
actress. Since that film, when filling in the answer to the
profession question on any legal document, I can
unflinchingly write "actress".

You see, up until working with John Schlesinger, I
always answered the question in a twisted way, being too
embarrassed to say what I did professionally. In fact, I've
noticed that I have only felt comfortable defining myself
professionally by the activity that I have most recently
abandoned!

For example, my first job was as a journalist which, at the
time, seemed too big a title for me. So, on legal documents,
I always said that I was a student. When I became a model,
I did not feel beautiful enough to be entitled to that
professional definition, so I would write journalist — the
job I had just quit to become a model! When I became an
actress, I felt way too shy about that definition of myself —
an actress was someone as elevated as my mother, Ingrid
Bergman, not me. At that point, I felt just fine writing
model on the legal documents.

Today, I'm a businesswoman and, yes, this seems like
a ridiculous definition of myself to me. So instead I write
down actress and think fondly of John Schlesinger who
gave me the courage to use the word.

with my daughter
Elettra

47
BRUCE WEBER
Bellport, Long Island, 1999

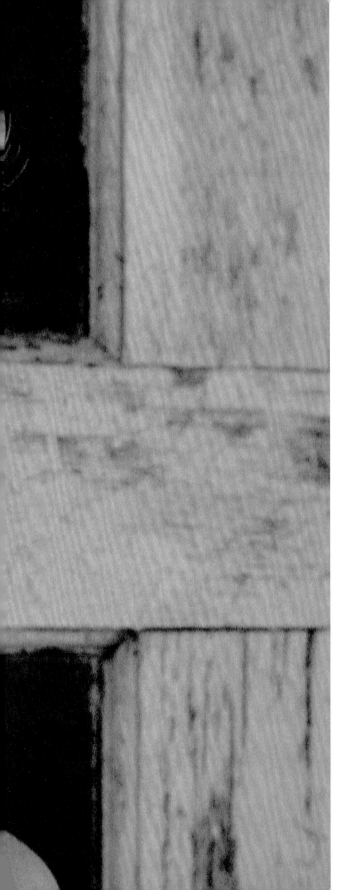

48
ELLIOT MARKS
As Perdita Durango in David Lynch's Wild at Heart,
publicity shot, 1990

*Some models become actresses. Some actresses become models.
It's a fine line which is crossed and blurred all the time.*
ARTHUR ELGORT

Perdita Durango is the best example in my life of modeling
applied to acting. Her looks and attitude were inspired by
the self-portraits of painter Frida Kahlo. As Perdita Durango,
I tried to convey what I felt when looking at Frida's paintings — the uncomfortable duality of being both attracted
and repulsed at the same time.

49
BRIGITTE LACOMBE
During shooting of The Siege of Venice, *Moscow, 1990*

50
BRIGITTE LACOMBE
During shooting of The Siege of Venice, *Moscow, 1990*

51
IKÉ UDÉ
Cover of aRude #16, New York City, 1999

I love to embellish and color the events in my life until
I lose sight of what really happened. Even as a child, my
grandmother always asked me "verita o fantasia?" — "truth
or fantasy?" If you want to eliminate my grandmother's
kindness and put it more bluntly, I lie. I always did. Not big,
far out lies, but not exactly reality either.

Fashion photography lies just like I do. It does not capture
reality nor total, exaggerated, impossible fantasy. Fashion
photography captures something in between the truth and
lies. It searches for a "colored" reality — one that is possible,
one that is better. My lies are just the same — not real, not
false, just an enhanced, tinted truth. That might be the reason
why fashion photography and I get along so well.

Isabella's renown owes to her perfection as a type and grace in
attitude. Due to her confidence, she's exquisitely free from that
perishable vanity that often afflicts great beauties. Photographing
Isabella was more of a mutual collaboration than anything else.

Iké Udé

52–54
ERIC BOMAN
New York City, 2001

This series of photographs is a nod to *National Geographic* and homage to cultural differences. I wanted to show how make-up can be used for transformational purposes and how fun it can be. I hate that people only think of make-up in terms of covering blemishes and wrinkles. This approach is so depressing! It is the fantasy aspect of fashion and cosmetics that is so appealing to me.

Photographer Eric Boman is my neighbor both in the city and the country. He was one of the first photographers to shoot me during my modeling career. We have remained very close, perhaps partly because we share the same blood — we are both half Italian and half Swedish — and perhaps also because we share the same love of dressing up!

55

BRIGITTE LACOMBE
Paris, 1990

I can always recognize Brigitte's photos regardless of
who is in the picture. First, there is the black-and-white —
Brigitte's black-and-white, I mean! Then the marble-like
skin and the intense but serene expressions — this is what
Brigitte tries to capture over and over in all the faces that
come before her lens. She sorts through all emotions and
captures the one she is longing for, I suspect.

When you meet Brigitte, she is a bit like her photos —
soft, kind, intense and warm. But as you get to know her
better, you sense an ever existing melancholy, an uneasiness,
a kind of anxiety. She doesn't photograph these feelings.
Photography to her may be like a surgeon's intervention
cutting out all that is bad and leaving only what's good.
I once asked her, "Why do you always do black-and-white
and not color?" She answered, "Black-and-white is kinder."

In 1990, a year after the fall of the Berlin wall, Gorbachov
was in power in Russia. I lived in Moscow for three months
working on a film. Brigitte came to visit. Photographing,
acting and modeling often creates an opportunity for travel,
often to countries that I or Brigitte would not dare go on
our own! Adventure, more than professional, financial or
career considerations, is at the core of a lot of my decisions.

56
BRIGITTE LACOMBE
Paris, 1990

57 (overleaf)
ARTHUR ELGORT
Lancôme advertisement, Madame, *March 1988*

Theater director Robert Wilson who recently cast me in one of his productions called me a prism in *Flare Magazine*. He said, "she is made up of many characters — the worldly, sophisticated and very intelligent professional and the highly eroticized woman."

   Arthur Elgort, for years one of the principal photographers for Lancôme's advertising campaigns, seems to have captured these qualities in this 1980s image. For 14 years, I was the model for the cosmetics house of Lancôme and for 14 years, I portrayed an idealized woman that fits the definition that Bob has of me. Thank you, Bob! Perhaps it is because Arthur and I were able to create images that projected such a wide range of qualities that they continued to appeal to so many people for so many years.

BILL KING
New York City, 1985

with my baby daughter
Elettra

59
STEVEN MEISEL
Italian Vogue, *New York, 1990*

Steven's photos transcend fashion. For him clothes are just
an accessory to the image he's trying to capture. What he
is after is the archive of images that are mysteriously stored
in all our brains.

   I guess if there was an X-ray machine that could photograph our thoughts, we would find that we all share a lot of
images. Is this what is called the collective unconscious?
Is this what images are... individual frames that sum up an
entire event for all of us? If that's so, that's what Steven
Meisel is after.

STEVEN MEISEL
With Madonna for her book Sex, *1992*

oh Madonna!

STEVEN MEISEL

For Dolce & Gabbana, "Gli anni 40," Fall/Winter 1989/90
New York City, 1990

I never grasped what was serious and artistic about fashion
until I saw Dolce & Gabbana's clothes. I come from a world
of filmmakers and artists where fashion was always regarded
as frivolous. At its worst, fashion was considered a waste
of money — at its best, a shallow case of someone's personal
taste, but no more than that.

When I first saw Dolce & Gabbana's clothes it was as if
I saw my Italian background interpreted not in a song, a film
or a painting but in clothes. The thick, chaste bras of the
Sicilian woman, shirts worn tight over the voluptuous breasts
of the Italian mamas, lots of lace and of course, the black —
layers and layers of black.

Black has always been worn a lot in Italy, a testimony
to the dramatic history of the country. Traditionally, black is
the color of mourning. Traditionally, black is the color
that denies fashion. And fashion, being frivolous, is not
allowed to a woman in mourning.

But, what Dolce & Gabbana saw hidden behind the
layers of black clothes was the restless spirit of the Italian
woman — their humor, playfulness and seductive ways.
Dolce & Gabbana captured that spirit, emphasized that
irreverence and made it into their own fashion signature.
Never have I seen so much psychology, subtlety, and irony
in fashion.

Steven Meisel hired me to shoot one of the first ad
campaigns for Dolce & Gabbana. Their clothes were a great
inspiration to my posing, my attitude, my acting in front
of Steven's camera. Domenico Dolce, Stefano Gabbana and
I became friends and since this first shoot we have kept
up an ongoing collaboration.

One year, I don't know why, Steven Meisel did not shoot
the campaign. Michel Comte was hired instead. Throughout
the shooting Domenico kept whispering, "It's like having a
new girlfriend but deep down you miss the old one." The
following year, Steven was back shooting the campaign,
but I was not hired. I missed it.

64
BRUCE WEBER
With son Roberto in a red toy Ferrari,
Bellport, 1999

It was my brother Roberto who, by slapping my father
Roberto in the face, convinced him to give up racing cars.
He was only three years old when he took this matter into
his hands. He had witnessed my mom's agony at waiting for
dad to come home safely. Enzo Ferrari remained my dad's
friend and built for us children this mini Ferrari for our
amusement. Bruce took this photo of my son, also named
Roberto, and myself in my family's toy Ferrari.

65
BRUCE WEBER
Fashion photograph for Yves Saint Laurent,
New York City, 1981

Bruce took my first modeling photo for British *Vogue*. I was
very afraid — I was convinced that Bruce's original eye saw
me as beautiful but was sure that *Vogue* was going to send
me home. Grace Coddington, the editor on the shoot, was
kind and encouraging. She did not send me home. She had
been a model herself and was stunning in her own right.
Andie McDowell and Rosemary McGrotha were the other
two models at this shoot and I thought I had never seen
more beautiful women. I kept wondering what I was doing
there and what Bruce saw in me. Whatever Bruce did see in
me, it worked. As soon as my photos were published, I got
many requests from different magazines and photographers.
Bruce indeed launched me as a model. We worked a lot
together over the years and we became friends.

66
PAOLO ROVERSI
Room 811, Chelsea Hotel, New York City, 1992

67
PAOLO ROVERSI
Room 811, Chelsea Hotel, New York City, 1992

Paolo's photos are "struggenti." In the dictionary,
"struggente" is translated as "all-consuming" but that
is just part of the meaning. "Struggente" is the
constant ache caused by the joys and sorrows of life.
You've heard it in Neapolitan songs and it is to that
music that Paolo and I work together on a set. Paolo's
photos are dark, mysterious and out-of-focus. They are
images not about reality but that are in our minds when
we are remembering things from the past or are longing
for something to appear in a dream.

68
PAOLO ROVERSI
Room 811, Chelsea Hotel, New York City, 1992

69–71
MICHEL HADDI
New York City, 1994

I'm told that I speak with my hands.
Once I played a German woman in a
movie and the director made me sit
on them. After having lived in New
York for nearly 30 years, I now think
of myself as a cultural hybrid. I didn't
think that my hands would still give
away my Italian heritage!

72
JAMES BALOG
Sally and Isabella, California, c. 1993

James Balog takes pictures for magazines such as *National Geographic*. For one assignment, he posed animals that were on the endangered species list on a white seamless background like one does for a fashion shoot. Taking the animals out of their normal environment resulted in a chilling message — we are about to see the last of these creatures.

I think I sent Balog a congratulatory note on this series. Then, I don't remember the details, but somehow I ended up in Balog's car driving out of Los Angeles south to Brian McMillan's Hollywood Animal Actors residence. The business card from the residence — which I kept — shows a grandmother, mother, daughter, granddaughter, and great grand-daughter chimpanzee (above).

In the pictures he took of me there, Balog wanted to do a photographic essay on the differences and similarities between man (me) and our closest rela-tive, the chimpanzee. The final results show that the chimp has very effective and dramatic expressions, but I am less successful in my attempt at being "just a human being." In my mind, I had to be Eve, the first woman, a prototype with no context. Yet in these photographs I seem to come across as a con-temporary woman. I wonder how that was possible when I was naked and wearing no make-up. I really don't know what betrays my attempt to be timeless — maybe it's just that stupid haircut.

73
ANNIE LEIBOVITZ
"Drink Milk" advertising campaign, New York City, 1993

Annie took this photograph for the very popular American "Drink Milk" advertising campaign. This shot was an easy one to do, but Annie is demanding. For her, just posing pretty and model-like won't do. Being spontaneous isn't enough. Her portraits aren't intimate or revealing. They are obvious, big mise-en-scènes where clothes, make-up, background, and props all work together to define the subject in the full context of his or her life. When Annie put together a collection of her work in her first book, I realized that she was like Proust — one of the most important portraitists of our age and society.

74

ANNIE LEIBOVITZ

Isabella Rossellini and David Lynch, New York City, 1986

The first time I worked with her, Annie wanted a close-up of director David Lynch with me naked, floating around his head as if I were a thought of his. The image would have portrayed very precisely the public image of our personal relationship — me as the lover/muse, he the thinking genius. I did not want to do it. I did not want to take my clothes off for the sake of Annie's and David's art and then repent doing it for the sake of my family.

Instead, this is the strange photo that emerged from that session. It began by accident when Annie "saw" the image she wanted as David was trying on his sweater. Incredibly, she found another way of capturing exactly the same perception of us that she wanted with the original concept. David's covered face seems symbolic of his dark, surrealist mind and me, bare faced, the interpreter of his mysterious thoughts.

75

ROBERT MAPPLETHORPE
New York City, 1988

When Robert Mapplethorpe took this picture of me, he was already very sick. He was very thin and looked like a concentration camp prisoner. His hair was lifeless and his eyes were feverish, shiny, sad and a bit crazy…or so they seemed to me. I had never worked with him or even met him before. I knew of his photos, of course: the flowers, the vases, and you know his most famous works…that big black model with the biggest cock ever and the gay sado-masochistic photos which created such a sensation and scandal.

I was surprised he wanted to photograph me. He had been commissioned to do a book on women — everybody knew he was dying of AIDS and I guess there was a curiosity to see how Robert Mapplethorpe would photograph us regular gals. When Robert was taking my photograph, I was worried that I was a bit of a boring subject for him and he intimidated me though he was very kind and solicitous.

He also seemed shy. I remember looking up on a shelf and keeping my eye there on a row of beautiful vases, some of which I had seen in his photos. I did not know what to talk about with Robert, I was shy too. Then Robert died. Years later, some of his photos came up on an auction. The one of me sold for $5000 but "Helmut and Brook" (fistfucking) went for $20,000.

HERB RITTS
Donna Karan advertisement, New York City, 1999

Donna Karan's clothes are sexy but not sexist. She manages
to design clothes that underline a woman's power without
undermining her and she does this as a mission. This austere
photo of Herb's captures the sexy, masculine femininity
that I associate with Donna — strength without artifice.
I consider Donna a fashion suffragette.

BRUCE WEBER
*Isabella Rossellini with Viggo Mortensen
for American* Vogue, *Malibu Beach, 1987*

Among my all-time favorite photographs is this black-and-white portrait Bruce and I did for American *Vogue*. The idea behind the photo was to make it look like an accident — to look like a frame of a film, full of emotion and intensity even if not perfectly framed or in focus. Bruce hired an actor and made me do improvisation with him — he was to be my boyfriend and we were to argue. I am an actress besides being a model, so it was relatively easy for me to argue with this guy who I'd never met. We were to ignore the camera, forget Bruce, strike poses and catch the best light…all of which a model knows how to do well. Bruce wanted only emotions and for us to forget the rest so I argued and argued with this guy I did not know under the blazing California sun. Diana Vreeland used to say, "There is no beauty without emotion." This photograph of Bruce's proves this statement to be true.

I love working with Bruce because he is always searching, always pushing, always experimental. I try to be the same way — to do new things, to stretch and to search for new visual definitions of fashion photography.

78

ANTON CORBIJN
New York City, 1993

I am not used to working with portraitists. Is that what you
call a photographer who does portraits? There is nothing
that embarrasses me more than having a photo taken of me
as me — I only love it when I can be someone else. All shy-
ness, embarrassment and self-consciousness are shed when I
can pose as someone else. In that situation, my brain gives
me a million ideas of what to do, what expressions to use,
what attitudes to strike etc. But I knew Corbijn's work and
I was curious to meet him so I went to the appointment.
I guess this photo makes me look like I am in hiding with
sunglasses on and a scarf around my head. I look a bit lost
at what to do in front of the camera, as just myself.

*I cannot remember exactly how it all got together but there
was the idea of an Italian looking immigrant to the States and
Isabella knew how to make that look convincing by using a scarf
and doing her own make-up in my little room at the Mayflower
as there was no budget. She was the more professional of the
two of us, I have to admit, and I am grateful for her input and
turning up in the first place.*

                                              ANTON CORBIJN

Italian looking immigrant? Really?

WIM WENDERS
With Martin Scorsese, Monument Valley, 1978

Martin Scorsese, my husband at the time, and I were sitting in the back seat of Wim Wenders' convertible. Wim took this photo of us after rescuing us from the desert.

Our car had broken down in the middle of nowhere under the blazing, hot sun. Martin and I had stood for hours on the highway hoping for a car or a truck to come by so we could hitchhike a ride to any place with a phone, some shade and a drink. I cannot tell you how relieved, pleased and surprised we were when we recognized our rescuer to be the German filmmaker Wim Wenders. Wim was traveling with his wife, and like Martin and I, they intended to go through Monument Valley in Utah where John Ford had shot most of his famous Westerns.

Both Wim and Martin were film buffs and tremendous fans of John Ford. Wim would stop the car often and they would cross fingers in front of their eyes mimicking the framing of a shot and search for the exact location of scenes from Ford's films. They recognized every backdrop, every mountain, stone and hump in the desert. They even discovered that Ford had cheated on some of his reverse shots in order to get a better background behind the close-ups for the actors! They were moved to be in the location where (as they explained Ford's importance to me) America's "mythology" had been created.

I was stunned at how and what a director's eyes could see. They scan every frame of film to decode how to recreate emotions. They see not only actors' faces and their expressions but composition, colors, juxtaposition of images, camera moves, rhythms, light, shadows and then on top of it remember it all. Do you know that Martin can even sniff a film and tell if the emulsion is from the 1940s or 1960s and if it is Kodak or Fuji?

Once Martin and I took a boat trip from Naples to Salina, an island north of Sicily, and he woke up from his nap and saw a rock in the middle of the blue sea. He recognized it immediately as the one in the backgrounds of a Monica Vitti close-up in *L'Avventura* by Michelangelo Antonioni. I have never met anybody like Martin.

UMBERTO MONTIROLI

As Dorothy Vallens in David Lynch's Blue Velvet,
publicity shot, 1986

This is an image from *Blue Velvet*, the film I'm most known
for. When it came out, it was very controversial. I got hurt
and scared by the reaction of the public and the press to the
film but now I am proud and happy that I was in it. Time
takes care of a lot!

81

KURT MARKUS
Mirabella, *May 1991*

Kurt Markus is known for beautiful photos of cowboys.
I live in New York and in this urban environment one for-
gets that there are cowboys in America. The prairies, the
horses, the saddles, the boots, the lassos — these are all part
of Kurt's world.

   Kurt came to New York to shoot for the fashion magazine
Mirabella. He was extremely shy and during our shoot, he
started to photograph me right away before I was finished
with hair and make-up. When I began actually posing for
him, invoking the sexy glances I'd shamelessly learned to
throw at the camera as a fashion model, he reacted as if he'd
gotten an electric shock. I still don't know if his reaction
was a sign that he liked or was embarrassed by my poses.
What I did discover though was that he liked unusual things
about me — like the back of my neck. This is one of my
favorite pictures of me.

"What I like best about her is that I can talk to her...man to man"
                    Luciano De Crescenzo, *writer/philosopher*

biography

Isabella Rossellini grew up in Paris and Rome. At the age of 19, she moved to New York, where she became a translator and later a reporter for RAI Italian Television. Her popular segments led to appearances as New York correspondent for the weekly Italian comedy show "L'altra domenica," with Roberto Benigni (*Life is Beautiful*).

At the relatively advanced age of 28, Rossellini began a modeling career when she was photographed by Bruce Weber for British *Vogue* and by Bill King for American *Vogue*. She has since worked with the industry's most distinguished photographers, from Richard Avedon to Steven Meisel, from Helmut Newton to Peter Lindbergh, from Norman Parkinson to Eve Arnold. She has appeared on the cover of such magazines as *Vogue*, *Elle*, *Marie Claire*, *Harper's Bazaar*, and *Vanity Fair*. An exhibition of photographs of Rossellini, "Portrait of a Woman," was held in March 1988 at the Musée d'Art Moderne de la Ville de Paris.

She made her cinematic debut in 1979 in Paolo and Vittorio Taviani's *Il Prato* (*The Meadow*). Her American film debut was opposite Mikhail Baryshnikov and Gregory Hines in Taylor Hackford's *White Nights* (1985). In 1986, she starred opposite Dennis Hopper as Dorothy Vallens, the tortured lounge singer in David Lynch's haunting and controversial *Blue Velvet*.

Other films include the romantic comedy *Cousins* (opposite Ted Danson), and two more films with David Lynch, *Zelly and Me* (directed by Tina Rathbourne), and *Wild at Heart*. In 1992, Rossellini was featured in Bob Zemeckis' *Death Becomes Her*, starring Meryl Streep, Goldie Hawn and Bruce Willis, and Peter Weir's *Fearless*, co-starring Jeff Bridges and Rosie Perez. In 1993, she starred in *The Innocent,* directed by John Schlesinger.

She played the role of Big Nose Kate in Lawrence Kasden's *Wyatt Earp* with Kevin Costner and Dennis Quaid, and appeared in *Immortal Beloved* opposite Gary Oldman. Most recently, Rossellini starred as the two-timing girlfriend in *Big Night*, co-directed by Campbell Scott and Stanley Tucci, which won Best Screenplay at the 1996 Sundance Film Festival; and in Abel

Ferrara's *The Funeral* (opposite Christopher Walken, Chris Penn and Annabella Sciorra). The portrait of the Jewish Hasidic mother in *Left Luggage* directed by Jeroen Krabbé won a special award at the Berlin Film Festival in 1998.

For television, most notably Rossellini starred as the goddess Athena in the mini-series *The Odyssey: The Last Elephant* (opposite John Lithgow); *The Frightening Frammis* (starring Peter Gallagher); and *The Gift* (Laura Dern's directoral debut). Other recent television roles were as the wife of accused Lindbergh baby kidnapper Bruno Hauptmann (Stephen Rae) in *Crime of the Century,* for which she received a Golden Globe award nomination; and a two-episode arc of the series *Chicago Hope*, for which she was nominated for an Emmy award. In 1998 she starred in the mini-series *Merlin*, with Sam Neil and Miranda Richardson. In 1999 she starred in the mini-series *Don Quixote* opposite John Lithgow. This past summer of 2001, she starred opposite Christian Clavier, Gerard Depardieu, and John Malkovich in the upcoming French-American television mini-series *Napoleon*.

Her modeling and acting career also led Rossellini into the world of cosmetics. Beginning in 1982, she was exclusive spokesmodel for the international cosmetics brand Lancôme for 14 years. In 1990, Lancôme launched its very successful fragrance *Trésor*, which was Rossellini's first involvement with product development. In 1995, Isabella began a collaboration with the Lancaster Group to develop her own brand of cosmetics, Isabella Rossellini's *Manifesto*, which launched internationally in May 1999. In May 2000 her fragrance *Manifesto* was launched and is now sold in 28 countries worldwide.

Rossellini's self-described fictional memoirs *Some of Me* were published in the USA in 1997. The book has since also been published in Italian, German and French language editions. Also in 1997, the George Eastman House (USA) honored Rossellini for her work in preserving the films of her parents, Ingrid Bergman and Roberto Rossellini.

She lives in New York City with her son, Roberto and her daughter, Elettra.

acknowledgements

Of course, I am infinitely grateful to all the photographers who lent their photographs to this book and all the make-up artists, hairdressers, and stylists who contributed so much to the creation of these images. Most of the time, we had lots of laughs and great fun at the shoot and for that I am even more grateful than for their work in making me look so pretty.

Graphic artist Thomas Elsner helped with his severe and clean layouts. I love everything clean. I even love to clean and fix my house. Order gives me a feeling of accomplishment and when everything is in ist place, I can allow myself to think forward – into the future. Thanks, Thomas. Monique Kouznetzoff, thank you too for helping retrieve old photos from your archive.

But most of all, I am grateful to Paige Pedersen and Wayde Binder who did more than this book. They are my guardian angels. I loved putting this book together with the publisher, Lothar Schirmer, Paige, and Wayde. It was an informal, enthusiastic process which gave us many wonderful hours together.

Isabella Rossellini

photo credits

© Miles Aldridge 2002: 28, 30/31, 32/33; Sergio Alocci / ©Vogue, Condé Nast Publications, Inc.: 41; © Kevyn Aucoin 2002: 49; © 1982 Richard Avedon: 23, 24; © James Balog 1996: 121; © Eric Boman / H & K: 94, 95; courtesy of Jeff Bridges and Rose Gallery, Santa Monica / © 1992 by Jeff Bridges: 68, 69; © Michel Comte 2002: 50, 53; © Anton Corbijn: 133; © Patrick Demarchelier: 20; © Arthur Elgort 2002: 100/101; © Fabrizio Ferri 2002: 35, 36, 37, 38; © Oberto Gili 2002: 4, 70, 72/73; © Michel Haddi 2002: 119; © Mary Hilliard: 75; © Dominique Issermann 2002: 27; © Bill King Estate 2002: 62, 103; Photograph by Brigitte Lacombe: 90, 91, 97, 98; © Annie Leibovitz / Contact Press Images, 2002: 122, 125; © Peter Lindbergh / Creations & Visions, N.Y., 2002: 13, 14/15, 16; © David Lynch: 46/47; © Magnum / Focus 2002: 42, 43, 65, 66/67; "Isabella Rossellini, 1988" © The Estate of Robert Mapplethorpe. Used with permission: 127; © Kurt Markus 2002: 139, back cover; © Steven Meisel 2002: front cover, 104, 107, 109, 110,111; © Sheila Metzner 2002: 78, 79; © François Nars 2002: 19; Irving Penn © 1997 Condé Nast Publications Inc.: 76/77; courtesy of private collection, New York: 7, 45, 88/89, 120, 137;© Jim Rakete 2002: 84; © André Rau 2002: 57, 58, 59; © Herb Ritts - Fahey/Klein Gallery: 128; © Paolo Roversi 2002: 114, 115, 117; © Francesco Scavullo 2002: 60, 61; Schirmer/Mosel Archiv/ © Horst P. Horst-Archiv, Gerd Elfering: 54/55; © Iké Udé 2002: 93; © Ellen von Unwerth 2002: 82, 83; © Max Vadukul 2002: 80/81; © Bruce Weber 2002: 87, 112, 113, 131; © Wim Wenders 2002: 134/135.

Many people provided help in obtaining pictures and permissions. We thank all of them: Jay Aaseng, Asymmetrical Productions; Sandy Altermatt, Michel Comte Studio; Jerôme Bartau, Belminda Ferreira, Lancôme; Tanith Berkeley, Sheila Metzner Studio; Launa Beuhler, The Robert Mapplethorpe Foundation, Inc.; Lina Bey, Steven Meisel Studio; Angelika Blechschmidt, German Vogue; Thomas Bonnouvrier, Ellen von Unwerth Studio; Anke Degenhardt, Camera Work; Carla Ghiglieri, Alexandra Agnello, Studio G; Anna Hägglund, Studio Luce; Caroline Herter, Herter Studio; Nicky Hulme, Jeff Bridges Studio; Janet Johnson, Brigitte Lacombe, Inc.; Corinne Karr, Global Creative Management; Margot Klingsporn, Peter Hillmer, Sabine Schmidt, Olga Neufeld, Focus; Monique Kouznetzoff, Sonia Henry, H & K; Leslie Morrison Lambert, Little Bear, Inc.; Griffin R. Lauerman, Herb Ritts Studio; David Leverton, International Photography Sales; Wendell Maruyama, Patrick Demarchelier, Inc.; Janet McClelland, Bill King Estate; Saskia Middelburg, Middelburg Pictures; Jocelyn Miller, Max Vadukul Studio; Leigh Montville, Michael Stiers, Condé Nast Publications; Barbara Münzing, Eye.D; Pascale, l'office; Sandra Rubalcava, Victoria Varela, Trade, Inc.; Liz Rosenberg, Warner Bros. Records; Kim Sion, Natalie Doran, Smile Management; Jeffrey D. Smith, Bernice Koch, Contact Press Images; Marla Ulrich, Wenders Photography; Michael Van Horne, Art + Commerce Anthology, Inc.; Justin White, Richard Avedon Studio; Lea Russo, Rose Gallery; Brigitte Woischnik, Foto Factory; Marisa Zanatta, Stefana Persona, Industria Produzioni.

Design: Thomas Elsner

Schirmer Art Books is an imprint of Schirmer/Mosel Verlag GmbH, Munich.
For trade information please contact:
Schirmer Art Books, John Rule, 40 Voltaire Rd., London SW4 6DH, England
or Schirmer/Mosel Verlag, P.O.Box 221641, 80506 München, Germany
Fax 089/338695

Reproductions: NovaConcept, Berlin
Typesetting: Fotosatz Huber, Germering
Printing and binding: EBS, Verona

ISBN 3-8296-0057-7
A Schirmer/Mosel Production
www.schirmer-mosel.com